ALICE

Life Behind the Counter in Mel's Greasy Spoon

(A Guide to the Feature Film,
the TV Series, and More)

By Barry M. Putt Jr.

Alice: Life Behind the Counter in Mel's Greasy Spoon (A Guide to the Feature Film, the TV Series, and More)
© 2019 Barry M. Putt Jr. All Rights Reserved.

All illustrations are from the author's personal collection, unless otherwise noted. All illustrations are copyright of their respective owners and are also reproduced here in the spirit of publicity. While we have made every effort to acknowledge specific credits whenever possible, we apologize for any omissions.

No part of this book may be reproduced in any form or by any means, electronic, mechanical, digital, photocopying or recording, except for the inclusion in a review, without permission in writing from the publisher.

Published in the USA by BearManor Media
4700 Millenia Blvd.
Suite 175 PMB 90497
Orlando, FL 32839
www.bearmanormedia.com

Printed in the United States of America
ISBN   978-1-62933-426-4 (paperback)
        978-1-62933-427-1 (hardcover)

Book and cover design by Darlene Swanson • www.van-garde.com

Contents

                Acknowledgements vii
                Introduction ix

Chapter 1:   The Feature Film *Alice Doesn't Live Here Anymore* 1
Chapter 2:   The Cast and Crew of *Alice Doesn't Live Here Anymore* 15
Chapter 3:   The Characters in *Alice Doesn't Live Here Anymore* 43
Chapter 4:   *Alice Doesn't Live Here Anymore*—Fan Quiz 51
Chapter 5:   Creating the TV Series *Alice* 53
Chapter 6:   The Cast of *Alice* 77
Chapter 7:   The Crew of *Alice* 101
Chapter 8:   The Characters in *Alice* 109
Chapter 9:   The World in *Alice* 123
Chapter 10: *Alice*—Episode Log 137
Chapter 11: *Alice*—Fan Quiz 241
Chapter 12: Creating the Spin-off TV Series *Flo* 253
Chapter 13: The Cast of *Flo* 257
Chapter 14: The Characters in *Flo* 273
Chapter 15: The World in *Flo* 277
Chapter 16: *Flo*—Episode Log 281
Chapter 17: *Flo*—Fan Quiz 297

Alice...

Chapter 18:	More about *Alice Doesn't Live Here Anymore, Alice,* and *Flo*. 301	
Chapter 19:	Fan Quiz Answer Guide 313	
	Further Reading 325	
	Index. 327	
	About the Author 355	

From one *Alice* fan to another.

Acknowledgements

THIS BOOK WOULD NOT have been possible without the help of many people.

A sincere thank you goes to Daniel Calandro, electronic resources librarian at the Mercer County Community College Library, for providing invaluable assistance in locating and retrieving the majority of the articles and books that I reviewed during the research phase of writing this book.

I truly appreciate the assistance of Sungmin Park, reference librarian at the Mercer County Community College Library, for enthusiastically conducting research and creating source bibliographies, both of which were essential during the development of the book.

I thank Melissa Thomas, head of interlibrary loans and periodicals at the Franklin Township Public Library, for her help in locating several sources that were used in the creation of this book.

My gratitude goes to Gina Gold, for conducting social media research that was needed during the development of the book.

I appreciate the assistance of the Special Collections Research Center, Swem Library, at the College of William and Mary (Linda Lavin Papers); the Cinematic Arts Library at the University of Southern California; the Lilly Library at Indiana University; and the Bowling Green State University Library for providing research materials that I reviewed during the initial phase of writing this book.

A large thank you goes out to David Barry Plunkett who told me about his scrapbook, his experiences at tapings of the series *Alice* and *Flo*, his interactions with various actors associated with the series, and for providing photographs that were used in the book.

I am grateful to Joyce Bulifant, Lucy Lee Flippin, David Silverman, and Christopher Tayback who discussed their experiences related to the TV series *Alice* and *Flo*.

An earnest thank you goes to Liz Astrof for providing information associated with the possible reboot of *Alice*.

I appreciate Ben Ohmart and the staff at BearManor Media for their help and guidance during the creation and publication of this book.

A special thank you goes to Steve Halvorsen for taking the photo of Mel's Diner in Phoenix, Arizona, that was used in the book.

I offer a heartfelt thank you to Rachel D. Barrett, a gifted teacher and friend, for her unwavering support of my writing career.

Finally, I would like to thank my parents, Judie and Barry Putt, for their support during the writing of this book.

Introduction

THE TV SITCOM *ALICE*, which was based on the feature film *Alice Doesn't Live Here Anymore* (1974), premiered on CBS in 1976 during a time of social evolution for women in the United States. Alice Hyatt was a single mother, striking out on her own for the first time. She was eager to engage in life and love and aspired to work professionally as a singer. Through it all, she sought to help her fellow man whenever possible.

The role of mothers on television has evolved over time. During the 1950s, most TV moms focused on their homes and families. They dealt with inner family issues. This changed in the 1960s with the character Laura Petrie in *The Dick Van Dyke Show*. Laura was a homemaker, but she thought for herself and had a degree of sexual attraction not seen until that time. More advancements were made for TV mothers in the early 1970s when the series *Maude* came along. The show dealt with women's sexual issues, including birth control, unwanted pregnancy, and menopause. Having a career became important for female characters, as was seen with Ann Romano, a divorced ad executive, in the series *One Day at a Time*. Alice Hyatt was part of this new breed of TV mother. She was a hero for her generation and generations to come.

Alice aired for nine seasons. The 202 episodes that comprise the series can be seen regularly in syndication, on DVD, and through internet streaming services including Amazon Prime Video. The sitcom has a large fanbase and continues to resonate with people to this day.

Alice: Life Behind the Counter in Mel's Greasy Spoon tells the story of how the feature film *Alice Doesn't Live Here Anymore* and the series *Alice* and *Flo* were developed. It is based on verified information from a variety of sources. In researching this book, I interviewed various people associated with the series, including Christopher Tayback, the son of Vic Tayback (Mel in *Alice*); David Silverman (writer, seasons 7–9 for *Alice*); Lucy Lee Flippin (Fran in *Flo*); Joyce Bulifant (Miriam in *Flo*); and *Alice* enthusiast David Barry Plunkett. The pages that follow will give you insight into the creation of the film and TV series, test your *Alice* trivia knowledge, and make you smile as you remember the many humorous and sometimes touching situations the film and shows depicted as Alice and her friends journeyed through life together.

Barry M. Putt Jr.
June 2019

CHAPTER 1:

The Feature Film *Alice Doesn't Live Here Anymore*

IN 1973, A YOUNG college professor who taught English at California State University became disgusted with an uninspired movie he saw on television. The experience prompted him to write a gritty, provocative screenplay that he hoped could be produced for the big screen. His name was Robert Getchell. The title of his script was *Alice Doesn't Live Here Anymore*. The story focused on a thirty-five-year-old housewife, Alice Hyatt, whose life in Socorro, New Mexico is turned upside down when her husband is killed in a traffic accident. After sorting through her options, she decides to return to her hometown, Monterey, California, with her eleven-year-old son and resume the singing career she started there as a young adult. On the way, she runs out of money in Tucson, Arizona and is forced to take a job waitressing in a small café. As Alice struggles to save, so she can resume her journey to Monterey, she falls in love and ultimately decides to remain in Tucson and pursue her goal of singing there.

Getchell's script was inspired by the sexual revolution. The story dealt with issues in the forefront of people's minds, especially women, who were redefining their societal roles. An important quality found within films set during the sexual revolution is that female heroines became the masters of their destinies and triumphed over the men who stood in their way. This was true of Alice Hyatt. In the film, she makes her own decisions and deals with their consequences. In the end, she is the one responsible for her happiness in life.

After Getchell finished writing the screenplay, he found an agent. The agent thought the story had great potential and began to market it. A short time later, movie producer Peter Thomas optioned the script. Female centered films were not in demand at the time. Thomas searched for a production partner for a year with no results. At that point, the option ran out and he returned the rights to the screenplay to Getchell. The script was then optioned for three months to longtime TV producer David Susskind. At the same time, Ellen Burstyn was completing work on *The Exorcist* (1973). Warner Bros. was sending her scripts to consider for her next project. She was disappointed that the women in the screenplays she was reading were all running from something and not forging their own paths. Her agent, Tony Fantozzi, gave her the script for *Alice Doesn't Live Here Anymore*. She found it to be bold and engaging and immediately decided that she wanted it to be the next film she starred in.

The studio encouraged Burstyn to direct the production herself. She wasn't interested in that, however, so she initiated a search to find a director. Francis Ford Coppola recommended that she take a look at Martin Scorsese's film *Mean Streets* (1973). She thought it was intriguing and decided to take a meeting with Scorsese. During their discussion, Burstyn told him that she liked his directing work but found it to be male focused. She questioned how much he knew about women. Scorsese said that he had not yet focused on women in his film work. It would be a new avenue for him and one he was eager to explore. Burstyn admired his honesty and the breadth of skill he had as a director. These qualities, along with Scorsese's enthusiasm about the project, led her to select him to direct the movie.

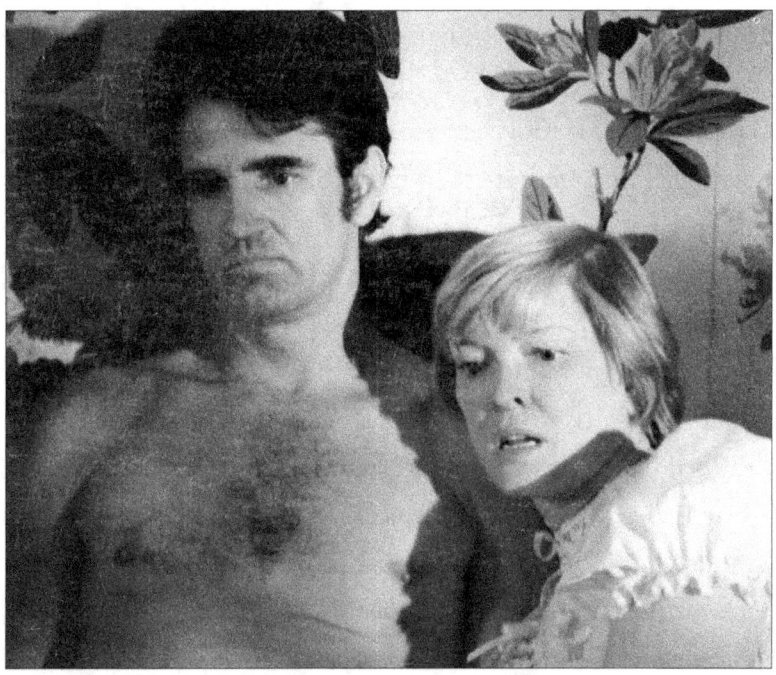

Billy Green Bush and Ellen Burstyn in a scene from *Alice Doesn't Live Here Anymore*

In addition to *Mean Streets,* Scorsese had made several significant independent feature films prior to working with Burstyn including *Who's That Knocking at My Door* (1967) and *Boxcar Bertha* (1972). *Alice Doesn't Live Here Anymore* was his first studio picture. He wanted viewers of the movie to learn something about themselves and their own relationships by the time they finished watching it. To achieve this, he recrafted aspects of the script and infused the character of Alice with some of his own emotional conflicts. Doing so filled her character with a greater degree of emotional truth, which ultimately hit home with audiences.

Ellen Burstyn was officially the first actor cast in *Alice Doesn't Live Here Anymore*. She had recently got divorced and was raising her twelve-year-old son on her own, which paralleled her character's situation in the film. After her divorce, Burstyn realized that for most of her life she had felt trapped in the role of housewife and the duties associated with it. It took her, as it did Alice, some time to move past her issues and find happiness in being on her own. These similarities made it easy for her to relate to Alice.

Burstyn had studied acting with Lee Strasberg at the Actors Studio. She encouraged Scorsese to cast as many actors who had trained there as possible because doing so would assure a certain level of authenticity within their performances. Scorsese was familiar with the studio through his work with alumnus, Harvey Keitel, and readily agreed with Burstyn's request. In addition to Keitel, Scorsese cast Actors Studio members Diane Ladd, Billy Green Bush, and Vic Tayback in the film.

At the time, Kris Kristofferson was a well-known country singer with a gold single entitled "Why Me?" He was also a box office draw. Scorsese initially wasn't interested in considering him, but when Burstyn suggested it, he changed his mind. Kristofferson was estranged from his children from a former marriage, which enabled him to identify with the character of David he was playing in the film who was in a similar situation.

The role of Alice's son, Tommy, was challenging to fill. Scorsese used Marion Dougherty Associates in New York to assist with casting the part. They saw over three hundred boys. Scorsese didn't find what he was looking for there. Sandy Weintraub, associate producer on the film, encouraged him to audition one particular boy: Alfred Lutter III. She said that Lutter was shy yet wanted to be a standup comedian. Scorsese had him improvise with Burstyn. They had great chemistry and really got into the improvs, spontaneously coming up with compelling, character-driven moments. He thought that Lutter was ideal for the role and cast him.

By the time Jodie Foster auditioned for the part of Tommy's friend, Audrey, she was already a well-known child star. She had long hair when she went to audition but decided to cut it short after she was cast. This forced Scorsese to have to transform her character into more of a tomboy than the script had originally called for.

Burstyn's son, Jefferson, played Tommy's best friend, Harold, in the Socorro scenes. Her friend and fellow actress, Lelia Goldoni, was cast as Alice's close friend Bea. Their real-life connection gave authenticity to their relationship in the scenes they appeared in together.

During preproduction, Scorsese discussed the storyline with Burstyn and other cast members. When needed, he would videotape improvisations of scenes with the actors to explore situations more fully. Scorsese gave new drafts of scenes to Getchell, who would polish them or craft entirely new scenes according to the structure that Scorsese constructed from the improvs. The bulk of the improvisations were between Burstyn and Lutter. As the production moved forward, other cast members became involved in this process as well.

Many wonderful moments came out of Scorsese's use of improv. During rehearsal, Lutter told him a gorilla story *ad nauseam*. The story eventually made its way into an improvisation with Burstyn and then later into the film. Another moment that grew out of improvs was the scene in David's kitchen where Alice tells David about her childhood. The bathroom scene at Mel and Ruby's Café was developed using this process as well. In the end, almost everything that was shot was based on a combination of Getchell's screenplay and Scorsese's improvs with the actors.

Alice Doesn't Live Here Anymore, like Scorsese's earlier film *Mean*

Streets, uses pop music to ground the world of the story in a realistic context. Characters don't burst into song to convey their feelings as they had in traditional movie musicals. Instead, the music in *Alice Doesn't Live Here Anymore* gives insight into who Alice is as a person. In the opening scene, young Alice sings a few bars of the song "You'll Never Know." This moment represents the aspiring performer within her. Later in the film, the songs Alice chooses to sing in preparation for her act, such as "Where or When," "When Your Lover Has Gone," and "Gone with the Wind," all deal with lost love and new beginnings. They reflect on Alice's personal life and were included in the script to provide insight into what she is going through at different points in time.

The importance of music can also be seen in Tommy's character. He listens to "Roll Away the Stone" by Mott the Hoople in the film because rock 'n' roll was popular when the movie was made and consistent with what American kids of his generation listened to. Tommy cranked up the music in order to block out the world and his problems.

Burstyn requested to do her own singing and piano playing in the film. Her mother had belittled her ability to sing when she was a child, which created a mental block within her. She was determined to overcome her apprehensions and spent six months taking lessons to brush up on her music skills before principal photography began. In her 2007 autobiography, *Lessons in Becoming Myself*, Burstyn confessed that although the final recordings were spliced together and included augmentation, she did all her own singing and was proud of it.

Warner Bros. gave Scorsese a $1.6 million budget to produce the movie. It was shot in eight weeks during the spring of 1974. Except for the opening scene, all filming was done on location in and around Tucson. Labor laws limited child actors to a four-hour workday. The rest of the cast put in fourteen hours each day, six days a week. Working on location for such a concentrated amount of time kept all actors immersed in the world of the story.

The opening scene is set on a farm in the rural US and shot in bleak, hazy tones. Scorsese crafted it as an homage to MGM's *The Wizard of Oz* (1939). Alice dons a dress similar to the one Dorothy wears. Her relationship with her family has qualities comparable to the relationship Dorothy has with her family. Both characters sing a song that reflects on their longing for more than what they have. In the end, Alice and Dorothy come to appreciate a renewed understanding of home and a new sense of belonging.

The opening scene was shot toward the end of production at the Gower Street Columbia lot in Los Angeles. The set cost $85,000 to construct and was used only once before being disassembled. Scorsese had two days to shoot the scene. The welfare worker looking after Mia Bendixsen, who played the eight-year-old Alice, was a strict overseer. She made sure Bendixsen went to school for the legally required amount of time each day. She opposed Bendixsen's saying the lines "Blow it out your ass" and "Jesus Christ." Scorsese was firm that those specific words needed to be said because they defined her character. The matter put him at odds with the welfare worker. Luckily, one take of the scene had been shot before the dialogue became an issue. Scorsese decided to withdraw from the conflict and simply inserted the existing take into the film instead.

Scorsese opted to employ moving camerawork throughout the production. He felt it was the most authentic way to capture the state of confusion of most of the characters in the story. The only times Scorsese used a fixed camera was when characters were seen in stable situations, such as Alice's affectionate interplay with David in his kitchen. In the scene in which Alice says goodbye to her close friend Bea and leaves Socorro with Tommy, the camera pans slowly then hesitates interrupting its own movement. Scorsese requested this be done to create a mood of indecision, helping emphasize how conflicted Alice is about leaving.

Jodie Foster was available to work on the film for only two four-hour days. Scorsese had to move at a fast pace to shoot all of her scenes within that time. He felt that she did a great job, but he wished that he had more time to do improvs with her, which could have produced even stronger results than what had been achieved.

Alfred Lutter III and Ellen Burstyn in a scene from *Alice Doesn't Live Here Anymore*

Since Lutter was new to acting, the preproduction improvs helped to immerse him in the world of the story and his character, which gave his work a deep sense of psychological realism. Burstyn admired his ability to be in the moment. She found him to be smart yet hard to handle at times because he lived his character on and off screen.

There are several moments in the film that were thought up on the same day they were shot. This is true of the scene in which Alice returns to the hotel dressed in a new outfit. Everything in the scene was scripted except for when Tommy slams the door in her face. That aspect is based on an improv done moments before the shoot. In another instance, an improvised scene clocked in with an initial running time of fifteen minutes. It was eventually whittled down to three minutes for the final film. In such scenes, Scorsese kept the camera angles simple to streamline the shooting and editing process.

In the film, Burstyn drew from her relationship with her real-life son. This was true of the scene in which Alice insists that Tommy jot down everything that is going wrong in his life. A similar situation had occurred in Burstyn's life. When her son was unhappy and refused to see anything positive, she sat him down and demanded he write down every awful thing he was going through.

The scene in which Harvey Keitel's character, Ben, flies into a violent rage in Alice's motel room was choreographed and extensively rehearsed before it was filmed. Since the action takes place in a small space, Scorsese decided to do all cinematographic work using a handheld camera. Doing so made filming in such an intimate location easier. The only improv in the scene occurs when Ben tells Alice that if she doesn't mess with the scorpion, it won't mess with her. Everything else was scripted. According to Burstyn's autobiography, she found Keitel frightening in the scene. She emoted what she was actually feeling in the moment. Working on that section of the film was a draining experience for her because it had to be shot several times from different angles. Burstyn tried to distance herself from what was happening in the scene during breaks in filming, but she ultimately found that difficult to do. By the time she finished shooting the scene, she was emotionally distraught.

Burstyn and Ladd knew each other prior to working on *Alice Doesn't Live Here Anymore*. Burstyn had been cast in a couple roles for which Ladd had auditioned. Being reunited after losing these parts created some tension between them. Scorsese used that energy to the film's advantage in the scene in which their characters argue and then forge a friendship.

Diane Ladd in a scene from *Alice Doesn't Live Here Anymore*

Ladd incorporated elements of people she knew into the character of Flo. Her childhood friend, for instance, used to put gum on her nose and behind her ear to save for later. Ladd's father used to say, "Grandma is slow and moves like dead lice." Ladd felt that both of these would make her character truer to life, so she used them in an improv. They were later incorporated into the film.

After the bathroom scene at Mel and Ruby's Café was shot, Ladd told Scorsese that she and Burstyn could do a better job in the scene if he let them reshoot it. Scorsese was reluctant to do so for budgetary reasons, but eventually he agreed. The work the actresses did during the reshoot was so much more emotive than the original takes that Scorsese used only the reshot footage in the film.

In addition to Burstyn's son being in the film, other cast members' family members made appearances. Ladd's seven-year-old daughter, Laura Dern, was featured in a diner scene eating an ice cream cone at the counter; William A. Shea Jr., Ladd's ex-husband, sat beside her. Vic Tayback's brother lived in Arizona at the time the film was being shot. Tayback got him a brief role in a scene at the diner as well.

The climax of the film, which occurs in the diner, had been in development since work on the film began. One draft of the script had Alice and David get back together, while another had Alice break up with him. No matter what was drafted, it didn't feel right to Scorsese. During rehearsal, Kristofferson decided to improvise that his character would take Alice to Monterey if it meant so much to her. He was willing to relinquish power to her in the situation. Diner patrons clapped at Alice's acceptance, which signified a triumphant moment in her journey. Scorsese felt that this shift fulfilled Alice's objective and made the story feel complete, so they used it.

Getchell wrote several versions of the final scene, including one in which Tommy kills himself. Other drafts had him fleeing to

Monterey alone and then returning to Tucson with Alice. Burstyn wanted her character to go to Monterey and establish a home there, while Warner Bros. insisted that the film end with a romantic connection. They had just released a movie that didn't end happily, and it hadn't done well at the box office. The studio told Scorsese that if *Alice Doesn't Live Here Anymore* didn't have a happy ending, they wouldn't release it. Scorsese took all this into consideration and ultimately decided to end the movie with a bonding moment between mother and son. In this scene, Alice comforts Tommy and tells him that Tucson is their home now: it has everything they've been looking for, they are comfortable there, and they have a sense of family and an opportunity to grow. All parties agreed that this was a satisfying way to conclude the film for both the lead characters and the audience.

The "Monterey" sign that appears during the final moments in the movie was shot by coincidence. Scorsese contemplated removing it but then decided it should be seen. He felt the sign represented Alice and Tommy finding their "Monterey" in Tucson.

Alice Doesn't Live Here Anymore was the first of Scorsese's films in which he wasn't involved in the majority of the editing. This was due to the fact that he was simultaneously working on two other projects, which put limitations on his time. While Scorsese did edit a few sections of the movie, he asked his friend, Marcia Lucas, to edit most of it for him.

The initial cut came in at three hours, sixteen minutes. It was the longest initial cut of any film Scorsese had made until that point. Warner Bros. encouraged him to remove the opening scene with Alice as a girl. Scorsese felt that that moment was essential and refused to be associated with the film were it cut. The studio rethought its position and agreed to keep the scene in. Outside of this incident, Warner Bros. allowed Scorsese to craft the final version of the film on his own. The initial cut contained a large amount of character development, most of which Scorsese eventually decided was unnecessary. He regretted having to remove moments that related to Alice's husband, Donald, because they gave insight into how he had become the person he was. But Scorsese felt these aspects needed to be cut to keep the story advancing at a steady pace.

By the time the film was ready for previews, the production had surpassed its budget by over a million dollars, coming in at $1.72 million. This was attributed to the need for additional shooting and Scorsese's taking ill for a time, which slowed down production. Preview audiences felt that several early scenes relating to Alice's marriage weren't needed, so Scorsese had them cut. After these adjustments were made, the movie was deemed complete. It was released on December 9, 1974. Overall, the film received positive reviews. It went on to gross over $21 million. Warner Bros. asked Getchell to write a novelized version of the story as a tie-in to the movie. The novel closely follows the story established in the film. However, in the novelization, Alice's married life is set in Ponca City, Oklahoma. This is consistent with early drafts of the screenplay but not the final version of the film, where the location is Socorro. The novel also provides some additional insight into the main characters. It was published in paperback soon after the movie was released.

The film *Alice Doesn't Live Here Anymore* and the people associated with it received many accolades after the movie's release. The film was nominated for the Palme d'Or at the 1975 Cannes Film Festival. It won a British Academy of Film and Television Arts (BAFTA) Award for Best Film. Burstyn was nominated for the Golden Globe Award for Best Actress in a Leading Role and won both an Oscar and a BAFTA for best actress in a leading role. Ladd was nominated for a Golden Globe Award and an Academy Award for Best Supporting

Alice...

Actress; she won a BAFTA for her portrayal of Flo. Getchell was nominated for an Oscar for Best Original Screenplay and a WGA Award for the same. Scorsese was nominated for a BAFTA Award for Best Direction. This recognition was proof that the story was relevant, well-crafted, and resonated strongly with its audience.

CHAPTER 2:

The Cast and Crew of *Alice Doesn't Live Here Anymore*

Ellen Burstyn *(Alice)*

Ellen Burstyn was born Edna Rae Gillooly in Detroit, Michigan, in 1932. She had two brothers. Her parents divorced when she was young. After that, her mother and stepfather raised her. Burstyn was six years old when she first performed on stage: as Little Miss Muffet at St. Mary's Academy, a boarding school in Windsor, Ontario.

She dropped out of high school during her senior year due to failing grades and took a job modeling clothes in a local department store. A few years later, Burstyn married salesman William Alexander and moved to New York City, where she got a job as a dancer on *The Jackie Gleason Show*. When her involvement with the series ended, she took the stage name Erica Dean and started to pursue acting. By that point, her marriage to Alexander was failing. They divorced in 1957. That same year she was cast in the lead role in the Broadway play *Fair Game*.

In 1958, she married director Paul Roberts. Her career began to flourish, and she was cast regularly in guest parts on TV shows including *Gunsmoke*, *Perry Mason*, and *Dr. Kildare*. In 1961, Burstyn adopted a son. Soon after, her marriage to Roberts became strained, and they got divorced.

Alice...

Ellen Burstyn

In 1964, she married actor Neil Burstyn and took his last name professionally. A few months later, she was cast in the film *Goodbye Charlie* (1964), which featured Debbie Reynolds, Walter Matthau, and Tony Curtis. When filming ended, Burstyn realized that she was unhappy with how her career was going. In an effort to change it, she started taking private acting classes at the Actors Studio with Lee Strasberg. She found working with him to be an invaluable experience.

In 1971, she was cast in *The Last Picture Show*. Her performance in the film garnered her an Academy Award nomination for Best

Supporting actress. Not long after, Burstyn's relationship with her husband broke down. He was a schizophrenic and had started acting violently toward her. His erratic outbursts ultimately led them to divorce.

In 1973, Burstyn starred in *The Exorcist*. It was a demanding role that took nine months to shoot. The following year, she played the lead role in *Alice Doesn't Live Here Anymore*, for which she won an Academy Award and a BAFTA.

After *Alice Doesn't Live Here Anymore*, Burstyn starred in *Same Time, Next Year* (1975) on Broadway. She won a Tony Award for her performance and reprised the part in the 1978 film adaptation of the play, for which she was nominated for an Academy Award for Best Actress. The exposure led to a steady stream of other movie roles. In 1986, Burstyn got her own TV series, *The Ellen Burstyn Show*, which ran for one season on ABC. She starred in several more TV shows, including *That's Life*, *The Book of Daniel*, and *House of Cards*.

Diane Ladd *(Flo in the feature film, Belle in the TV series)*
Diane Ladd was born in Meridian, Mississippi, in 1935. She initially wanted to pursue a career in law and was awarded a scholarship to Louisiana State University while still in high school. At the same time, she was cast in the lead role in her school play. She wound up liking theater so much that she declined the scholarship and moved to New York City to pursue a career in acting.

A few months after arriving in New York, Ladd was hired for a short-term job in the chorus of a show at the Copacabana nightclub. After that work concluded, she was cast in a tour of the play *A Hatful of Rain* (1957). That was followed by several supporting roles in off-Broadway shows, including *Orpheus Descending* (1957).

Alice...

Diane Ladd

In 1960, Ladd married actor Bruce Dern. They had a daughter and forged a life together while pursuing their careers. When their daughter was almost two, she died in a drowning accident. Ladd was heartbroken yet determined to have another child. In 1967, her second child, Laura, was born. The following year, Ladd was cast in her first Broadway production, a play entitled *Carry Me Back to Morningside Heights* (1968). The play lasted for only seven performances, including one preview, but being on Broadway was a major step forward for Ladd's career. Not long after the show concluded, her relationship with her husband started to decline, and they decided to get a divorce.

In 1969, Ladd married her second husband, William A. Shea Jr. She continued to act in supporting roles in films and appeared in the soap opera *Secret Storm*. In 1974, she was featured as Ida Sessions in the classic neo-noir film *Chinatown*. A few months later, Ladd was cast as Florence Jean Castleberry in *Alice Doesn't Live Here Anymore*. She received Golden Globe and Academy Award nominations for best supporting actress and won a BAFTA in the same category.

In 1976, Ladd and Shea divorced. Soon after, CBS executive, Alan Shayne asked her to reprise the role of Flo in the TV series *Alice*. She was under contract with NBC at the time, though, and unable to pursue the opportunity. The part went to Polly Holliday instead. Holliday found great success with it and eventually left the show to star in her own series based on the character. By that point, Ladd's contract with the competing network had expired, and she was invited to be a regular member of the cast on *Alice* playing the Southern waitress Belle Dupree. She appeared in twenty-two episodes, crafting a determined, humorous, and engaging character. Ladd won a Golden Globe Award for Best Supporting Actress in a Series, Miniseries or Motion Picture Made for Television for her work on the show. At the end of her second season on the series, she decided to move on to pursue other opportunities.

During the 1980s and '90s, Ladd was cast in a steady flow of guest and supporting parts in films and TV series, including *The Love Boat*, *Something Wicked This Way Comes*, and *Father Dowling Mysteries*. She won an Independent Spirit Award for Best Supporting Female for her performance in the movie *Rambling Rose* (1991) and was nominated for Primetime Emmys for her work in guest roles in the TV series *Dr. Quinn: Medicine Woman*, *Grace Under Fire*, and *Touched by an Angel*.

In 1999, Ladd married Robert Charles Hunter. A few years later, she authored the memoir *Spiraling Through the School of Life: A Mental,*

Physical, and Spiritual Discovery (2007) and, later still, a collection of short stories entitled *A Bad Afternoon for a Piece of Cake* (2016). She continued to appear in film and TV roles after that. Many of these productions also featured her daughter, Laura Dern. They included *Kingdom Hospital*, *Enlightenment*, and *Chesapeake Shores*.

Vic Tayback *(Mel in the feature film and the TV series)*
Vic Tayback was born in 1930 to a working-class family in Brooklyn, New York. His father worked as a fry cook and his mother as a seamstress to support their three children. When Tayback was old enough, he sold magazines and made deliveries for a dry-cleaning business to help the family get by.

Tayback's parents eventually moved the family to Los Angeles in search of prosperity and an easier lifestyle. After completing high school, Tayback attended Glendale Community College. He quit during his first semester and joined the United States Coast Guard. He served with them for four years during the Korean War.

When he returned from the war, Tayback attended the Frederick A. Speare School of Radio and TV Broadcasting and planned to become a sports announcer. During his first year there, a director offered him a lead role in the play *Stalag 17* (1951). Tayback was reluctant to accept the part until friends prodded him to give acting a try. He wound up loving it and transferred to the Actors Studio, where he immersed himself in the study of the craft.

After Tayback completed his training at the Actors Studio, he started to go on auditions while supporting himself as a cab driver and with short-term office work he obtained through the temp agency Kelly Services. In 1959, he cofounded a small theater called Company of Angels. In one of the company's productions, he met Sheila McKay. They wed in 1962. Two years later, they had a son.

During this time, acting jobs came in slowly until Tayback was hired to appear in a TV series pilot that featured Sid Caesar. The series was never picked up, but the exposure helped Tayback get steady television and commercial work.

Vic Tayback

During the 1960s, Tayback was cast in numerous guest roles on shows such as *Gunsmoke, Bewitched, Mission Impossible,* and *The Monkees.* In 1973, he played a main part as Captain Barney Marcus in the series *Griff.* That was followed by his iconic portrayal of the gruff short-order cook Mel Sharples in *Alice Doesn't Live Here Anymore.* The success of the movie led the public to take note of him. Tayback

Alice...

was the only actor from the film to reprise his role on an ongoing basis in the TV series *Alice*.

Tayback was a big fan of horse racing. He owned several racehorses and loved betting at the track. He was personable and endeared himself to the rest of the cast on *Alice*. Tayback was always there when Linda Lavin or Polly Holliday needed a supportive hug or when Philip McKeon needed to talk over a personal problem.

In 1980, at the height of his stardom, Tayback lent his time and likeness, in the role of Mel, to a cookbook entitled *Recipes for Busy People*, which was published jointly by Kelly Services and Warner Books. The book contained three hundred recipes culled from more than ten thousand that Kelly Services employees in the US and Canada had submitted for a chance to be included in the publication. Warner Books selected the top ten recipes and featured them in the Busy People's Recipe Contest Cook-Off that was held in Hollywood. Tayback's own chili recipe was served to attendees while he and several food editors judged the contest. They used a rating system to rank each recipe's appearance, taste, texture, ease of cooking, and creativity and selected two grand winners.

After the series *Alice* ended, Tayback continued to act in shows including *The Love Boat*, *Tales from the Darkside*, and *Murder, She Wrote*. In 1990, he made his final appearance in the series *MacGyver*. He died of a heart attack later that year at the age of sixty.

Mia Bendixsen

Mia Bendixsen *(Alice, age eight)*

Mia Bendixsen was born in 1964. She made her debut as an actress when she was six-years old in the TV series *Medical Center*. Bendixsen went on to appear in *Gunsmoke, Mod Squad, The Bob Newhart Show, Barnaby Jones,* and *Adam-12*. In 1974, she portrayed eight-year-old Alice in *Alice Doesn't Live Here Anymore*. She followed this performance with a guest appearance in an episode of the TV series *Little House on the Prairie* and a supporting role in the film *Prophecy* (1979). In 1982, she played the pregnant girl in the ladies' room in *Ladies and Gentlemen, the Fabulous Stains*. That was her last part for almost thirty years. In 2010, she reemerged briefly to play the role of Cassidy Lane in the TV movie *Where's My Man*.

Alice...

Alfred Lutter III

Alfred Lutter III *(Tommy)*

Alfred Lutter III was born in 1962 in Ridgewood, New Jersey. He got his start as an actor playing Alice's eleven-year-old son, Tommy, in *Alice Doesn't Live Here Anymore.* He went on to play a young version of Woody Allen's character, Boris, in the film *Love and Death* (1975). That was followed by the part of Ogilvie in the popular children's film *The Bad News Bears* (1976). In mid-1976, Lutter reprised the role of Tommy in the pilot episode of *Alice.* When CBS picked up the show for a test run, producers decided to recast the part with actor Philip McKeon. Soon after, Lutter was hired to play Alvin Tanner in the 1977 TV series *Family.* He then performed the role of Ogilvie again in *The Bad News Bears in Breaking Training* (1977). Lutter retired from the entertainment business and focused on his education, eventually earning a master's degree in management and engineering from Stanford University. He later became chief information officer of a computer information systems company in Southern California.

Kris Kristofferson *(David)*

Kris Kristofferson was born in 1936 in Brownsville, Texas. After graduating from high school, he aspired to be a writer and got a bachelor's degree in literature from Pomona College in Claremont, California. He was awarded a Rhodes Scholarship at Oxford University where he earned a postgraduate degree in English literature and then married his longtime girlfriend, Frances Mavia Beer. They had two children. Early in their marriage, Kristofferson began to write songs. Family pressure led him to join the US Army. While stationed in Germany, he performed with a band. He was offered a position teaching literature at West Point but decided to leave the military to pursue a career in songwriting. His family disowned him over this decision.

In the early 1960s, Kristofferson moved to Nashville and got a job sweeping floors at Columbia Recording Studios. The position enabled him to get a demo tape of his music into the hands of Johnny Cash, who agreed to record his song "Sunday Mornin' Comin' Down." Kristofferson was awarded Songwriter of the Year at the Country Music Awards for the recording.

In 1967, Kristofferson released his first single: "Golden Idol." It was followed by more singles and ultimately full albums. By 1969, his relationship with Beer had become strained, and they got a divorce. The following year, Kristofferson began to pursue a career as a film actor. His first role was as the Minstrel Wrangler in *The Last Movie* (1970). Around that time, he met and married singer Rita Coolidge. They had one child. More film roles followed. In 1972, Kristofferson's album *Jesus Was a Capricorn* reached number one on the US country music charts. He and Coolidge then collaborated on the album *Full Moon* (1973), which hit number one on the US country music charts as well.

Kris Kristofferson

In 1974, Kristofferson was cast as David in *Alice Doesn't Live Here Anymore*. That was followed by a starring role as John Norman Howard in Barbra Streisand's *A Star is Born* (1976). A few years later, his relationship with Coolidge began to cool. They divorced in 1980. In 1983, Kristofferson married Lisa Meyers. Between 1983 and 1994, they had five children. TV and film work continued to come Kristofferson's way including leading roles in *Amerika* (1987), *Christmas in Connecticut* (1992), *Planet of the Apes* (2001), *Jump*

Out Boys (2008), *Best Friend from Heaven* (2018), and many others. Throughout his life, Kristofferson maintained simultaneous careers as an actor and a singer and continued to be in demand in both fields.

Billy Green Bush

Billy Green Bush *(Donald)*

Billy Green Bush was born William Warren Bush in Montgomery, Alabama, in 1935. As an adult, he moved to Los Angeles to pursue a career as an actor. In 1963, Bush landed his first acting job playing a doctor in an episode of the series *Stoney Burke*. He followed this performance with guest roles in popular shows including *The Outer Limits*. In 1967, he married Carole Kay Campbell. They had three children. During the early years of his marriage, Bush was featured in many mainstream films, such as the 1971 release *Five Easy Pieces*. For most of his parts, he was cast as sheriffs and police officers.

In 1974, he got to perform a more villainous role as Alice's husband, Donald, in *Alice Doesn't Live Here Anymore*. Around this time, his twin daughters, Lindsay and Sidney Greenbush, began to star alternately as Carrie in the TV series *Little House on the Prairie*. His son, Clay Greenbush, played a student in many episodes of the show as well.

Bush went on to play guest roles in series including *The Incredible Hulk*, *The Dukes of Hazzard*, *Hill Street Blues*, and *Matlock*. These appearances were followed by his portrayal of Elvis Presley's father, Vernon, in the movie *Elvis and Me* (1988). He reprised the part in the 1990 TV show *Elvis*. By 1991, his relationship with Campbell had faded, and they got divorced. Bush made his final acting appearance portraying Sheriff Ed Landis in the film *Jason Goes to Hell: The Final Friday* (1993).

Valerie Curtin *(Vera)*

Valerie Curtin was born in 1945 in New York City. Both of her parents were actors. Curtin got her start on TV, playing a nurse in an episode of the 1971 series *The New Dick Van Dyke Show*. That was followed by a guest role on *Happy Days*. The same year, she was cast as Vera in *Alice Doesn't Live Here Anymore*. She maintained a writing career while acting and wrote for TV series including *The Mary Tyler Moore Show* and *Phyllis*.

In 1975, Curtin married director and writer Barry Levinson. Soon after, she starred in the first pilot for the sitcom *Three's Company*. The version she appeared in was shelved. A second pilot was then written. It replaced her character with a new one played by Joyce Dewitt. The network picked up the version of the pilot that featured Dewitt. The series went on to become a hit.

In the late 1970s, Curtin and Levinson cowrote the screenplay for the film *. . . And Justice for All* (1979). It received an Academy Award nomination for Best Original Screenplay. In 1982, they teamed up again to write the semiautobiographical film *Best Friends*. Marriage troubles during that time led them to get a divorce.

Valerie Curtin

From 1982 to 1988, Curtin starred as Judy Bernly in seventy-eight episodes of the sitcom *Nine to Five*. In 1984, she, Barry Levinson, and Robert Klane cowrote the script for *Unfaithfully Yours*, which was based on Preston Sturges's screenplay for the 1948 movie of the same name. Curtin went on to appear in episodes of *Frasier, Party of Five, The District, ER,* and *Out of Practice*.

Alice...

Lelia Goldoni

Lelia Goldoni *(Bea)*

Lelia Goldoni was born in 1936 in New York City. When she was a teenager, she studied acting at the Actors Studio. Soon after completing her training, she began her film career by performing in uncredited roles. The first of these was as Consuelo Valdés in *We Were Strangers* (1949). In 1960, she married actor Ben Carruthers. The marriage didn't last; the two divorced that same year. Goldoni moved on to guest star in TV series including *The Lloyd Bridges Show, Espionage, Secret Agent,* and *Doctor in Charge.*

In 1974, Goldoni was cast as Alice's close friend Bea in *Alice Doesn't Live Here Anymore.* More acting work followed, including parts in the 1978 remake of *Invasion of the Body Snatchers,* the miniseries *Scruples, Cagney & Lacey,* and *Homefront.* In 1993, Goldoni produced and directed the documentary *Genius on the Wrong Coast* about the life of dancer-choreographer Lester Horton. Afterward, she continued to perform in guest roles in numerous TV series and the film *The Next Cassavetes* (2019).

Jodie Foster *(Audrey)*

Jodie Foster was born in Los Angeles as Alicia Christian Foster in 1962. She started working in TV commercials at the age of three. By the time she was six, she and her brother were cast in guest roles on the TV series *Mayberry RFD*. The success Foster found in that series led to a steady stream of acting work for her. She had simultaneous, recurring parts on *My Three Sons*, *The Courtship of Eddie's Father*, and *Bob & Carol & Ted & Alice*. After appearing in these series, she was cast in the film *Alice Doesn't Live Here Anymore*.

In 1976, Foster played a child prostitute in Martin Scorsese's *Taxi Driver*. She received a National Society of Film Critics Award for her work in the production. This part showed her range as an actress and proved that, in addition to spunky children's roles, she could play more layered, mature parts. Later that year, she was cast in a costarring role in the popular Disney movie *Freaky Friday* (1976).

In 1980, Foster graduated from high school at Le Lycée Français de Los Angeles as valedictorian. She took a break from acting to attend Yale University. During her freshman year, she was stalked by John W. Hinckley Jr., who later tried to assassinate President Ronald Reagan. Foster did all she could to put the experience behind her and focus on earning a degree in literature. She wound up graduating magna cum laude.

Alice...

Jodie Foster

After completing her education, Foster resumed her acting career and starred as a rape victim in *The Accused* (1988). She won her first Academy Award for her performance in the film. She followed this part with another major role as FBI agent Clarice Starling in *The Silence of the Lambs* (1991), which earned her a second Academy Award.

As her popularity with audiences grew, Foster opened her own production company and strove to transform how Hollywood represented women by producing and acting in films that contained unique roles and offered new perspectives on the female characters they depicted. This was true of the 1994 film *Nell*, about a small-town female doctor, and *The Baby Dance* (1998), which looked at motherhood, class issues, and adoption.

In the mid-1990s, Foster started dating production manager, Cydney Bernard. They had two sons. During this time, Foster worked on several more films, including *Panic Room* (2002), *Flightplan*

(2005), and *The Brave One* (2007). The couple's relationship eventually deteriorated, and they broke up in 2008.

In 2014, Foster married photographer Alexandra Hedison and reduced her film work so she could spend more time with her family. The projects she took on going forward were sparse yet always had something new and important to say about people and the world.

Harvey Keitel *(Ben)*

Harvey Keitel was born in 1939 in Brooklyn. He was expelled from high school when he was fifteen because of his unruly behavior. A few months later, he joined the United States Marine Corps and became a part of President Eisenhower's Operation Blue Bat, which fought against communism in Lebanon. Keitel found his time in the military to be life changing. The discipline he acquired while there gave him a sense of honor and self-esteem that served him well going forward in life.

After Keitel was discharged, he supported himself as a court reporter for several years. During that time, he became interested in acting. Although his parents didn't support his pursuit, Keitel studied acting with Stella Adler and Lee Strasberg at the renowned HB Studio in New York City. It wasn't long before he was cast in off-Broadway shows in notable theaters, including La Mama Experimental Theatre Club and Caffe Cino.

In 1967, Keitel auditioned for Martin Scorsese's first feature-length film: *Who's That Knocking at My Door*. He was cast in the lead role, beginning a longtime association between the two. Keitel went on to be featured in Scorsese's *Mean Streets*, *Alice Doesn't Live Here Anymore*, and *Taxi Driver*. Afterward, he moved on to work with other directors—first in independent films and then in Hollywood, where Francis Ford Coppola took note of his talent and selected him

Alice . . .

to play Captain Willard in *Apocalypse Now* (1979). During the first week of filming, Coppola felt that Keitel wasn't right for the part and recast him. This ended Keitel's stint in Hollywood movies for a while. He refocused on independent film work.

Harvey Keitel

In the 1980s, Keitel started dating actress Lorraine Bracco. They had a daughter. He appeared in several European films during that time, including *Death Watch* (Germany, 1980) and *La Nuit de Varennes* (Italy, 1982). When he returned to the United States, he was cast in supporting roles in the romantic drama *Falling in Love* (1984) and the comedy *Wise Guys* (1986). In 1988, he reteamed with Scorsese and played Judas in the controversial film *The Last Temptation of Christ*.

In 1991 Keitel reemerged into mainstream Hollywood movies playing the role of sympathetic detective, Hal Slocumb, in *Thelma and Louise*. That was followed by a part in *Sister Act* (1992). These films' success gave Keitel broad exposure. He then starred in Quentin Tarantino's *Reservoir Dogs* (1992). The two went on to collaborate on several more movies, including *Pulp Fiction* (1994) and *From Dusk till Dawn* (1996).

By the mid-1990s, Keitel's relationship with Bracco had ended. In 2000, he started dating San Diego pottery instructor, Lisa Karmazin. They had a son in 2001. The couple broke up a few months after his birth. Later that year, Keitel married actress Daphna Kastner; they also had a son. Since then, Keitel has worked steadily as a film actor in movies such as *The Grand Budapest Hotel* (2014), *The Irishman* (2019), and *The Painted Bird* (2019).

Robert Getchell *(Screenwriter)*

Robert Getchell was born in Kansas City, Missouri, in 1936. He earned a degree in English from the University of Missouri in 1965. After graduating, he set out to become a teacher. By 1970, he was working as an English literature professor at California State University. Three years later, Getchell decided to try his hand at screenwriting, which resulted in the screenplay *Alice Doesn't Live Here Anymore.*

Not long after he completed the script, a movie producer optioned it and set it on its way toward production. The film did well at the box office and earned him an Oscar nomination and a BAFTA Award for Best Original Screenplay. Getchell's next film, the music-filled *Bound for Glory* (1976), based on the autobiography of folk singer Woody Guthrie, earned him a second Oscar nomination.

Alice...

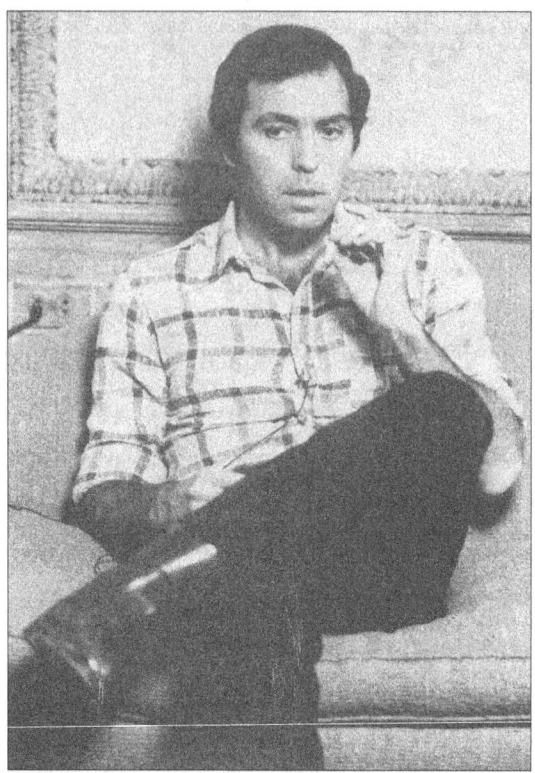

Robert Getchell

In 1976, Getchell adapted *Alice Doesn't Live Here Anymore* into the TV sitcom *Alice*. It ran for nine seasons. In 1980, *Alice* was spun off into the comedy series *Flo,* which centered on the colorful character Florence Jean Castleberry and her life in Cowtown, Texas. It ran for two seasons.

In 1981, Getchell wrote the script for the film adaptation of Christina Crawford's book *Mommie Dearest*, about life with her adoptive mother, the actress Joan Crawford. In 1985, Getchell scripted the musical biopic *Sweet Dreams*, which explored the life of singer Patsy Cline. He went on to do an adaptation of Olive Higgins Prouty's 1923 novel *Stella Dallas*. Getchell's version was the third time the story had been adapted for the screen. The film was released in 1990 as *Stella* and had modest success at the box office. In 1993, Getchell penned the screenplay for the movie *The Point of No Return*. A remake of Luc Besson's *La Femme Nikita* (1990), it debuted at number two at the box office. That same year, Getchell wrote a film version of Tobias Wolff's memoir, *This Boy's Life*. He then cowrote the screen adaptation of John Grisham's highly popular legal thriller *The Client* (1994).

After completing work on *The Client*, Getchell moved away from screenwriting and resumed his career teaching literature at the University of Missouri and Miami University in Oxford, Ohio. He remained in the academic world for the rest of his work life and passed away on October 21, 2017.

Martin Scorsese *(Director)*

Martin Scorsese was born in Flushing, Queens, New York, in 1942. His parents were actors who had emigrated to the United States from Italy. When acting jobs were sparse, they supported the family by working in Manhattan's Garment District. Scorsese and his brother were raised Catholic. Asthma prevented Scorsese from playing with the neighborhood children, so the family saw movies to entertain him and his brother instead. This was how Scorsese developed his passion for cinema.

In the early 1960s, he attended New York University and started a relationship with fellow student Laraine Marie Brennan. During that time, he earned a bachelor's degree in English followed by a master's degree in filmmaking. He graduated in 1965 and then married Brennan. A few months later, they had a daughter.

Alice...

Martin Scorsese

Scorsese made several short films in the mid-1960s, including the dark-comedy *The Big Shave* (1967). He saw moviemaking as a form of self-expression and was drawn to films that spoke to the director's unique vision. Scorsese used naturalism in his work to portray characters as they really were. He exposed a character's rawness, brutality, and unfiltered self, which made him unique as a director.

In 1967, he directed his first feature film: *Who's That Knocking at My Door*. It was based in part on his life and starred a young actor, Harvey Keitel, whom Scorsese would work with throughout his career. In 1971, Scorsese got divorced from Brennan. The following year he made *Boxcar Bertha* (1972), which was considered his first important film. After that he directed and cowrote *Mean Streets* (1973), with Keitel and Robert De Niro as stars.

Mean Streets was highly autobiographical and dealt with a situation from Scorsese's childhood. It contained specific themes that would become synonymous with Scorsese's work going forward including: the mafia, masculinity, and Catholic guilt. The movie also established his filmic style, which included constantly keeping the camera in motion. *Mean Streets* garnered a lot of attention and enabled Scorsese to make his first major studio picture—*Alice Doesn't Live Here Anymore*—the following year.

Although the script for *Alice Doesn't Live Here Anymore* was originally fictitious, Scorsese infused subtle elements of his own life into it. The film became a major success upon release and enabled Scorsese to do additional big-budget movies.

In 1976, Scorsese married Julia Cameron. They had a daughter. The couple split up less than a year into their marriage. At the time, Scorsese was directing the controversial film *Taxi Driver* (1976). The movie sparked a longtime collaboration with writer Paul Schrader. It was awarded the Palme d'Or at the Cannes Film Festival and received four Oscar nominations. Scorsese's next production was the big-budget musical *New York, New York* (1977). He intended for it to be a tribute to his hometown. The movie wasn't received well by critics, who felt it didn't live up to Scorsese's previous work. The poor reaction sent Scorsese into a depression. He struggled on to direct *The Last Waltz* (1978), a documentary about The Band's last concert.

In 1979, Scorsese married Isabella Rossellini. The marriage and the production of *The Last Waltz* did little to boost his spirits. Scorsese continued his downward emotional spiral, concerned that he'd never be a successful filmmaker again. Urged by others, he devoted all his energy to making the true story *Raging Bull* (1980). It received high praise upon release and was selected as the number one American sports film by the American Film Institute. The movie received eight Academy Award nominations and became a turning point in Scorsese's career.

After a few years, Scorsese's relationship with Rossellini weakened, and they divorced. Despite his personal struggles, Scorsese made several outstanding films during this period, including *The King of Comedy* (1982) and the dark comedy *After Hours* (1985). In 1985, he married Barbara De Fina. Soon after, Scorsese directed *The Color of Money* (1986). The film was a sequel to *The Hustler* (1961) and starred Paul Newman and Tom Cruise. Scorsese then teamed with Michael Jackson to make a music video of Jackson's hit song "Bad" (1987). It was shot in a New York City subway station. The box office success of *The Color of Money* enabled Scorsese to gain the status he needed to take on *The Last Temptation of Christ* (1988), a project that had been a passion of his for some time. It was released in 1988 to a mixture of controversy and praise. He received an Academy Award nomination for Best Director for the film.

In 1990, he directed *Goodfellas*. It was nominated for six Academy Awards and was considered one of his best movies. In 1991, Scorsese got divorced from De Fina and started to work on *Cape Fear*. The film was a remake of J. Lee Thompson's 1961 movie of the same name which was based on the 1958 novel *The Executioners* by John D. MacDonald. The success of Scorsese's version of the film led him to do a period adaptation of Edith Wharton's novel *The Age of Innocence* (1993). It was a personal project, but it didn't fare well at the box office. Scorsese shook off the criticism and went on to make *Casino* (1995). It received mixed reviews but was a financial success. Next, he worked on *Kundun* (1997), about the life of the fourteenth Dalai Lama, Tenzin Gyatso. In 1999, Scorsese married Helen Schermerhorn Morris, and they had a daughter.

In 2002, Scorsese directed the $100 million epic *Gangs of New York*. It was the first of several collaborations he would do with Leonardo DiCaprio. Scorsese received his first Golden Globe Award for Best Director for the film. The movie also received ten Academy

Award nominations. Soon after, Scorsese started work on the film *The Aviator* (2004). It was a true story about Howard Hughes and featured DiCaprio in the lead role. The movie was nominated for six Golden Globe Awards and received eleven Academy Award nominations. It wound up winning three Golden Globes and five Oscars. A few years later, Scorsese and DiCaprio worked together again on the film adaptation of *Shutter Island* (2010), which became Scorsese's highest-grossing film.

In the 2010s, Scorsese started to work in new media forms beginning with directing the pilot episode of the HBO series *Boardwalk Empire*. After that, he directed the 3-D adventure movie *Hugo* (2011), which was nominated for eleven Academy Awards, winning five, and won two BAFTAs. For his next project, Scorsese teamed once again with DiCaprio on the biographical dark comedy *The Wolf of Wall Street* (2013). The movie was nominated for five Academy Awards. Scorsese widened his scope even more after that and became executive producer for *The Third Side of the River* (2014) and *Revenge of the Green Dragons* (2014). He continues to be an influential force in the film industry today.

Kris Kristofferson and Ellen Burstyn in a scene from *Alice Doesn't Live Here Anymore*

CHAPTER 3:

The Characters in Alice Doesn't Live Here Anymore

Alice (Graham) Hyatt

As a child in Monterey, California, Alice loves going to see movie musicals. Afterward, she stands under the locust trees in her neighborhood and sings the songs she has heard in the shows. Her love of singing prompts her to want to be a vocalist. When she is 19, Alice gets a job singing at the Rathburn Hotel in Monterey for a few days. Soon after, she meets navy man Donald Hyatt. They date briefly and then get married.

After their wedding, they move to Socorro, New Mexico. A couple years later, Alice gives birth to their son, Tommy. Donald isn't that talkative during their marriage and grows less communicative as time goes by. His reticence prompts Alice to develop a closer bond with Tommy than with him. When Donald doesn't speak during meals, Alice strikes up conversations with an imaginary friend in an attempt to prompt him to engage. It doesn't work, which leaves Alice feeling ever more disconnected from him.

By the time Alice is thirty-five, there is a deep divide between her and Donald. Even so, she remains committed to him. After his unexpected death, Alice is forced to examine her life and determine

Alice . . .

what she wants to do. She had been happy in Monterey and decides to return there and pursue her dream of becoming a singer.

Alice was a decent singer. She inherently connected with the songs she sang and brought out the meaning within them for her audience. She has been away from singing for so long, however, that it takes a lot of practice to build up her confidence again. She is determined to make it happen, though, and she does.

On the way back to Monterey with Tommy, Alice runs out of money. This forces her to stop briefly in Albuquerque so she can earn money to get her and Tommy back on the road. During that time, Alice gets a job as a lounge singer and starts seeing an eager young man named Ben. He fulfills her sexually where Donald was unable to because he focused only on his own needs. Not long into their courtship, Alice learns that Ben is a womanizer and has a violent temper. This is a big turnoff to her. She and Tommy hit the road fast to get away from him.

By the time they reach Tucson, their money has run out again. Alice is forced to take a job as a waitress at Mel and Ruby's Café. She sees this as a real low point in her life. Alice meets a rancher named David there. They start dating. She is embarrassed by Tommy's crude language when the three of them are together because she fears that David will not think highly of her skills as a mother. She finds her coworker Florence's rough personality and language to be repulsive. Once she gets to know Florence, though, they become friends. In the end, Alice decides to stay in Tucson and sets up a new life for her and Tommy there.

Tommy Hyatt

Tommy is Alice's eleven-year-old son. He is rebellious, blunt, and likes to play jokes to get attention. From a young age, Alice speaks to him like an adult, which leads him to respond to her in the same manner.

One of Tommy's teachers calls him "motormouth" because he talks so much. Tommy's closest friend is Bea's son Harold. They get along decently, but Tommy is jealous of Harold because he has a guitar.

Tommy initially doesn't have a lot of faith that Alice can make a living as a singer. As her vocals improve through practice, his confidence in her ability grows as well. Once they are on the road, Tommy becomes restless from being cooped up in the motel while Alice is out all day looking for work. To curb his boredom, he makes obscene phone calls to random women and watches TV for hours on end. Alice manages to save money and buy him a guitar. It means a lot to him. He starts to practice when he is alone and longs to learn as much about the instrument as he can.

After Tommy and his mother arrive in Arizona, his life changes. He is thrilled to be able to take guitar lessons there. He meets two friends: the young rebel Audrey and the fatherly rancher David, who has eyes for Alice. Audrey takes Tommy on daring, antisocial adventures, including several shoplifting jaunts and drinking binges. David gives him the opportunity to ride horses, practice the guitar with him, and learn about various aspects of farm life.

Tommy appreciates the new family that forms when Alice and David start to date. Their relationship brings a degree of stability into his life that hadn't existed in a long time. Despite some friction in their relationship, Tommy, Alice, and David's bond has all the right ingredients to enable Tommy to someday become a productive, responsible citizen.

Donald Hyatt

Don is a thirty-six-year-old navy veteran. He is Alice's husband and works as a deliveryman for the Coca-Cola company in Socorro. He likes to eat lamb and watch *The Dean Martin Show*. During his marriage to Alice, he becomes less and less talkative. His lack of communication creates a major breakdown in their relationship. He is more concerned about his needs than his family's. He frequently grows tired of his son, Tommy, and threatens to hit him if he won't stop talking. He is killed in an accident while on the job.

Bea

Bea is a housewife in her mid-thirties. She lives near Alice in Socorro. They are close friends for most of the time Alice lives there. Bea is married to Ken. They have one child, a son named Harold, who is about Tommy's age. Bea enjoys bowling and is in the same league as Alice. She never misses an episode of the soap opera *All My Children*. She is in love with the character of Jeff on the show. Bea is a bit dull but is a good friend to Alice.

Ben Eberhardt

Ben is twenty-seven years old, good-looking, and knows the effect he has on women. He fills bullet cases with powder for a living. He can be loving yet flip into a violent rage when he feels he is losing control of his life. His wife, Rita, is pregnant with their second child. Their first child, George, gets sick a lot. Even though Ben is married, he is lonely, which drives him to seek the affection of other women. When he discovers that Rita has told Alice that they are married, he fears that Alice will no longer want to see him. Ben's insecurity about the situation sends him into a rage. His outburst is an unfortunate pattern that is sure to repeat as he moves forward in life.

Mel Sharples

Mel is single, has heavy eyebrows, and wears a sailor's cap. Hair covers his forearms and sprouts from under the neck of the clean, white

T-shirts that are part of his everyday attire. He has a gruff demeanor yet backs off when his employees are in a crisis. Mel and his grandmother ran Mel and Ruby's Café until her death eleven years before Alice arrives in town. He took over the business after her death and has run it ever since. The restaurant does good business and is packed with customers every day.

Florence Jean Castleberry

Florence is a fifty-two-year-old, physically fit blond. She likes to use crude expressions that she picked up from her father. She wanted to become a dancer when she was growing up, but her legs were too short, so she wound up working as a waitress instead.

Florence is married with two children: a boy and a girl. Her daughter needs $4,000 worth of dental work, but Florence doesn't have money to pay for it. Her husband sits at home all day watching TV. He stopped speaking to her when JFK was assassinated but has never told her why. All Florence knows is that he isn't crazy about her working at Mel and Ruby's Café. She has been employed at the restaurant for over eleven years before Alice starts working there. Despite her gruff exterior, she is sensitive to other people's problems. This is brought out when she and Alice become friends.

Audrey Prinson

Audrey is a rebellious teenage tomboy. Her real name is Doris, but she prefers to be called Audrey. She meets Tommy when they take guitar lessons together. She thinks Tucson is filled with weird people and likes to point out examples of it to Tommy. She claims that her mother is a prostitute who turns tricks after 3:00 p.m. at the Ramada Inn every day. Her father left them two years ago. Audrey didn't get along with him. He used to whip her with a belt.

Alice . . .

Most days Audrey spends alone without parental supervision. She craves attention from her mother but never receives it. In an effort to get her mother to notice her and to curb her own boredom, Audrey becomes adept at shoplifting. She brings Tommy along sometimes. Other times, they hang out at Audrey's house and get drunk on cheap wine. Audrey and Tommy are eventually caught shoplifting and taken into custody. Audrey's mother picks her up from a juvenile facility afterward but doesn't show any concern for her, which can only serve to increase the distance in their relationship going forward.

Vera
Vera is a quiet, lanky waitress who has worked at Mel and Ruby's Café for several years. She gets frazzled easily during the lunch and dinner rushes. This leads her to get customers' orders mixed up. She rarely speaks except to patrons of the restaurant.

Vera enjoys reading suspense novels, including *The Bride Screamed Murder* by Terry Molloy. She is thoughtful and lets Tommy borrow her copy of the book. When she doesn't take the bus to and from work, her burly, mustached father, Duke, drives her on the back of his motorcycle. Vera has a brother who Florence thinks is a good catch because he is sexy and has a new Chrysler.

David Barrie
David is a thirty-eight-year-old loner who owns a large farm a few miles outside of Tucson. He is quiet and rugged and wears blue work shirts and jeans all the time. He worked for six years to save enough money to purchase his farm. He was married with two children at that time. Soon after he acquired the farm, his wife left with the children and divorced him. She claimed that they both had grown to

want different things in life and from their relationship. That made them incompatible.

Two years after David's divorce, Alice and Tommy come to town. David meets them while eating at Mel and Ruby's Café. He and Tommy become fast friends. They enjoy doing father-and-son activities together, including playing the guitar and singing. David shows Tommy how to ride and shoe a horse and how to milk a cow as well.

David is attracted to Alice and gets her to take notice of him when he picks Tommy up to do things together. He doesn't like the bad language and unruliness that Tommy sometimes exhibits. His dislike of Tommy's behavior comes to a head one day during an argument that turns physical. Ultimately, everything is ironed out. David shows his commitment to Alice by agreeing to set his farm aside and help her pursue her singing career. His selflessness in this regard means a lot to her and helps strengthen their relationship.

CHAPTER 4:

Alice Doesn't Live Here Anymore— Fan Quiz

1. What is the name of the restaurant where Alice works as a waitress?
    a. Mel's Place
    b. Mel and Ruby's Café
    c. Mel's Diner

2. What is the opening scene in *Alice Doesn't Live Here Anymore* based on?

3. Alice's husband, Donald, works for the _____ Company.

4. How does Donald die?

5. Who actually plays the piano while Alice sings in the bars?
    a. Duke Ellington
    b. A studio musician
    c. Ellen Burstyn

Alice...

6. What does Ben do for a living?

7. True or false: Mel and Ruby's Café is in Phoenix, Arizona.

8. How far does Alice live from Mel and Ruby's Café?

9. True or false: Alice meets David at the laundromat.

10. What does Mel's tattoo say?

11. Does Mel employ others besides Alice, Flo, and Vera in the restaurant?

12. What does Alice's brother call her?
    a. Al
    b. Alison
    c. Alicia

13. How old is Tommy?

14. What picture hangs on David's living room wall?

15. _____ is advertised on a poster in the diner.

CHAPTER 5:

Creating the TV Series Alice

AFTER THE SUCCESS OF *Alice Doesn't Live Here Anymore*, TV producer David Susskind hired Robert Getchell to adapt the movie into a sitcom. In creating the series, Getchell made several modifications to the story to make it work better for television. Instead of Alice wanting to return to Monterey, California, as she does in the film, in the series she heads to Hollywood with Tommy to find work as a singer. The location of the show was transferred from Tucson to Phoenix. In the series, a lack of money and car trouble force Alice to set up life in Phoenix and get a job waitressing at Mel and Ruby's Café. The name of the restaurant was changed to Mel's Diner starting in episode two of the first season. Alice speaks favorably about her deceased husband to Tommy in the sitcom—a contrast with the film, in which she loves her husband but thinks him difficult to connect with on an emotional level.

After Getchell completed the pilot script for *Alice*, casting got underway. Susskind's fellow producer, Bruce Johnson, reached out to Ellen Burstyn about reprising her role in the series only to learn that she wasn't interested. This prompted him to search for another actress to play the part. Linda Lavin had worked for CBS for several years by that point, most recently being featured in a few episodes of

Alice...

Barney Miller. Her contract with the network was about to expire. CBS executives Perry Lafferty and Alan Shayne didn't want to lose her, so they gave her a chance to try out for the role.

During Lavin's audition, Lafferty, Shayne, and Johnson were drawn to how she could show two emotions at the same time. She was able to grin yet be filled with concern. Her ability to do this assured them that she was the right actress for the part. They hired her soon after. Lavin found the series' concept engaging, especially how Alice and Flo bonded and supported one another. Such a dynamic hadn't been explored on TV before. Lavin saw Alice and Flo as survivors. Their relationship was an important part of the success of the show. Lavin longed to gain a deeper understanding of her character. She had never been a waitress or had a child, so she conducted some research to help her understand Alice's motives. In the process, she spoke with feminist Gloria Steinem about women in the workforce. Their discussion led Lavin to conclude that Alice's first responsibility was to support her son and herself. She planned to play the character in an authentic and dignified manner.

With Lavin confirmed for the lead role, the producers focused on securing actors for the other main parts. Audrey Mass, a coproducer on the film, contacted Vic Tayback about reprising his role as Mel. Tayback had doubts about the series. Not long after their discussion, Mass died. Tayback felt that would be the end of the show. However, Warner Bros. continued to pursue him. Tayback eventually agreed to do the pilot if the network would meet his salary requirements. They declined at first but ultimately accepted his terms. Once contracts were signed, Tayback became concerned that the other characters would overshadow his. These fears were quickly put to rest when he realized that his role was a pivotal one in the series.

Diane Ladd was asked to recreate the role of Flo on the show. She had to turn the offer down, though, because she was under contract with NBC. This forced producers to search for another actress to play the character. When Polly Holliday's agent called her to say she was under consideration for the part, Holliday thought back on her brief experience working as a waitress at a Howard Johnson's in New York City. It was the most difficult work she had ever done and gave her a deep respect for both the profession and the character of Flo. She decided to incorporate her knowledge into her portrayal when she auditioned. She colored her hair and punched up her Alabama accent in an effort to secure the part. The producers loved what she did and hired her immediately.

When Beth Howland auditioned for the role of Vera, she thought the part was challenging to play because there wasn't much substance to latch onto. The producers were drawn to her scattered portrayal of the character, which made them certain she was right for the role. Howland was thrilled to be cast. She had never worked as a waitress, so she went to coffee shops and observed the environment. She understood that the show centered on Lavin, but it took a strong performance by each member of the main cast to make the series work. She looked forward to the experience.

After Alfred Lutter agreed to reprise his role as Tommy, casting was complete. At that point, members of the production staff went to Phoenix in search of a business that had a unique sign that the show could feature. They spotted one outside a restaurant called Chris' Diner. The owner, Christine Harris, was asked whether she would change the name on the sign to Mel's. She agreed. The footage in the opening credits consists of scenes specifically shot to narrate how Alice wound up working in the diner. Clips from various episodes are also included. Toward the end of season two, the diner sign was incorporated into the opening as well.

Lyricists Alan and Marilyn Bergman and composer David Shire were hired to write the show's theme song, "There's a New Girl in Town." The track tells of the emotional journey that led Alice to Phoenix and Mel's Diner. Various versions of the song were sung by Lavin throughout the course of the series. The Bergmans were a prolific songwriting team that had created theme songs for shows including *Maude, Good Times,* and *Brooklyn Bridge.* They were also lyricists on Barbra Streisand's film *Yentl* (1983) and her thirty-sixth studio album, *Walls* (2018). Shire had composed music for TV series including *Tales of the Unexpected* (1977), *Flying High* (1978), and *Darkroom* (1981).

After the pilot was shot, executives weren't convinced that the series would succeed. They ordered a test run of four additional episodes to give the show a chance to develop and requested that Lutter be recast. They thought he was too old to play the part on an ongoing basis. Philip McKeon, a child actor from New York, and Vic Tayback's son, Christopher, were top contenders for the part. The role ultimately went to McKeon. Being cast as Tommy was a life-changing experience for him and his family. They gave up their life in New York and moved to California to support his career. McKeon worked on *Alice* for the next nine years. He found it to be a wonderful experience. From his perspective, his fellow actors were like surrogate parents to him. They were there when he needed to talk and even threw him birthday parties. Tayback took Christopher and McKeon to baseball games, horseback riding, and later to the track to bet on horses.

As the initial episodes of the series moved into production, producer Bruce Johnson hired Arnold Kane as the sole staff writer. Kane wrote some of the scripts for the first season; independent writers hired on a per-episode basis wrote the rest. In addition to scripts, Kane wrote bios for each character to help the actors and independent writers craft their characters and scripts.

Once the additional four episodes of the show had been completed, Shayne and other network executives watched them. They found the new installments to be dull and uninspired. CBS didn't want to give up on *Alice*, though, and granted Shayne time to address the network's concerns. Shayne decided to bring in TV comedy director John Rich to help invigorate the series. Rich requested that all singing be cut from the show. He also wanted every scene to be a battle between the characters. The cast found this approach challenging to deal with because they longed to have comradery between them. Rich treated each episode like a theater performance and told the actors they had one chance to get it right in front of the studio audience. While the absence of singing didn't help the show, Rich's philosophy of live performance energized the actors' delivery. In the end, Shayne wasn't satisfied with the results of Rich's approach and looked for others to help craft the series.

By this point in production, the cast had become concerned about the show's future. Howland found the character of Vera to be clumsy and unintelligent. It made her feel bad to play the role. She wasn't sure how such a person could keep her job. She had always seen Vera as the most dedicated worker in the diner. She might live in her own dimension, but she was not stupid. Howland expressed her concerns to the producers. In an attempt to flesh out the part, the show's creators had a writer develop an episode entitled "Good Night, Sweet Vera." It centered on Vera's trying to commit suicide. Although the episode was nominated for an Emmy, it did little to bring depth to Vera's character or ease Howland's mind about portraying the role.

Tayback had similar apprehensions about his character. All Mel did was yell. Tayback talked with the producers about having more than only one emotion to play. Despite their conversations, no changes were made. Reviews of the series emphasized the show's limits. The December 18, 1976 edition of *TV Guide* described the writing on the series as "gagwriting . . . to show off the writers, not the characters." Network executives, including Shayne, were disheartened by the ongoing issues associated with the show and continued to search for ways to get it on a solid track.

Holliday made it a point not to see *Alice Doesn't Live Here Anymore*, because she wanted her portrayal of Flo to be original to her and not influenced by the movie. She used what she called "puzzle solving" to understand her character. This entailed reviewing the script and constructing a background for her character based on it. The dialogue in the *Alice* scripts stated that Flo was born in the South. Holliday combined different traits and attitudes from people she knew growing up in Alabama to craft Flo's persona. To help her look the part, she donned a wig and chewed gum. The dialogue her character spoke in the script made it clear that Flo didn't have much education. She had dropped out of school to enter a marriage that didn't last. She had remarried twice since then. Her lack of education made her question her abilities. She took the waitress job because it was what her education level afforded her. She compensated for her lack of self-confidence by masking her doubt with a strong exterior. Her mothering nature toward Alice suggested that Flo was the oldest sibling in her family. Holliday had seen women like Flo working as cashiers and at truck stops and understood them. They tended to be engaging and extroverted and had great senses of humor. The writers on *Alice* found the backstory Holliday created for her character to be rich with detail. They incorporated most of it into episodes of the show, which helped to make the series more engaging overall. Even with Holliday's contributions, the program had additional issues that needed to be worked out.

When Holliday first encountered the phrase "kiss my grits" in an *Alice* script, she questioned why Flo was saying it and what it meant.

The writers had created it, and it was not an authentic expression from the South. The audience loved the phrase, however, which led Holliday to embrace it.

Studio audience tickets for the August 11, 1982 and June 21, 1983 tapings of *Alice (Photo provided by David Barry Plunkett.)*

Despite the problems the series' creators faced, the first season deals with important issues, including stereotyping and valuing others. In the episode "Alice Gets a Pass," Mel's longtime friend Jack Newhouse, a former football player who retired to make Italian Westerns, comes for a visit. He and Alice go out a few times. He eventually reveals to her that he is gay. As his time in Phoenix comes to a close, he and Alice affirm their friendship. Later, in a mother-and-son talk, Tommy is surprised to learn about Jack's sexual orientation. Tommy's peers had described gay men to be different from what he has found Jack to be. The experience helps Tommy understand that the misconceptions he heard are not true. He winds up valuing Jack as an individual.

The series was taped in front of a studio audience on Tuesday evenings on a soundstage at Warner Bros. Studios in Burbank. Studio audience tickets stated that more tickets were distributed than the studio had the capacity to hold, which meant people interested in being in the audience needed to arrive early to be sure they were admitted. According to *Alice* enthusiast David Barry Plunkett, there were two types of tickets: VIP and general admission. Celebrities and family and friends of the cast received the VIP tickets. The public received the general admission tickets. VIP ticketholders were seated first, followed by as many general ticket holders as could fit into the remaining seats.

An emcee welcomed the audience prior to the taping of each episode. He went over some basic rules and then introduced the producer and director. The cast then came out one at a time through the appropriate bathroom door on the diner set and waved to the audience. Writers were on set during each taping in case a joke needed to be revised at the last minute. After an episode was recorded, the audience was dismissed. The cast remained and did retakes of small moments the director thought needed to be redone. They also recorded close-up reaction shots.

During the first season, four sets of producers came and went as the network attempted to work out the kinks in the series. Cast members were the last to know about these changes, which left them feeling uncertain about the direction the show was taking. After production for season one came to a close, producers told McKeon that he would no longer appear on the series. Over the summer, producer

Chris Hayward brought the program back into production for several episodes. These installments of the series are set entirely in the diner and feature only Mel and the waitresses. Mel wears a blue shirt in them instead of his standard white T-shirt. This approach did little to invigorate the show and was quickly scrapped.

The first season drew a large female following because it was one of the few programs that depicted women's lives in the workforce. Many concerns that were at the heart of the women's movement were dramatized in episodes of the show. Key figures in the movement took note of this and invited Lavin to speak at their events. The invitations took her by surprise, but she embraced the importance of the issues at hand. She eventually became a leader for the Commission on Working Women and attended a rally in front of the White House in Lafayette Park, where she spoke about equal pay for equal work. The Commission on Working Women brought its message to presidential candidates at the time, requesting that they end gender-based job segregation and equalize pay. They encouraged candidates to address daycare needs for working women, battle sexual harassment and bullying at work, and enhance Social Security benefits for women. Due to the work of women's advocacy groups and television series like *Alice*, advancements were made in the depiction of women on TV and in the treatment of women in the workforce.

As season two got under way, Shayne had one of his team members ask comedy veterans Madelyn Davis and Bob Carroll Jr., whether they would be interested in coming on board as the new producers of the series. Davis and Carroll had been longtime writers for Lucille Ball. They started with her on her 1948 radio series *My Favorite Husband* and wrote for all her TV series and specials, including *I Love Lucy*, *The Lucy Show*, *Here's Lucy*, *Lucy Calls the President*, and *Life with Lucy*. They readily accepted the network's offer. Before getting started, CBS requested that Davis and Carroll write a sample script for the series to verify that they were a good fit. They agreed to do so and wrote a teleplay entitled "A Semi-Merry Christmas" as their sample. Network executives wound up disliking the script, which surprised Davis and Carroll. Davis reached out to Shayne and asked what they should do. They thought the script was good. Shayne wanted them involved with the show. He discussed the situation with the studio and then told Davis and Carroll that their script would be used. He warmly welcomed them aboard as the series' new producers.

Madelyn Davis and Bob Carroll Jr., the producers of *Alice* from season two to season nine

When Davis and Carroll took over production of *Alice*, several episodes of the second season had already been shot. Studio executives hadn't found any of them engaging. The new season was set to premiere in five weeks. Davis and Carroll immediately sprang into action, assembling a strong team of writers to get production on track. These writers included industry veterans Arthur Marx, Robert Fisher, Vic Rauseo, and Linda Morris.

Davis and Carroll reviewed every aspect of the series and searched for ways to make the show stronger and more enjoyable for the audience. The characters were the show's heart. Davis and Carroll talked with the main cast members about their impressions of the parts they played. Tayback wanted his character to have more depth. Mel was tough, but underneath he cared. Davis and Carroll understood his concerns and brought out a softer side in Mel, which made him more endearing to the audience. Tayback was pleased to see this change.

Davis and Carroll felt that Vera's character was one-dimensional, so they looked for ways to flesh her out. Carroll told *TV Guide* in 1979 that there were traces of Gracie Allen, Edith Bunker, and Stan Laurel in Vera. He and Davis worked to safeguard, not parody, the childlike quality in her character. They toned down her slapstick tendencies and gave her more depth. She even began to stand up to Mel when he tried to dominate the waitresses. The studio audience showed their approval of this change by clapping when she took a stand, affirming that the series was moving in a positive direction. Vera's self-confidence grew so much that she even played poker against local card-game aficionado Mel and won. That episode was Howland's favorite because it showed that there really was substance within Vera's character.

According to Davis's 2005 book, *Laughing with Lucy: My Life with*

Alice...

America's Leading Lady of Comedy, by the time *Alice* hit the airwaves, things had eased up a bit in TV broadcasting. Shows could include "three hells and a damn" in an episode if the writers deemed them necessary to the telling of the story. They had to be peppered in throughout the script, though. This was a major advance from the 1950s, when the word "pregnant" wasn't considered acceptable for on-air use.

Davis and Carroll decided to update the diner set to make it more appealing. They started by adding brown stools with backs at the counter. The door previously marked "restrooms" was now the women's room. The room that had "private" written across it was now the men's room. A store room was added behind the kitchen. There was no longer a window over the grill. The pay phone that had been behind the counter was moved to the wall near the women's room. The plaza sidewalk outside the diner's main entrance became a street with a parking lot adjacent to it.

Davis and Carroll brought Marc Daniels in to be the series' primary director. The trio had worked together on *I Love Lucy*. Daniels was exacting about his process and made sure that everything that went onscreen adhered to real-world logic. In the first episode he directed, a customer ordered breakfast on one page of the script and paid their bill on the next. He altered this scenario so there was a plausible reason that the customer would do such a thing. Although other directors worked on the series, Davis and Carroll gave Daniels the most challenging scripts because they knew he would pay attention to detail and make every moment in the episode work.

During the series, Davis was able to work with many actors she admired. In season two, for instance, she brought George Burns in for the episode entitled "Oh, George Burns!" It was one of Davis's personal favorites. The episode was inspired by Burns's recent hit movie *Oh, God!* (1977). He was in his late eighties at the time yet still had a great aptitude for remembering his lines. On the flip side, Davis mentioned in *Laughing with Lucy* that memorization didn't come easy for Tayback. Even though he ran lines each week with a neighbor, he still had to write his dialogue on food props throughout the set, including vegetables and hamburger rolls. In one episode, he forgot and ate his lines. Despite this, Davis found him to be a wonderful actor to work with.

Davis and Carroll instilled in every writer who worked on the series their unique style of comedy writing, which they had honed since working on *My Favorite Husband*. Each episode of *Alice* needed to build to a big-block comedy scene at the end that contained sustained physical humor. This was Davis and Carroll's trademark. It brought great success to every show they worked on.

Beginning in season two, the writing process on *Alice* became more structured. Each individual writer or writing team would present five or six story ideas to Davis and Carroll, who in turn gave the writers feedback. The writers then had a week to outline a script. Davis and Carroll gave feedback on the outline. The writers were expected to have a draft of the script completed within the next two weeks. Revisions followed. Once a script was ready, it was scheduled for production.

An average production started with the main cast doing a table reading of the script. The writers received notes regarding some story aspects and jokes that weren't working well. By this point in the script development process, feedback was generally minor. Over the course of the next few days, the director would block out each scene with the actors. This was followed by a costume and makeup session as well as dry runs of the episode with the camera operators. When major special effects were used on the show, like the wrecking ball that destroys the diner in one episode, the effect would only be done once, during the actual taping of the episode.

Alice...

Many late-seventies sitcoms were recorded before a studio audience. "Sweetening" was used in postproduction to punch up the laughter. Davis and Carroll always used big jokes in *Alice* that got strong laughs from the studio audience, so the "sweetening" process wasn't used much during their tenure on the series.

Linda Lavin, Beth Howland, Polly Holliday, and Vic Tayback in a scene from episode 50 (3.2), "Car Wars"

As the third season began, Vera got a boyfriend and was given the last name Gorman. Howland was glad to see her character continue to gain more definition. She felt that these changes made Vera more palatable to play and more relatable to the audience.

Davis and Carroll increased the number of celebrity guest appearances during this season in an effort to grow their audience. Guests included comedian Martha Raye, who portrayed Mel's mother in the episode entitled "Mel Grows Up." The staff wanted to dress her in glasses, but she declined, saying that eyes were everything when it came to comedy and she didn't want to hide hers. She was right. The audience loved her quirkiness. Raye was so engaging that the producers invited her back a dozen times over the course of the series to reprise her role. They even found ways to highlight Raye's talents as a singer in several episodes.

Beth Howland, Linda, Lavin, and Polly Holliday in a scene from episode 84 (4.12), "Good Buddy Flo"

During season four, the show's use of special effects increased. The episode entitled "Good Buddy Flo" is a solid example of this. The script called for Flo to test drive a truck while Alice and Vera sat next to her for moral support. Flo ultimately discovers that she can't stop the truck and is forced to crash it through the front of the diner. During rehearsal, Holliday drove the truck around the studio lot to get comfortable with it while the production staff created a

Alice...

breakaway version of the entrance wall to the diner. Lavin was apprehensive about crashing through the set wall. Davis was accustomed to testing stunts for Lucille Ball on *I Love Lucy*, so she agreed to don a wig and waitress uniform and do the stunt for Lavin during the taping. Lavin ultimately decided to perform it herself. The stunt went off without a hitch. The crash shocked the audience and received a lot of laughs.

Another important change that began in the fourth season was that Lavin started to direct two episodes of the show per year. She wound up directing ten in all. During many of the episodes she directed, her character would appear briefly at the start of the show and then leave. This enabled Lavin to focus on directing instead of acting. She was one of just a few women directing for TV at the time. Most female directors were unable to sustain careers in the male dominated field due to gender inequality issues. Lavin's directorial work on the show led her to serve on the Directors Guild of America's women's committee, which focused on increasing opportunities for women in the profession.

The opening credits during this season began to feature a clip with Tayback, McKeon, Holliday, Howland, and Lavin sitting in a bathtub. This was shot specifically for the credits and was a riff on the situation from the episode entitled "Cabin Fever". The scene in the actual episode features Mel's girlfriend, Marie (Victoria Carroll), in the bathtub instead of McKeon.

Holliday left the show midway through the season to star in the spin-off series *Flo*. Davis and Carroll wanted to replace her with another Southern waitress. By that point, Diane Ladd's contract with NBC had expired. Davis and Carroll brought her in to originate the role of hearty Southerner Belle Dupree. Belle had worked as a waitress for Mel in the past and had come to town to pursue a career as a singer-songwriter. When that didn't pan out, she started working as a waitress at the diner.

In the fifth season, the series celebrated two milestones. The first was that cast member Philip McKeon turned sixteen. The second was the show's hundredth episode. After the taping of the hundredth episode concluded, the studio held a party to celebrate both occasions. According to a December 1, 1980, article in *People* magazine, the producers went all out for the celebration, ordering duck pâté, shrimp omelets, and chocolate cream cake from Rococo, a well-known, high-end caterer in Los Angeles.

That same season, Davis and Carroll had the unusual opportunity to do a casting call for guard dogs for the episode "Dog Day Evening." In the episode, Mel is concerned about security at the diner, so he hires dogs to watch it overnight. At one point, Dobermans were auditioned. Their trainer had them act on cue. He told Davis and Carroll that the dogs could wear false teeth to look more threatening if necessary. Davis and Carroll had never heard of such a thing for dogs. Ultimately, German Shepherds were hired, and no false teeth were used.

In 1981, Diane Ladd won a Golden Globe Award for her portrayal of Belle in the series. Despite this, she decided to leave the show because she felt that her part hadn't evolved as she hoped it would. Her final appearance consisted of one scene in an episode in which Belle calls the diner and tells her coworkers that she has taken a job in Nashville as a backup singer.

With the third waitress role once again open, Davis and Carroll started looking for a replacement. When Celia Weston was hired for the part, she didn't want to come across as a copy of Belle or Flo. She told Warner Bros. that she had an idea about the character she wanted to portray. It would be based on a fictitious Southerner, Verlene Mahaffey, that she invented while playing with her siblings as a child. The producers were receptive to the idea. They named her character Jolene and agreed to base her on Verlene. Lavin and Howland were extremely welcoming and supportive of Weston. They even had flowers delivered to her after her first show. Weston went on to appear in ninety episodes of the series—the same number Holliday had been in.

Beth Howland, Celia Weston, and Donald O'Connor in a scene from episode 118 (6.2), "Guinness on Tap"

As the series progressed, the makeup of the staff became more diverse, with women employed as camera slates, performers, directors, and production assistants. Davis was proud to see this shift in the work environment. By coincidence, five people employed on the series were from Davis's home state of Indiana. These included a production assistant, a customer in the diner, the audience warm-up comedian, a carpenter, and actor Forrest Tucker, who guest-starred in an episode as Flo's father.

Tayback was dedicated to his role in the series. He didn't let the chronic pain he felt from a herniated disc in his back stop him from working. He had a hospital bed installed in his dressing room so he could rest when the cast was on break. Tayback was in so much pain during one episode that he was unable to stand. Still, he refused to stop working. His scenes were reblocked to make it easier for him to endure the discomfort. Whenever he appears in that episode, he is seen leaning on something, usually the diner counter. At another point, he spent nine days in the hospital for triple bypass surgery. He returned home with improved health, eager to get back to work on the show.

Alice ranked among the US's top fifteen most-watched TV series for the majority of its original run. As season seven drew to a close, the show fell to number forty-one. Davis and Carroll took note of this decline and looked for ways to reinvigorate the series. The following year they brought in new concepts, including having Lavin play a double role as Alice and Vera's landlord, Debbie Waldon, and having Vera get married. They also had a crossover episode with characters from CBS's *The Dukes of Hazzard* and had the cast of *Alice* get trapped in a hot air balloon in the sky. Davis and Carroll's innovations paid off as the show ranked as the twenty-fifth most-watched series by the end of its eighth season.

Alice...

As the eighth season came to a close, Lavin was ready for the series to end. The network wanted to renew the show for another season. Lavin didn't want to disappoint them, so she agreed to stay on for one more year. The other main cast members agreed that after another season it would be time to move on to other opportunities.

During season nine, *Alice* fell to number fifty-eight in the ratings. Despite this drop, the episodes produced were filled with some wonderful moments and covered important topics, including suicide, prejudice, and career transitions.

Philip McKeon and Linda Lavin in a scene from episode 191 (9.5), "Tommy's Lost Weekend"

The episode "Tommy's Lost Weekend" explored teenage drinking and how Tommy's social use of alcohol had turned into an addiction. It was a serious topic handled in a responsible yet humorous way. Behind the scenes, McKeon endured a four-hour-long process as makeup artists cemented a Mohawk-like wig to his head for use in a scene in which Tommy's hair is revealed to have been "altered" by a fraternity member. That episode was nominated for an Emmy Award.

The final episode of the series featured an exciting new beginning for each of the main characters. In it, Vera announces that she is pregnant. Jolene terminates her employment at the diner so she can open a beauty parlor. Alice gets a job as a singer and is about to move to Nashville. Mel sells the diner to a developer who plans to turn the property into a parking lot. As a going-away present, Mel gives each of the waitresses a check for five thousand dollars—money derived from the profit he makes in selling the diner. The gift shows that Mel truly has a generous heart and cares about Alice, Vera, and Jolene.

Celia Weston, Philip McKeon, Linda Lavin, Beth Howland, and Vic Tayback on the set of *Alice* after the taping of the final episode, 202 (9.16), "Th-th-th-that's All Folks"

Alice...

Working on the last episode of the show was an emotional experience for the cast. Many of the performers had to hold back tears during rehearsal. Family and friends made up the bulk of the studio audience during the taping. They gave the cast members a standing ovation when they took their final bows.

By the time the series came to a close, all of the main actors had new projects lined up. Lavin, Howland, and Weston planned to refocus on their work in theater. Lavin also formed her own production company and planned to produce TV movies and series. McKeon, Tayback, and Kaplan continued to work in TV for years to come. For the rest of Lavin's life, she was recognized on the street for her portrayal of Alice. The series has aired in the UK, Germany, Russia, Spain, and Italy and been dubbed into German, Russian, Spanish, and Italian, showing that workforce issues relating to women have a universal reach.

Linda Lavin

CHAPTER 6:

The Cast of *Alice*

Linda Lavin *(Alice)*
Linda Lavin was born in Portland, Maine, in 1937. Music was a big part of her childhood. According to her mother, who had been an opera singer and hosted a local radio show, Lavin sang her first song, "Three Little Fishes," while still in her crib. When she was a child, her family moved to a suburb of Boston. Lavin's mother encouraged her to study to become a professional concert pianist. Although she was itching to act, Lavin focused on the piano until she was fifteen. While in high school, she spent each June, July, and August singing in the chorus of summer stock musicals in Camden, New Jersey.

After graduating from high school, Lavin wanted to pursue a career in show business, but her parents urged her to continue with her schooling before starting a career. She attended the College of William and Mary and majored in drama. During her freshman year, she was featured as Margot Mary Wendice in the school production of *Dial M for Murder* (1954). Lavin's appearance in the play was highlighted in the college newspaper because first-year students rarely got cast in lead roles.

Upon completing her degree, Lavin moved to New York City and worked as an office temp to support herself as she auditioned for stage roles. Since she didn't have an agent, she could only audition for the chorus. She tried out with hundreds of others at each audition, hoping for a break. During this time, she developed a nightclub act and performed in several intimate venues in Greenwich Village.

In 1962, Lavin was cast in the chorus of the Broadway musical *A Family Affair*, directed by Hal Prince. Prince took note of her during rehearsals and gave her a speaking role in the show. Soon after, Lavin made her television debut in *The Doctors and the Nurses*. In 1966, she was featured in the Broadway musical *It's a Bird . . . It's a Plane . . . It's Superman*. Lavin played the girlfriend of Clark Kent's rival: gossip columnist Max Mencken. She sang "You've Got Possibilities" by Charles Strouse and Lee Adams in the show, which became a hit. In 1967, Lavin received an Outer Critics Circle award for her performance in the off-Broadway play *Little Murders*. She was then cast in the stage drama *Cop-Out* (1969), on the set of which she met her husband, costar Ron Leibman. This was followed by a lead part in Neil Simon's *Last of the Red Hot Lovers* (1969).

By the early 1970s, Lavin wanted to focus on television. It was a challenging time for her because she was a New York actress, and Hollywood producers weren't sure how to cast her. She was hired for a small role as a wisecracking neighbor in the pilot for the TV series *Jerry*. Though the show never advanced beyond the pilot, Lavin's work in it garnered her the attention of CBS programming chief Fred Silverman, who signed her to a development contract. When *Alice Doesn't Live Here Anymore* was adapted into the sitcom *Alice*, Lavin was cast in the lead role.

In 1979, Lavin received a Golden Globe Award for her work in the series. Her professional life was blossoming. However, her personal life had become strained. By 1980, her relationship with Leibman deteriorated to the point that the couple decided to divorce.

In 1982, Lavin met and married actor Kip Niven and assumed the role of stepmother to his two young children, whose mother had died in a car accident.

In 1985, the *Alice* series ended. Lavin returned to Broadway in Neil Simon's play *Broadway Bound* (1986), winning a Tony Award for Best Actress for her performance in the show. After that, she focused on film and TV, producing and acting in several movies, among them *A Place to Call Home* (1987) and *I Want to Go Home* (1989). In 1990, Lavin's relationship with Niven ended, and she filed for divorce. She charged him with mental and emotional cruelty, excessive spending of her wealth, and adultery. It was an emotional trial, but she was determined to reclaim her life and ultimately did.

In 1992, Lavin produced and starred as Edie Kurland in the sitcom *Room for Two*. In the show, Edie is a recent widow who decides to move from her hometown of Dayton, Ohio, to live near her daughter, Jill (Patricia Heaton), in New York City. Jill gets her mother a job on the talk show she produces. Each episode ends with some on-air words of wisdom from Edie, which philosophize about life and how viewers can grow by reflecting on their own experiences.

In 1997, Lavin founded the Linda Lavin Arts Foundation to support education in the arts. The organization worked to boost confidence in troubled urban teenage girls. Soon after, she returned to Broadway and starred as Mrs. Van Daan in *The Diary of Anne Frank* (1997) and Marjorie in *The Tale of the Allergist's Wife* (2000). She received Tony nominations for her work in both productions.

In 2005, Lavin married entertainer Steve Bakunas. They moved to Wilmington, North Carolina, and ran the Red Barn Studio Theatre. Both Lavin and her husband directed plays there each year. During this time, Lavin connected with musical director Billy Stritch and developed a cabaret show. Her five-piece band included Bakunas on drums, Daniel Fabricant on bass, and Stritch on piano. The show featured songs that told the story of Lavin's life and career. Songs included "The Boy From," a humorous tune featured in the off-Broadway show *The Mad Show* (1966); "Tacaremba la Tumba del Fuego Santa Maliga Zacatecas lo Onto del Sol y Cruz?," a comedic number with a rhythm reminiscent of "The Girl from Ipanema"; Steely Dan's "Between the Raindrops"; and Hugh Prestwood's "The Song Remembers When." Lavin's cabaret show started touring the US that year and played in venues from Los Angeles's Vitello's Supper Club and Catalina Bar & Grill to New York City's Café Carlyle and Birdland.

In 2010, Lavin was nominated for a Tony Award for her performance in the Broadway show *Collected Stories* (2010). Soon after, she and her husband transferred management of the Red Barn Studio Theatre to other theater professionals and moved to New York. In 2012, Lavin recorded *Possibilities*, an album featuring songs from her cabaret show. That same year, she starred on Broadway in *The Lyons* (2012) and received a Tony nomination for her work. In 2013, she was cast in the TV series *Sean Saves the World* as the lead character's mother. That was followed by a featured role in the sitcom *9JKL* and a part in the movie *Nancy Drew and the Hidden Staircase* (2019). As of 2019, she and her husband operate a bed and breakfast in upstate New York and continue to tour with her cabaret show.

Vic Tayback *(Mel)*
See page 20.

Beth Howland *(Vera)*
Elizabeth "Beth" Howland grew up in Brookline, Massachusetts. She was shy and overweight when she began first grade in a Catholic school. She liked the nuns there, however—particularly Sister Gretchen, who

gave her encouragement when she performed in school plays. During that time, Howland started to train as a singer and studied dance at the Hazel Boone Studio. She graduated from high school at the age of sixteen and moved to New York City with a ballet dancer friend to pursue work in the entertainment industry.

Beth Howland

Alice...

Not long after arriving in New York, Howland was cast in the Broadway production of *Once upon a Mattress* (1959). That was followed by *Bye Bye Birdie* (1960). While working in *Bye Bye Birdie*, Howland started dating fellow cast member Michael J. Pollard. They eventually got married and had a daughter named Holly.

In 1967, Pollard got a sudden dose of fame from his performance as C.W. Moss in the hit film *Bonnie and Clyde*. Success came so fast to him that it made Howland jealous. That put a strain on their marriage and contributed to their divorce.

In 1970, Howland was cast in the Broadway musical *Company*. She played Amy, a jittery bride-to-be, and sang the rapid-fire patter song "Getting Married Today." TV executive Alan Shayne attended a performance of the show. He was impressed by her work and invited her to Hollywood.

When Howland arrived in California, money was so tight that she had to bring her daughter everywhere she went, including to auditions, rehearsals, and tapings. She and Holly had a close relationship though, which made the day-to-day process of Howland's acting career a positive experience for both of them. In 1973, Howland landed a part in the sitcom *Love, American Style*. Additional work followed over the next few years, including roles in *The Mary Tyler Moore Show*, *Little House on the Prairie*, and *Eight is Enough*. Howland preferred dramatic parts but generally found herself being cast in comedic ones. She was glad to have the work and embraced the roles that came to her.

In 1976, Howland was under serious consideration for a role in a TV series pilot at CBS. After four on-camera screen tests, she didn't get the part, but network production executive Shayne kept his eye on her. A few months later, Howland auditioned for the role of Vera in *Alice*. She thought it was a challenging part to play because of its lack of definition. Producers loved her interpretation of the character and offered her the role.

Vera was the first major TV role that Howland played. She was glad to see the character evolve as the series progressed. The show brought her into the limelight and made her known to TV audiences throughout the country.

After *Alice* ended, Howland and fellow actor Jennifer Warren co-produced a documentary entitled *You Don't Have to Die* (1988). The piece centered on a boy's triumphant battle with cancer. It received an Academy Award for Best Documentary, Short Subjects. Howland then guest starred in several series including *Sabrina, the Teenage Witch*, *Chicken Soup for the Soul*, and *As Told by Ginger*.

During her career, Howland received four Golden Globe nominations for Best Performance by an Actress in a Supporting Role in a Series, Miniseries or Motion Picture Made for Television. In 2002, she retired from the entertainment business and married actor Charles Kimbrough. They lived a quiet and contented life together for over a decade. After a battle with lung cancer, Howland died on December 31, 2015. In respect for her wishes, no service was held in her honor.

Polly Holliday *(Flo)*

Polly Holliday was born in Jasper, Alabama, in 1937. She adored her father. He drove a truck for a living and took her on the road with him once per week. Her parents divorced when she was young. It hit her hard—as did the fact that her father remarried. Not having a consistent father-daughter relationship made Holliday withdraw into herself. She was rather shy in school and saw herself as a loner. She enjoyed music and focused on learning to play the piano during this time.

Alice...

After completing high school in the late 1950s, Holliday attended Alabama College at Montevallo and later obtained a degree in music from Florida State University. She had intended to become a music teacher. While in college, however, she discovered that she had a talent for acting and began to pursue it. After completing her education, she joined the Asolo Repertory Theater in Sarasota, Florida. Over the next seven seasons, she performed in more than sixty productions, including many Molière plays and Restoration comedies.

In 1973, Holliday moved to New York City. Theater producer Joseph Papp cast her in Alice Childress's play *Wedding Band* (1966) at the Public Theater. Afterward, she did television commercials to get by while looking for other acting roles. Her big break came when she was cast in the play *All over Town* (1974), written by Murray Schisgal and directed by Dustin Hoffman. The following year, Hoffman was involved with the film *All the President's Men* (1976). He introduced Holliday to Alan Shayne, who was handling casting for the movie. He gave her a role in the production.

A few months later, Holliday got an audition for the part of Flo in the sitcom *Alice*. By then, Shayne had become an executive with CBS. *Alice* was one of his first assignments with the network. Shayne and Bruce Johnson, the series' initial producer, loved Holliday's audition and immediately hired her for the role.

Holliday infused the character of Flo with qualities of people she had seen in diners when traveling with her father and with traits she had honed while playing the comedic characters at Asolo Rep. The richness she brought to the part helped endear her to television audiences. Playing the character was a milestone in her life and gave her career a considerable boost.

Despite her success, Holliday remained grounded. She lived in a modest apartment and drove a 1972 Chevrolet. She felt it was in good condition and so found no reason to get a new car. She shopped at the Los Angeles–based discount store Pic 'N' Save as well. She was not one to partake in the social side of Hollywood. She lived a modest life similar to how she was raised from her Depression-era mother and never married.

Polly Holliday

Alice...

After four seasons on *Alice*, the character of Flo received a spin-off series called *Flo*. According to the Nielsen ratings, *Flo* debuted as the number one most watched program during its first week on the air. The series finished in the top ten most watched programs of the season. Holliday was instrumental in the show's development and worked closely with the writers, producers, and directors to shape it. She was nominated for an Emmy for Outstanding Lead Actress in a Comedy Series for her portrayal of Flo. The series lasted for two seasons. Soon after it ended, Eileen Brennan, a lead actress in the television series *Private Benjamin*, was injured in a car accident, and Holliday was written into the series to play a role comparable to Brennan's until Brennan was able to return.

In 1984, Holliday was cast as the villainess Ruby Deagle in the hit film *Gremlins*. The movie's success brought her more work in Hollywood and eventually back to Broadway, where she played Big Mama in the 1990 revival of Tennessee Williams's *Cat on a Hot Tin Roof*. Holliday was nominated for a Tony Award for her performance in the play.

In 1995, Holliday played Momma Love in the television series *The Client*, which was based on the John Grisham novel and the screen adaptation by Robert Getchell. Holliday went on to feature as Lillian Patterson in the sitcom *Home Improvement*. She eventually retired from the entertainment business and settled into a quiet life outside the limelight.

Diane Ladd *(Belle)*
See page 17.

Celia Weston

Celia Weston *(Jolene)*

Celia Weston was born in Spartanburg, South Carolina, in 1951. As a child, she loved creating quirky characters and accents with her sister. Verlene Mahaffey, a woman with a thick Southern drawl, was her family's favorite of the characters she made up. Weston enjoyed playing Verlene for the family whenever possible.

Weston was athletic and lettered in field hockey and basketball in high school. She also wrote for the school newspaper and was a cheerleader. After graduating, Weston attended Salem College in North Carolina and pursued a degree in art and psychology.

Alice . . .

She eventually moved to New York City, where she was cast in a Westchester production of Woody Allen's *Play It Again Sam* (1969). She thought that the role would be her big break, but no acting work followed from it. She was forced to work as a cocktail waitress to support herself.

In 1977, Weston began to study acting with Uta Hagen and Herbert Berghof at HB Studio. In 1979, she made her Broadway debut in *Loose Ends*. The following year she was featured in Edward Albee's play *The Lady from Dubuque* (1980). The president of Warner Bros. television programming attended a performance of the show and was interested in auditioning her for a part in the series *Alice*. Soon after, Weston was flown out to Hollywood to audition and was cast in the role of Jolene. This was her first major part in a national TV program.

After *Alice* went off the air, Weston guest-starred on a variety of TV shows. In 1995, she appeared on Broadway in Tennessee Williams's *Summer and Smoke* (1948) and *Garden District* (1958). She was nominated for a Tony Award for her performance in *The Last Night of Ballyhoo* (1997). She followed this part with a supporting role as Aunt Joan in Paramount Pictures' *The Talented Mr. Ripley* (1999).

In 2003, Weston had a featured part in the miniseries *Out of Order*. She went on to have recurring roles in TV shows including *Memphis Beat*, *Modern Family*, and *American Horror Story*. In 2017, she played Aunt Ruth on Broadway in *Marvin's Room*. Since then, she has continued to act in theater, film, and television.

Philip McKeon *(Tommy)*

Philip McKeon was born in Westbury, New York, in 1964. When he was four, he started to work as a print model with his younger sister, Nancy, who later became known for her role as Jo in the sitcom *The Facts of Life*. McKeon was cast in his first television commercial when he was eight. His parents were supportive of his career but never pushed. They checked in with him from time to time to make sure he was doing what he really wanted to do. The answer was always yes. McKeon made his Broadway debut at the age of ten in *Medea and Jason* (1974). Linda Lavin attended a performance of the show and thought him talented.

Philip McKeon

In 1976, after the pilot of *Alice* was shot, the producers decided to recast the role of Alice's son, Tommy. Lavin recommended that they consider McKeon. He was brought in for an audition and ultimately got the part. Working on the show was a life-changing experience for McKeon and his family. They gave up their life in New York and moved to California to encourage their children's acting careers.

During the run of *Alice*, McKeon became close with his fellow cast members. They were like a second family to him. In addition to his work on *Alice*, he guest-starred on shows including *CHiPs*, *Fantasy Island*, and *The Love Boat*.

By the time *Alice* came to an end, McKeon was twenty years old. He had appeared in one hundred eight episodes of the series. He continued to find supporting roles in TV programs such as *Amazing Stories* and the miniseries *Favorite Son* and horror films such as *976-Evil II* (1991) and *Sandman* (1993). In 2005, McKeon coproduced the movie *The Jacket* that starred Adrien Brody. After that, he and his family moved to Texas, where he cohosted a weekday radio show for several years and enjoyed a more easygoing life.

Charles Levin *(Elliot)*

Charles Herbert Levin was born in 1949 in Chicago. He got his start in acting in the 1976 animated feature film *Everybody Rides the Carousel*. A steady flow of supporting roles in movies followed, including in Woody Allen's *Annie Hall* (1977), *Between the Lines* (1977), and *The Seduction of Joe Tynan* (1979).

In 1983, Levin was cast as Elliot Novak in *Alice*. He appeared in twenty-two episodes of the show. After the series ended, Levin was hired to play the gay cook in the pilot episode of *The Golden Girls*. Producers decided to cut his character from the show and made Estell Getty's character, Sophia, a regular instead. Many of her feisty lines in the series' initial episodes were originally written for Levin's character.

Life Behind the Counter in Mel's Greasy Spoon

Charles Levin

Levin went on to have recurring roles in TV shows including *Hill Street Blues*, *Karen's Song*, and *Capital News*. In 1990, he was cast in the Broadway musical *City of Angels*. More film and TV work came his way after that, including a recurring part in the series *NYPD Blue*. Levin's final acting role was as a geologist in the 1998 feature film *A Civil Action*. He was married to Katherine DeHetre until her death in 2007. They had two children. Levin passed away during the summer of 2019.

Alice...

Marvin Kaplan

Marvin Kaplan *(Henry)*

Marvin Kaplan was born in 1927 in Brooklyn. He graduated from high school at the age of sixteen and got a bachelor's degree in English from Brooklyn College. After that, Kaplan decided to move west to study drama at the University of Southern California. Not long after arriving in Los Angeles, he was cast in a small role in Molière's play *The Doctor in Spite of Himself* at the Circle Theater. Katharine Hepburn attended a performance of the show and was impressed with his acting ability. She got him an uncredited role in her next film, *Adam's Rib* (1949). Hepburn's enthusiasm for Kaplan's talent prompted him to quit school and pursue acting full-time. Within a few months, he was cast in movies including *Francis* (1950), *The Fat Man* (1951), *Angels in the Outfield* (1951), and *Behave Yourself* (1951).

In 1951 Kaplan was cast in a starring role as Alfred Prinzmetal in the radio sitcom turned TV series *Meet Millie*. He also appeared in shows such as *Make Room for Daddy* and *The Many Loves of Dobie Gillis*.

During the 1960s, Kaplan guest-starred in TV programs including *Petticoat Junction*, *The Mod Squad*, and *Love, American Style*. In 1973, he married Rosa Felsenburg. By 1976, things weren't working out between them, and they got divorced. Soon after, Kaplan was cast as the telephone repairman Henry Beesmeyer in *Alice*. He appeared in eighty-two episodes of the show.

In 1984, Kaplan began working with California Artists Radio Theatre. During his thirty-two-year association with the group, he wrote two radio-theater musicals and appeared in productions including *Alice in Wonderland*, *The Wizard of Oz*, and *A Midsummer Night's Dream*. He also continued to guest-star in TV series such as *MacGyver*, *Cagney & Lacey*, *ER*, *Becker*, and *The Garfield Show*.

By 2010, Kaplan was in his eighties and confined to a wheelchair. Despite this, he took on the role of executive producer and writer of feature films. His first movie, *Watch Out for Slick* (2010), was about a poorly planned kidnapping and its repercussions. Kaplan died on August 25, 2016. His final film, *Looking Up* (2016), was released a few weeks after his death.

Martha Raye *(Carrie)*

Martha Raye was born Margy Reed in 1916 in Butte, Montana. She first performed on stage at the age of three and toured the United States with her brother and parents in their show "Reed and Hooper." In her late teens, Raye was hired as the vocalist for orchestra leader Paul Ash's band. She sang with the group until 1934, when she was

Alice...

cast in the Broadway musical revue *Calling All Stars* (1934). A talent scout saw the show and encouraged her to go to Hollywood. She took the advice and headed west.

Soon after Raye arrived in California, she appeared in a short film entitled *A Nite in the Nite Club* (1934). Paramount Pictures took note of her work and signed her to a contract. She started to make feature-length movies with them, appearing in comic roles. Her debut was in *Rhythm on the Range* (1936).

Beginning in 1936, Raye appeared on Al Jolson's radio series *The Lifebuoy Program* (aka *Cafe Trocadero*). During that time, she became known for her endearing comedic style and her large mouth, which garnered her the nickname "The Big Mouth." More movie roles followed, including *The Big Broadcast of 1937* (1936), *College Holiday* (1936), *Waikiki Wedding* (1937), and *Double or Nothing* (1937).

Raye had an active personal life full of ups and downs. In 1937, she married makeup artist Bud Westmore. Six months into their marriage they realized they were not compatible and sought a divorce. In 1938, Raye started dating music conductor David Rose. After a brief courtship they wed. A year into their marriage their relationship fell apart. While they were in the process of getting a divorce, Raye began to date businessman Neal Lang. In May of 1941, after Raye's break up with Rose became final, she married Lang. Their relationship flourished for several years until poor communication and increasing disagreements made it sour. They divorced in the beginning of 1944.

Martha Raye

During World War II, Raye toured with the United Service Organizations Inc. (USO), entertaining US troops involved with the war effort. In 1944, she starred in the film *Four Jills in a Jeep*, which recounted her experience on the USO tour. That same year, Raye married dancer Nick Condos. They had one child, Melodye Condos, and remained together until June 1953.

By the mid-1950s, Raye had begun to appear in various TV programs. These led her to star in her own variety series called *The Martha Raye Show*, which ran from 1954 to 1956. In April 1954, she married dancer Edward Thomas Begley. Two years after they wed, their relationship deteriorated and they parted ways. While their divorce was in process, Raye started to date Los Angeles police officer Robert

O'Shea. After her separation with Begley became final in 1956, Raye tied the knot with O'Shea. The couple remained married until 1960.

Despite the difficulties in Raye's personal life, she had a strong and enduring career. In 1967, she returned to Broadway and starred as Dolly Levi in the musical *Hello Dolly* (1964). She was then cast as the comic villain, Benita Bizarre, in the 1970 children's show *The Bugaloos*. After that, Raye headlined in the Broadway musical *No, No, Nanette* (1971). Beginning in 1976, she played the part of Agatha for two seasons of the series *McMilan & Wife*. This was followed by a recurring role as Mel's beloved mother, Carrie Sharples, for six seasons of *Alice*. Raye's final film appearance was as the duchess in the 1985 made-for-TV movie *Alice in Wonderland*.

In 1991, Raye married for the seventh and final time: to her forty-two-year-old manager, Mark Harris. Not long after they wed, Raye was diagnosed with Alzheimer's disease. A few months later, doctors were forced to amputate her left leg below the knee and part of her right leg due to poor circulation. On October 19, 1994, at the age of seventy-eight, she died of pneumonia after a long battle with cardiovascular disease.

Dave Madden *(Earl)*

Dave Madden was born David Madden in 1931 in Sarnia, Ontario. He spent his early childhood in Michigan. After his father's death, his mother took a job on the road and sent him to live with his aunt and uncle in Terre Haute, Indiana. Shortly after settling into his new surroundings, Madden had a serious bicycle accident. While recuperating from it, he developed an interest in magic. He incorporated some of the tricks he learned during his recovery into a comedy act that he performed at various venues in town. After graduating from high school, Madden attended Indiana State Teachers College for one semester and then enlisted in the United States Air Force. He was deployed to Tripoli, Libya and became popular as an entertainer in shows on the base.

Dave Madden

On completing his stint in the air force, Madden earned a communications degree at the University of Miami and then began working in nightclubs. Frank Sinatra saw his show in Los Angeles and got him a brief job doing stand-up comedy on *The Ed Sullivan Show*. The exposure led Madden to be cast in a recurring role as Counselor Pruett on the 1965 TV series *Camp Runamuck*. In 1968, he appeared in several episodes of *Rowan & Martin's Laugh-In*.

1970 was a watershed year for Madden. He was cast as the harried talent agent Reuben Kincaid in the ultra-popular show *The Partridge Family*. The series brought him worldwide exposure. During its four-season run, he became a surrogate father of sorts to young actor Danny Bonaduce, who played Danny Partridge in the series. Madden had smoked cigarettes for many years by that point. In the episode "Each Dawn I Diet," Danny bets Reuben that he can't quit the habit. Madden took the opportunity to stop smoking on the show and in real life.

In 1974, he married Alvena Louise Arnold. They adopted a daughter and had a son. Madden's career continued to flourish with appearances on shows including *Happy Days*, *Starsky and Hutch*, *Barney Miller*, *The Love Boat*, and *Fantasy Island*. This was followed by a seven-season run as high-school basketball coach Earl Hicks on *Alice*.

In 1985, Madden's relationship with Arnold became strained and they divorced. Despite the challenges in his personal life, Madden went on to guest-star in such series as *Life with Lucy*, *Married with Children*, *The Ben Stiller Show*, *Boy Meets World*, and *Sabrina, the Teenage Witch*.

In 1998, Madden reconnected with his college sweetheart, Sandra Martin. They dated for a while and then got married. In the mid-2000s, Madden retired from a recurring role on the radio-theater series *Adventures in Odyssey* and focused on writing his memoir: *Reuben on Wry: The Memoirs of Dave Madden* (2007). As time went on, health issues began to affect him. He died of complications of myelodysplastic syndrome on January 16, 2014.

Victoria Carroll *(Marie)*

Victoria Carroll was born in 1941 in Los Angeles. Her father was a former vaudeville actor who became a publicity agent at 20th Century Fox. As a child, Carroll performed onstage with her family as "The World's Youngest Mind Reader."

Victoria Carroll

Upon completing high school, she supported herself through an art scholarship and started taking dance classes. She eventually found work as a dancer in Broadway shows. After two years on Broadway, Carroll returned to Hollywood, where she was cast in small parts in films including *My Fair Lady* (1964), *The Art of Love* (1965), and *How to Stuff a Wild Bikini* (1965). Afterward, she started to get guest roles in TV series such as *I Dream of Jeannie*, *Get Smart*, *Hogan's Heroes*, and *Marcus Welby, M.D.*

In the early 1970s, Carroll became a member of Vic Tayback's theater, the Company of Angels. Additionally, she was a founding member of the comedy improv group the Groundlings. Carroll's work with them enabled her to get more film and TV comedy roles. In 1977, she reunited with Tayback when she was cast in an uncredited role in an episode of *Alice* and later in a recurring part as Mel's girlfriend Marie. Carroll and Tayback had good chemistry and worked well together in the series.

In 1984, she married voice actor Michael Bell. Soon after, they had a daughter. At that point, Carroll began to focus more on voiceover work. She was hired for parts in series including *The Smurfs*, *Foofur*, *DuckTales*, and *The Mask*. She eventually became a painter, returning to acting sporadically when exciting roles came along.

CHAPTER 7:

The Crew of Alice

Madelyn Davis *(Series Producer)*
Madelyn Davis was born Madelyn Pugh in 1921 in Indianapolis, Indiana. She became interested in writing at the age of ten, when she wrote a full-length play. In high school she worked on the school newspaper and was a member of the fiction club. Davis earned a bachelor's degree in journalism from Indiana University. After graduation, she was hired as a writer at her local radio station WIRE.

During the height of World War II, Davis's family moved to California. Many writers were off fighting the war at the time, giving Davis opportunity. She was frequently the only woman on a team of writers. She started at NBC Radio and then moved to CBS, where she met Bob Carroll Jr. They had a strong camaraderie and decided to become writing partners. The alliance they formed lasted for more than fifty years.

In 1948, while writing for comedian Steve Allen's show, Davis and Carroll took interest in Lucille Ball's new radio sitcom, *My Favorite Husband*. They were so enthusiastic about the prospect of working with her that they paid Allen to script his own show for a week so they could have the time to write a sample episode for Ball's show. Producers loved their work and brought them in as main writers on Ball's new radio series.

Alice...

Davis and Carroll were instrumental in creating the TV series *I Love Lucy*. They loved dreaming up outlandish physical situations for Ball to become entangled in. Many times, Davis would try out the physical comedy stunts herself to make sure they worked before presenting them to Ball and the rest of the cast. For the majority of its run, *I Love Lucy* was the most-watched show on TV. Davis and Carroll were nominated for three Emmy Awards for their work on the series.

In 1955, Davis married TV producer Quinn Martin. They had one son. A few years later, the *Los Angeles Times* named Davis the Times Woman of the Year for her skillful writing for *I Love Lucy*. After the series ended, marital problems set in for her and Martin. They divorced a few years later. Davis and Carroll went on to write for Ball's next sitcom, *The Lucy Show*. In 1964, Davis married Dr. Richard Merrill Davis.

In 1967, Davis and Carroll created the sitcom *The Mothers-in-Law*. The show ran for two seasons. She and Carroll were then hired to write for Ball's new show, *Here's Lucy*. After that Davis wrote episodes of *Sanford and Son* and *Mr. T and Tina*. In 1977, she and Carroll reteamed to develop the comedy TV special *Lucy Calls the President*. That same year, they were hired to take over as producers of the sitcom *Alice*. They used the vast knowledge they had acquired while working with Ball to revamp the struggling series and make it a success. In 1979, Davis won a Golden Globe Award as producer for the show. She and Carroll were awarded a Laurel Award for TV Writing Achievement from the Writers Guild of America for their work as well.

In the mid-1980s, Davis wrote for the soap opera *One Life to Live*. A few years later, she again reteamed with Carroll to write and produce Ball's final sitcom, *Life with Lucy*. In 2009, Davis's husband passed away. Two years later, she received Indiana University's Distinguished Alumni Service Award. She died later that year in Bel Air, California.

Bob Carroll Jr. *(Series Producer)*

Robert Gordon Carroll Jr. was born in 1918 in McKeesport, Pennsylvania. He spent most of his childhood in Florida. After completing high school, Carroll studied French at St. Petersburg Junior College. During that time, he injured his hip in an accident and underwent surgery. While recuperating at home, Carroll penned a short comedy script about a man dealing with the good and evil sides of his conscience. He entered it in a contest sponsored by a local radio station and won. The victory gave him confidence in his storytelling ability and sparked his interest in script writing.

Not long after the contest, Carroll's family moved to California. His brother-in-law got him a job as a front-desk clerk at CBS. He was fired for requiring celebrities to sign in before entering the building. A short time later, Carroll landed a job doing publicity, which led him to write for Steve Allen's radio series. He met Madelyn Davis while working on the show. They got along wonderfully and decided to write together. They soon found work on Lucille Ball's new radio series, *My Favorite Husband*.

Carroll and Davis helped develop Ball's TV series *I Love Lucy*. They scripted thirty-nine episodes of the show per season. Writing so much each year made it challenging to come up with fresh ideas. They began taking notes on things they encountered in life and incorporated them into storylines for the show. One day they spotted a man twirling dough in a pizza parlor. Carroll and Davis were intrigued by his skill and thought that if they added Lucy's ineptitude at the task to the mix it would create a hilarious situation. They included that scenario in an episode. Another time, Carroll and Davis were unable to decide which movie to go see. They used that circumstance as the basis for an episode of the series as well. Carroll and Davis were nominated for two Primetime Emmy Awards for their work on *I Love Lucy*. During the height of their success, Carroll got married. Unfortunately, the marriage didn't last, and the couple wound up getting divorced a few years later. In 1967, he and Davis created the sitcom *The Mothers-in-Law*. The following year they were nominated for a Primetime Emmy Award for the work they did on Ball's subsequent show, *Here's Lucy*.

In the late 1970s, Carroll and Davis took over as producers on *Alice*. The changes they implemented led to the long-term success of the show. In 1980, the pair received a Golden Globe Award for their work. A few years later, Carroll married Darcy Jo Cooper. They had one daughter. Not long after, marital problems set in, and the couple divorced. In 1992, Carroll received the Laurel Award from the Writers Guild of America in honor of his achievements in writing for television. As the twenty-first century began, he helped Davis write her memoir, *Laughing with Lucy: My Life with America's Leading Lady of Comedy* (2005). He died two years later, after a short illness.

Arthur Marx *(Series Writer)*

Arthur Marx was born in New York City in 1921. He was the son of Groucho Marx, a member of the well-known comedy team the Marx Brothers. Until the age of ten, Marx lived on the road with his father and uncles as they toured the world on various vaudeville circuits. At the end of their tour, the family settled in California.

Marx was an avid tennis player and ranked nationally while still in his teens. In his first year of college, he won the National Freshman Intercollegiate Tennis title in Montclair, New Jersey. During World

War II, Marx joined the United States Coast Guard and was stationed in the Philippines. In 1943, he married Irene Kahn. They had two children. After leaving the coast guard, Marx became a script reader at MGM. His work at the studio sparked his interest in writing. Within a few years he was crafting screenplays for films including *Winter Wonderland* (1946) and *Blondie in the Dough* (1947) from the popular *Blondie* movie series, which ran from 1938 to 1950.

In 1954, Marx authored a biography about his father entitled *Life with Groucho*. By 1960, his relationship with Kahn had deteriorated and they got a divorce. Soon after, Marx met Robert Fisher. They became writing partners and wrote for the TV series *McHale's Navy*. In 1963, Marx married Lois Gilbert. He and Fisher then produced the sitcom *Mickey*, which starred Mickey Rooney. Their comedy *The Impossible Years* opened on Broadway the following year and ran for 670 performances. In the late 1960s, Marx and Fisher wrote several episodes of the show *The Mothers-in-Law*. Series creators Madelyn Davis and Bob Carroll Jr. enjoyed working with them and valued the high quality of their writing. After the show went off the air, Marx and Fisher returned to Broadway with a biographical musical about the Marx Brothers entitled *Minnie's Boys* (1970). It had a short run and then closed. In 1972, Marx published a follow-up book to *Life with Groucho* entitled *Son of Groucho*. He went on to pen biographies about other well-known actors, including Mickey Rooney, Red Skeleton, and Bob Hope.

In 1977, when Davis and Carroll took over as producers of *Alice*, they brought Marx and Fisher aboard as head writers. In 1982, Marx and Fisher cowrote the biopic *Groucho*, about Marx's father's life. They followed that project by writing for Lucille Ball's last comedy series, *Life with Lucy*. Marx then authored the book *Arthur Marx's Groucho: A Photographic Journey* (2001) and wrote the foreword for *The Guy's Guide to Dating, Getting Hitched, and the First Year of Marriage* (2007). In 2011, he revised *Minnie's Boys* and planned to mount a new production. He died before it could come to fruition.

Robert Fisher *(Series Writer)*

Robert Fisher was born in 1922 in California. He got his start as a TV writer in 1952, crafting scripts for the sitcom *Doc Corkle*. After that, he teamed with seasoned writer Alan Lipscott and wrote regularly for shows including *Willy, The People's Choice, The Donna Reed Show, Bachelor Father*, and *Make Room for Daddy*.

In 1961, Lipscott passed away. At that point, Fisher became the writing partner of Arthur Alsberg and then Arthur Marx. Fisher and Marx wrote for *McHale's Navy*. A short time later, their comedy *The Impossible Years* (1965) opened on Broadway. Fisher then teamed with Alsberg and cowrote the Broadway comedy *Happiness Is Just a Little Thing Called a Rolls Royce* (1968).

In 1970, he collaborated with Marx on the Broadway musical *Minnie's Boys*. When the show closed, Fisher and Marx returned to California and resumed a prolific TV career writing for *The Paul Lynde Show, Maude*, and *Good Heavens*. In 1977, Madelyn Davis and Bob Carroll Jr. hired them to write for the sitcom *Alice*. After Fisher completed his work on the series, he penned the novel *The Knight in Rusty Armor* (1987), a comic journey about one man's self-discovery. He died in Topanga, California, in September 2008.

David Silverman *(Series Writer)*

David Silverman is a TV writer and producer. In the early 1970s, he partnered with Stephen Sustarsic to script episodes of *The Jeffersons, One Day at a Time, Alice, Nine to Five, ALF*, and *Parker Lewis Can't Lose*.

During the 1990s, Silverman and Sustarsic focused on producing TV series including *Cleghorne*, *You Wish*, *Dilbert*, *Girlfriends*, and *Xiaolin Showdown*. They also developed new shows such as the animated comedy-adventure series *The Wild Thornberrys*, which ran for five seasons. In addition to writing, Silverman is a psychotherapist.

The cast of the TV series *Alice* including Polly Holliday, Vic Tayback, Beth Howland and Linda Lavin

CHAPTER 8:

The Characters in *Alice*

Alice Hyatt

Alice was originally from New Jersey. Her maiden name is Spivak. When she was eight, she got separated from her Brownie troop while they were in the forest. A squirrel led her back to the other girls. The experience taught her to value and marvel at nature.

After hearing Jo Stafford sing on an album, Alice knew she wanted to become a singer. Her biggest influences are Peggy Lee, Ella Fitzgerald, June Christy, Patti Page, Rosemary Clooney, and Billie Holiday. She loves performing songs from the Great American Songbook, especially anything written by Cole Porter or George Gershwin.

Alice starred in her high school's musical and was a cheerleader. She was voted the cutest knees. Her nickname was "Pudgy." Alice was honored when her voice teacher, Ruth, asked her to sing at her wedding. In college, she worked part-time in a dance studio. She formed a singing group called Alice and the Acorns and later moved to New York City. While there, she and her roommate, Julia Roberts, struggled to make it in show business. Alice eventually married a trucker, Don Hyatt. Julie went on to become a working stage director.

Alice and Don had a son named Tommy. After Don died in a truck accident, Alice's mother pressured her to marry a high school football coach she met in the frozen foods section of the grocery store. Alice wasn't interested in settling down and chose to leave New Jersey with Tommy to pursue a singing career in Hollywood. When their station wagon broke down near Phoenix, Arizona, Alice decided to take a full-time waitress job in town at Mel's Diner to make ends meet and look for singing work there. She was so nervous when she started at Mel's that she gave change for a fifty-dollar bill to a customer who had only given her a five.

Alice becomes close friends with Flo, Mel, Vera, Belle, and Jolene during the time she works with them. They help each other when challenging situations arise. Alice continually stands up for workers' rights when Mel treats the waitresses unfairly. She believes in self-improvement and takes various courses in night school. She is particularly interested in the study of psychology. She uses what she learns in class to try to improve her life and the lives of her friends. Alice is the go-to person when her friends have bad news they want to relay to someone. She always breaks the news for them, although she doesn't always want to have to do it.

She is a caring mother who has her son's best interests at heart. She teaches him to value people for who they are and not judge them by labels. She rejects bullying and feels that reasoning with people is the most effective way to handle challenging situations.

Alice sings at clubs several times while living in Phoenix. She even has an opportunity to go on a concert tour. She declines the tour, however, so that Tommy can live a stable life in one place until he is grown. Once he is in college, Alice takes an offer to move to Nashville and perform with a well-known singer named Travis Marsh.

Tommy Hyatt

Tommy is Alice's charismatic and precocious teenage son. He loves watching *Charlie's Angels* and thinking about attractive, young women. Although he is sometimes at odds with his mother, he appreciates her wisdom in the end and learns from it, which in turn strengthens their mother-son bond.

He loves trying new things, including learning to play guitar, hunting, and riding a dirt bike. When they first move to Phoenix, his closest friend is a local boy named Richie. Later, his closest friend is Roger. Roger lives in Tommy's apartment complex and is around his age. They hang out in Roger's apartment a lot. Tommy goes there for sleepovers once in a while as well.

In high school, Tommy pursues various career options, including acting. He is the varsity basketball team's top player. His skill lands him a scholarship to Arizona State University, where he plays for the Sun Devils. While in college, he becomes addicted to alcohol. Alice helps him realize that he has a problem and encourages him to take steps to overcome it. During his time in Phoenix, Tommy grows from a boy to a young man who towers over his mother at 6'2" tall.

Florence Jean Castleberry

Florence, or "Flo," as she is better known, hails from Cowtown, Texas. She is a sexy live wire who doesn't like to be idle for long or go without an evening date. She loves chewing gum and sometimes keeps it behind her ear. She wears her hair in a French twist with a modified beehive and a rinse.

Flo started dating when she was four. She has never liked public speaking. When she had to recite Henry Wadsworth Longfellow's "The Song of Hiawatha" in high school, she got so sick she had to go to the nurse's office. She had a wild side, however, which came out when she snuck into the boys' locker room as the football team was showering. She said, "Cheese!," and then snapped a picture while the team scrambled to hide behind a single small towel.

Flo dropped out of high school when she was in the tenth grade to marry a stock car racer named Big Daddy Dawson. They divorced because Flo learned on their wedding night that he wasn't going to be faithful to her. She has been married three times in all. Her third husband, Langley Moss, was a traveling Bible salesman. They were hitched for a year and then got divorced because he cheated on her too much.

Flo prides herself on her skill with men and being a five-time VFW jitterbug champion. She wanted to join the police force and become a meter maid but couldn't, since she never graduated from high school and was afraid that she'd fail if she took the police test. She was a waitress in Cowtown, Texas, before working at Mel's Diner.

Flo has one sister, Fran, and four brothers: Lonnie, Rhett, Edsel, and Jimmy-Joe. Except for Jimmy-Joe, she hasn't seen any of her family since she started to work at Mel's. Her mother and sister have lived their entire lives in the house the family grew up in.

When Flo was a girl, her father, Jarvis, took off, leaving the family with a mortgage to pay and a car up on blocks. He hit it big with an oil gusher but got involved with some ladies on the road, which distracted him from returning home. When he finally came home, the family didn't welcome him back, so he left. During Flo's time working at Mel's, her father comes to see her. It is a painful reunion, but they manage to make amends.

After working at Mel's Diner for many years, Flo tows her trailer back to Cowtown. She plans to leave it at her mother's house and get an apartment in Houston, where she will take a head hostess job at the Thundering Herd restaurant for three times as much as she earned at Mel's. When she arrives in Cowtown, she decides to purchase an aging bar and revamp it into a fun tavern she calls Flo's Yellow Rose. In doing so, she declines the head hostess job, choosing to live out of her trailer in her mother's backyard instead.

During Flo's first year back in Cowtown, she invites her entire family, including her father, who has been estranged from everyone except for her, to share Thanksgiving dinner together. It is a tense situation full of pain and misunderstanding. The family manages to work through their issues with Jarvis, however, and they find a way to reconnect.

Vera Louise Gorman

Vera grew up in Boston. Her family was originally from Ireland. As a child, she enjoyed music and learning how to play the clarinet. She also studied tap dance for six years.

Vera attended Walton High School. She was a drum majorette there for one football game. At that game, she threw her baton into the air and it knocked out the quarterback. That ended her career as a majorette. Vera went onto be the mascot for her high school chess team. She was voted Miss Congeniality in her senior year and graduated in 1962.

She attended college at the University of California, Berkley. She believed in world harmony and joined the peace rallies at school in hope of making a difference. At one of the rallies, she mistakenly hit a cop in the head with her purse and was arrested because of it. She was so upset by the situation that she quit school and moved back to Boston.

Vera started working as a waitress at Mel's Diner two years before Alice arrives. Mel thinks she is dingy, but her coworkers see her as a

Alice...

sweet, gentle soul. While working at the diner, she breaks the world record for continuous tap dancing. Soon after, Vera decides to pursue her dream of learning how to play the cello so she can perform with a string quartet. She takes lessons and is eventually invited to perform with a children's quartet. She is thrilled to have the opportunity.

She is an animal advocate who sets live turkeys free in Mel's Diner so they don't become Thanksgiving dinner. She loves pets. They are family to her. Over the years, she has had a canary named Piercy; three parakeets called Sammy, Clarence, and Tweety; two hamsters named Harold and Mitzy; and some goldfish called Starsky and Hutch. She saves up to buy a parrot named Birdie on layaway, but he dies just after she takes possession of him. The pet shop owner later reveals that Birdie was 106 years old, senile, and close to death when he sold him to Vera. He reluctantly refunds her money because of the bird's ill health at the time of sale. Vera also has a cat named Mel. She named him that because he is fat like Mel Sharples and loves to prowl the streets at night. He runs away after Vera tells him he will have to live with her boss, Mel Sharples.

Vera has never learned how to drive. That doesn't stop her from getting around, though. Her usual modes of transportation are walking and taking the bus. She loves movies and frequently attends Humphrey Bogart, Katharine Hepburn, and horror marathons. She is good with calculations and can scribble an equation in the air with her finger and come up with the correct answer faster than anyone else she knows.

As time goes on, Vera meets a kind police officer named Elliot Novak. They fall in love and marry. Soon after, they buy a large house. Vera eventually quits her job at the diner to have a baby.

Mel Sharples

Mel's full name is Melvin Emory Sharples, but everyone calls him Mel. He grew up in Brooklyn with his younger brother. His family had a dog named Buster. For years, Mel believed that Buster was a war hero, which his mother, Carrie, said to pacify him. In reality, she was forced to give Buster away because the apartment they were moving to didn't allow pets. She had also told Mel that his pet cat, Fluffy, ran off to become a movie star in Hollywood. She said that to ease his pain when Fluffy went missing.

As a kid, Mel dreamed of being a jockey. He enjoyed going to Coney Island. His father took him to Yankee Stadium once; it was the best time he ever had. In third grade, other kids teased Mel, calling him "Smelly Melly with the Jelly Belly." During a little league game in which Mel's team was losing thirty-four to nothing, Mel got up to bat anyway. In the process of swinging, he dislocated his shoulder. This incident proved that he wasn't a quitter, no matter the circumstances.

Mel attended a Catholic high school. He was mischievous during this time and became the class bully. He was called to the principal's office frequently because of it. At one point, he set fire to the shoe of his principal, Sister Mary Margaret, giving her a hot foot. His peers considered him well-dressed and a trendsetter. When Mel was in his mid-teens, he went on a date with a woman who was twice his age.

Though Mel planned to become a plumber after graduating high school, his plans changed when the Korean War began. He enlisted in the navy and became a cook on a ship. In his spare time, he took up boxing and won a championship. After he completed his time in the military, he returned home and attended college on the GI Bill. He worked as a cook in a hospital and then became co-owner of a diner in Brooklyn with his business partner, Jake Farley. Jake was a rigid taskmaster who made his waitresses work on Christmas Eve and Christmas Day. Mel idolized him.

Despite Mel's rough demeanor, he tries to be a good citizen by donating to the Red Cross and watching *The Waltons* on TV. He moved out of his family's home in Brooklyn when he was thirty-three. By then his father had divorced his mother and moved to Chicago. His younger brother was married with children and no longer lived at home either.

Mel decided to head west and bought the diner in Phoenix from Alfonzo "Slim" McDermic's estate. He got it for a bargain but needed to take out a GI loan to pay for it. He called it Mel's Diner.

Mel is a confirmed bachelor. He loves bowling, betting on horses, and poker night with the guys. During the time he owns the diner, he has numerous girlfriends. The steadiest of whom is Marie.

Mel's Diner is known for its famous chili. Mel takes great pride in that and even goes on Dinah Shore's television show to demonstrate how it's made. He keeps his secret ingredients to himself though. At one point, Mel tries unsuccessfully to mass-market his chili with the help of Art Carney. He becomes furious when his mother decides to include the chili recipe in a cookbook she is writing for publication. After some heated discussion with Mel, she decides to remove the recipe from the book and repair their strained relationship.

Mel eventually pays off the mortgage on the diner and later sells it for a huge sum of money. The profit he makes is so large that he gives each of his waitresses $5,000 from the sale as a thank-you before they part ways.

Belle Dupree

Belle hails from Mississippi. She is full of vim and vigor and likes to wear bell-shaped earrings and a necklace featuring a large cross made of coins. She worked as a waitress at Mel's Diner before Flo was employed there and has done a lot of traveling since.

While working as a cocktail waitress in Las Vegas, she met the manager for the country singer Wailin' Tammy Hawkins. Belle told him about a song she wrote called "Uncle Bud." She thought it would be a great piece for Tammy to record. Unfortunately, Tammy's tour was moving on to Phoenix, and Belle didn't have an opportunity to sing for the manager. Belle was so passionate about her songwriting ability that she quit her job in Vegas and followed Tammy's band to Phoenix to sing her song for the manager. When they finally connect, he is less interested in the song than in making advances. Belle, offended by his moves, tells him to get lost. With the songwriting opportunity gone, Belle is forced to start over again. She asks Mel for her old waitressing job back. He is in need of a waitress at the time and hires her.

During Belle's employment at Mel's Diner, she never gives up her pursuit of a songwriting career and peddles her songs whenever she can. Ultimately, she moves to Nashville, where her cousin Larry is starting a country-western band. When he offers her a job as one of his backup singers, she jumps at the chance and goes on tour with his band.

Jolene Hunnicutt

Jolene is from Myrtle Point, South Carolina. She is the only sister in a large family of brothers that includes Jess, Jasper, Jeremy, Jimmy, and Jake Jr. Jolene's favorite color is purple, and her favorite food is linguine. Her mother died when she was young, leaving her to assume household responsibilities. Jolene's grandmother had three teeth. This trait led her to be affectionately known as Granny Gums. Jolene's grandmother was related to Hazzard County's top, opportunistic, commissioner, J. D. "Boss" Hogg, who is featured in the TV series *The Dukes of Hazzard*.

Jolene is a talented athlete. Her longtime dream was to be a

Alice . . .

Formula One race car driver at the Indy 500. In high school, she won a trophy for being the most valuable player on her softball team. Her excellent pitching skills enabled her to strikeout the most opponents in one season and to pitch a perfect game. She was also the captain of the girls' basketball team. Her teammates called her "Hook Shot Hunnicutt."

She becomes acquainted with the diner when she takes shelter there in an attempt to escape from her trucking partner Burt's sexual harassment. Burt follows her in and insists that she continue to work with him. She refuses and throws plates at him to get him to leave. Mel is furious that she has destroyed diner property. Jolene thus agrees to work there temporarily to pay for the damage. Soon after, she becomes a permanent employee, remaining there for the next five years. She is the only waitress able to get away with ribbing Mel about his character and his cooking. Ultimately, she quits her job at the diner to open a beauty parlor.

Henry Beesmeyer

Henry is a longtime customer at Mel's Diner. He is stout and easygoing and wears large, thick glasses and a workman's uniform.

The day after Henry was born, his father ran off with another woman, forcing his mother to raise him on her own. He attended an all-boys high school, where he was cast in the role of Nanette in his senior-year production of *No, No, Nanette* because he had great legs. The director of personnel for the Phoenix phone company attended the performance. After the show, he offered Henry a job. Henry accepted. He has been employed for the company ever since. His dream is to be the first person to install phones on the moon.

Henry is married to a peculiar, controlling woman named Chloe. She isn't very affectionate or happy about how her life turned out.

Henry accepts the challenges in their relationship as a basic part of being married. Every year on their wedding anniversary, Chloe and her mother get together and sing sad songs. Chloe's mother bakes her a black cake as a reminder that she never wanted Chloe to marry Henry. Despite this, Chloe does love Henry. The hard edges of her personality soften when she discovers that she's pregnant. The increased affection that she shows Henry strengthens their relationship. Soon after, Henry and Chloe become parents to twin babies that they love very much.

Elliot Novak

Elliot is a Phoenix police officer. In high school, he was known as the fastest runner in school. He is also good at playing the piano and loves Rogers and Hammerstein.

He meets Vera while giving her a ticket for jaywalking. They wind up having several interests in common and start dating. After a brief courtship, they marry and buy an old house together.

During this time, Elliot has his sights set on becoming a detective. He and his partner, Maxwell, routinely go on stakeouts and undercover assignments. Elliot's success at his job ultimately leads him to be promoted to detective.

Earl Hicks

Earl is a frequent customer at the diner. After college, he attended law school for four months but then flunked out. At that point, he took a job as the basketball coach at Tommy's high school. He does double duty teaching history when the school needs an additional instructor. He occasionally uses his legal knowledge to help the workers and patrons at the diner.

Earl is currently divorced. During his marriage, his wife, Margie, got a basset hound. She named him Earl Jr. so the dog and her husband would be easier to call to dinner.

He meets Flo while eating at the diner. They date for a few months, but then decide just to be friends. Earl has dated other women on and off ever since.

Carrie Sharples

Mel's mother, Carrie lives in Brooklyn and occasionally visits him in Phoenix. She has an engaging personality, a witty sense of humor, and is a great cook to boot.

During Mel's adulthood, Carrie marries a man named Robby who is a few years younger than Mel. Mel resents the difference in their ages and refuses to call Robby "Father." Carrie eventually divorces Robby and writes a cookbook. She and Mel have a falling out when she wants to include the family's chili recipe in her book. Mel is concerned that publishing it would stop people from coming to the diner to buy his chili. The two smooth things out when Carrie agrees to remove the recipe from her book.

Carrie's pet name for Mel is "Chubby." She loves greeting him with that name and giving him a big, loving slug in the gut at the same time.

When Carrie is depressed, she goes on a cooking frenzy. Customers at the diner love everything she makes, especially her chicken potpies. They stand in a line that extends out the diner door just for a chance to purchase one.

Marie Massey

Marie is Mel's steadiest girlfriend during the time when he owns the diner. She is a bartender at the Café Chug-a-Lug, where the two meet. She briefly works as a waitress at the diner after Flo leaves.

Life Behind the Counter in Mel's Greasy Spoon

Mel asks her to marry him so he won't have to pay her to work there. When she learns that this is his motive, she quits. They eventually patch things up, but Marie never works at the diner again.

CHAPTER 9:

The World in Alice

THE FOLLOWING SAYINGS, FOODS, and locations from *Alice* define the characters and the town in which they live.

Memorable Sayings

Alice (of Mel): What a yak!

Belle: My little voice calls me Isabel.

Belle: Why don't you go chew on a hush puppy?

Carrie: You little dickens, you.

Flo: Ain't that a kick in the head.

Flo: Ain't that kicky.

Flo: Buffalo feathers.

Flo: Bull dingy!

Flo: Kiss my grits!

Flo: Kiss my honeydew.

Flo: Smell you, Princess Grace.

Flo: That horse's patoot.

Flo: That tears it!

Flo: That's a ring dang doo!

Flo: When donkeys fly!

Alice . . .

Jolene: Jump back.

Jolene: When pigs wear perfume.

Mel: Bag it, Belle.

Mel (of Jolene): Bottle it, Blondie/Bottle it, blond head.

Mel: Stow it!

Vera: In a rat's hat, Dumbo!

Vera: Silly Me.

Polly Holliday and Hans Conried in a scene from episode 69 (3.21), "The Last Stow It: Part 2"

Recurrent Pet Names and Terms of Endearment

Carrie (of Mel): Chubby.
Carrie (of Robby): Lover lips.

Flo (of Mel): Burger brain.

Jolene (of Vera): Shoe button.

Marie (of Mel): Barrel bottom.
Marie (of Mel): Bunny tummy.
Marie (of Mel): Cookie nose.
Marie (of Mel): Curly.
Marie (of Mel): Jelly belly.
Marie (of Mel): Melsie.
Marie (of Mel): Melsiekins.
Marie (of Mel): Sugar head.

Mel (of Marie): Cuddle cups.
Mel (of Marie): Honey bunny.
Mel (of Marie): Kitty paws.
Mel (of Marie): Lamb lips.
Mel (of Marie): Snookie Tookie.
Mel (of Marie): Tulip lips.

Vera (of Mel): Barnacle Belly.

Alice . . .

Victoria Carroll and Vic Tayback in a scene from episode 75 (4.3), "Mel Loves Marie"

Memorable Foods from Mel's Diner
Barney's Secret Sauce (used on burgers served at Barney's Burger Barn)

Tabasco sauce

Oregano

Black pepper

Cheap brandy

Tomato sauce

Carrie's Chicken Potpie

Delicious chicken pies that Mel's mother, Carrie, makes at the diner when she comes to town.

Life Behind the Counter in Mel's Greasy Spoon

Carrie's Lemon Pudding

A customer favorite that Mel's mother, Carrie, makes at the diner. Beware of imitations, especially the too-tangy version that Mel makes and that doesn't resemble lemon pudding at all.

Mel's Chili (as described in various episodes of the series)

Three pounds chuck steak

Tomatoes

Chopped onions

Green chili pepper

Various dried spices (Mel won't reveal what they are. It's a secret. Only he and his mother, Carrie, know.)

Cook thoroughly in skillet.

```
            "MEL'S CHILI"

2 lbs. lean ground beef
1 onion, chopped
2 cans tomato paste
6 cans water
1 clove garlic, mashed
Salt and pepper
1 large can chili beans
2 pkg. chili seasoning mix

Brown meat, add onion and saute until tender. Stir
in tomato paste, water, garlic. Simmer until thick--
about 2 hours. Add remaining ingredients and cook
about 15 minutes longer. Serve as is, or it is
delicious over spaghetti and topped with cheese.
```

"Mel's Chili" recipe card *(Photo provided by David Barry Plunkett.)*

The recipe card version of Mel's chili was sent to fans who wrote into the show. Try it! It might be good.

Alice...

Mel's Coffee
The secret to Mel's coffee is to use the grounds three times before throwing them out. Doing so gives the coffee a nice, weak flavor.

Tapioca Pudding
A customer favorite at the diner, according to Mel

Local Establishments
Antonio's
An upscale, candlelit restaurant whose garbage cans are known to contain the finest trash in town

The Appaloosa Club
A music venue in Phoenix

Barney's Burger Barn
A fast-food restaurant in direct competition with Mel's Diner

Benny's Beanery
A popular local eatery

Bibby's Appliance Store
A business that sells TVs and much more

Big Ed's Pizza Parlor
An Italian eatery

Big Herb's 24-Hour Filling Station
A gas station at which Vera works the night shift, pumping gas

The Biltmore Hotel
A large hotel that hosts top-of-the-line banquet events

The Boar's Nest West
Mel's Diner is transformed into this Southern-style chain restaurant for a month when the jovial schemer Boss Hogg comes to town and leases it.

Bob and Dale's Demolition
A wrecking company

The Boom Room
A club that specializes in stripteases

The Bread Basket
A bakery from which the diner purchases all its bread

Café Chug-a-Lug (also known as Chez Chug-a-Lug)
A small café where Mel's girlfriend, Marie, bartends

Café de Paris
A French eatery thought to be the nicest restaurant in town and where a dinner for two costs $50.00

The Camelback Inn
The hotel where most people choose to stay when they come to town

The Casbah
An upscale Middle Eastern restaurant

Alice . . .

The Cat's Meow
A cocktail bar where the waitresses wear only something around their necks

Cattle Baron Bistro
A seedy bar frequented by cattle thieves

Chateau Chihuahua
A French-Mexican eatery

Chez Pierre
An upscale French restaurant

Clem's Watering Trough
A Western bar

The Coconut Room
A bar that used to have burlesque shows

The Comstock Hotel
A local hotel

Connie's Hair Salon
A beauty parlor

The Crescendo Club
A restaurant that regularly features cabaret-style shows

Danny's Discount House
A store that sells discount jewelry

The Desert Bank
A commercial bank where Mel keeps a business account for the diner

The Desert Cinema
A local movie theater

Doobie's Drive-In
A restaurant with roller skating waitresses where Vera briefly works

Dry Gulch Saloon
A juice bar where Alice is hired as a singer

El Chiquita's
A nightclub that serves Mexican food

The Fin and Claw
A seafood restaurant

Freddy's Feedbag
A popular restaurant that takes business away from Mel's Diner by hosting a contest that offers its patrons the chance to win $100

Fred's Used Car Lot
An automobile dealership that sells previously owned cars

Alice...

The Funky Chicken
A fast-food joint that gives chicken-shaped hats to kids

Gillies Mortuary
A funeral parlor

Goldwater's
A lingerie store

Granny Annie's Kitchen
A highly regarded restaurant that wins an award for best home cooking from the Phoenix Restaurant Owner's Association

Hank's Health Club
A popular gym in town

Herman's Hitching Post
A small, rustic, Western club where Alice is hired to sing

The Hot Shot
A seedy club in Flat Rock, Arizona, where Alice was hired to sing

Howard's Department Store
A business that sells a wide variety of products, including VCRs

Jack's Fish House
A seafood restaurant

KBOB
A television station in Phoenix

KLMB
A Phoenix radio station where Vera works as an on-air host for a week

Leo's Roadside Restaurant
A singles bar

Lenny's Delicatessen
A deli with graffiti in the ladies' room written by lonely women. It sponsors a softball team in Phoenix.

The Little Palace Theatre
A local theater where Alice performs in a musical revue with Joel Grey

Marty's Munch-a-Rama
A popular eatery with plans to add a seventy-seat dining area to its existing restaurant

Mel's Diner
A diner with many loyal patrons who, although they put down the food, love eating there. It is run by Mel Sharples.

The Mesa Cinema
A movie theater where Vera sees a Katharine Hepburn marathon

The Mesa Inn
A hotel

Mother Goose Day School
A nursery school on the same street as Mel's Diner

Alice...

Omar's
An Armenian restaurant that serves shish kebabs

Papi's
A bar where Gertrude bartends

Pedro's Taco Stand
A Mexican eatery located a few blocks from Mel's Diner

The Phoenix Little Theatre
A professional theater in town where Alice's friend from New York, Julia Roberts, directs *Romeo and Juliet*

Phoenix Today
A magazine that focuses on life in Phoenix. Alice's boyfriend, Nick, writes for it

The Pink Pinna
The nightclub where Alice wins a disco contest

Pizza Haven
A local pizza parlor

The Pizza House
An Italian restaurant

The Playboy Club
A gentlemen's club whose waitresses wear bunny tails. It hosts live music every night.

The Pussycat Theatre
A movie theater that shows 3-D films

Quickie Burger
A fast-food restaurant

R. J. Caterer's
The largest catering business in Arizona

The Saddle Sore
A club at which Alice sings

Saint Mark's Chapel
A local chapel where Vera and Elliot get married

The Scotch and Sirloin
An upscale restaurant

The Starlight Room
A nightclub

Syd's Style Shop
A clothing shop with an inventory of over 3,000 men's suits

The Tidy House
A restaurant that is open late on Saturday nights

Alice . . .

The Topless Pancake House
An eatery that serves breakfast foods and more

Turf Paradise
A racetrack where Carrie and Tommy bet on horses

The Turnpike Carousel
A singles bar with barstools shaped like horses

Vinnie's House of Veal
A restaurant that features a revolving cow on the roof. The owner, Vinnie, is the chairman of the local restaurant association.

Vinnie's House of Veal West
A restaurant in Lake Havasu, Arizona, that hires Alice to sing for ten days

Vinnie's Place
A downtown bar run by Vinnie van Gogh

Watanabe's
A Japanese restaurant that goes out of business

The Wine and Whirl
A restaurant built on top of a tower. The building twirls while patrons eat.

Zacky's Fudge
A fudge shop near Jerome, Arizona, where Alice, Jolene, and Vera purchase five pounds of fudge

CHAPTER 10:

Alice–Episode Log

SEASON 1 (1976–1977)

Episode 1 (1.1): "Pilot" (Original broadcast date: August 31, 1976)

Writer: Robert Getchell

Director: Paul Bogert

Guest stars: Dennis Dugan, Jack O'Leary, and Arthur Space

Synopsis: Alice agrees to go out on a date with a diner patron after he mentions that he's a talent agent. All goes well until Alice realizes that he is actually a hosiery salesman.

(Note: This episode was written by Robert Getchell, who also wrote the screenplay for *Alice Doesn't Live Here Anymore*. Alfred Lutter III reprised his role as Tommy from the feature film in this episode. Linda Lavin sings "It Had to Be You." The restaurant is called Mel and Ruby's Café in this episode, a detail consistent with the feature film. That name is written on the window near the restaurant's entrance. It is visible a few times during the episode, including when Joel and Alice leave the diner together. The name of the restaurant was changed to Mel's Diner starting in episode 2 (1.2), "Alice Gets a Pass." "Pilot" was taped at CBS Television City in Hollywood. The rest of the series was taped at Warner Bros. Studios in Burbank. The set in this episode is different from the set that is used in the rest of season one.)

Linda Lavin and Polly Holliday in a scene from episode 1 (1.1), "Pilot"

Episode 2 (1.2): "Alice Gets a Pass" (Original broadcast date: September 29, 1976)

Writer: Martin Donovan

Director: Jim Drake

Guest star: Denny Miller

Synopsis: Mel encourages Jack Newhouse, his old college friend and a former pro football player, to go out with Alice. When Jack reveals to Alice that he's gay, she sorts through the situation and reveals that she would be glad simply to be his friend.

(Note: This was Philip McKeon's first episode in the part of Tommy. Denny Miller, best known for the role of Duke Shannon on *Wagon Train*, played Jack Newhouse. Starting with this episode, the name of the restaurant was changed from Mel and Ruby's Café to Mel's Diner. The new name of the restaurant can be seen written on the front entrance. Mistake: Alice never mentions moving during the series, yet various numbers for her apartment are given throughout the run of the show. In this episode, it is said that she lives in apartment 7.)

Episode 3 (1.3): "A Piece of the Rock" (Original broadcast date: October 6, 1976)

Writers: Art Baer and Ben Joelson

Director: Bill Persky

Guest stars: Jennifer Billingsley, Patrick Cranshaw, John Myhers, Lurene Tuttle, and Cletus Young

Synopsis: Alice is happy to discover that her husband, Don, had a life insurance policy, but she's upset when she learns that she is not the benefactor. She sets out to find the person listed on the policy instead of her.

Episode 4 (1.4): "Pay the Fifty Dollars" (Original broadcast date: October 13, 1976)

Writer: Lloyd Garver

Director: Bill Persky

Guess stars: Celeste Cartier, Patrick Cranshaw, Gordon Jump, Caren Kaye, Cliff Norton, and Louise Williams

Synopsis: The police mistake Alice for a prostitute when she sings at a seedy club. It takes all she can muster to fight the charges and be exonerated.

Alice...

(Note: In the first courtroom scene, the boom mic can be seen overhead between Alice and Vera when they are standing and talking to the sheriff. In the second court room scene, the boom mic can be seen overhead when the judge enters.)

Louise Williams, Linda Lavin, and Caren Kaye in a scene from episode 4 (1.4), "Pay the Fifty Dollars"

Episode 5 (1.5): "A Call to Arms" (Original broadcast date: October 20, 1976)

Writer: Lloyd Garver

Director: Jim Drake

Guest stars: Lew Gallo, Geoffrey Lewis, Jack Riley, William Neal Seals, and Emory Souza

Synopsis: Alice tries every tactic she can think of to get an obscene phone caller to stop contacting her.

(Note: The boom mic can be seen briefly in the apartment scene with Alice and Tommy. Actor Jack Riley appeared regularly in the role of Elliot Carlin in the sitcom *The Bob Newhart Show*. Geoffrey Lewis played Earl Tucker in the *Alice* spin-off *Flo*.)

Episode 6 (1.6): "The Last Review" (Original broadcast date: October 27, 1976)
Writers: R. S. Allen and Harvey Bullock
Director: James Sheldon
Guest stars: Victor Buono, Patrick Cranshaw, Brian Harvey, and Noble Willingham

Synopsis: Alice and her coworkers are concerned when a food critic dies in the diner shortly after eating Mel's chili.

(Note: The shadow from the boom mic can be seen overhead at the beginning of the first scene. When the food critic slides out of his seat after he dies, a cushion can be seen on the floor below him to pad his fall.)

Episode 7 (1.7): "Sex Education" (Original broadcast date: November 6, 1976)
Writers: Patricia Jones and Donald Reiker
Director: Bruce Bilson
Guest stars: Lara Parker, Michele Tobin, and Adam West

Synopsis: Alice is surprised to find a nude photo of a woman in Tommy's wallet and decides it's time to have a talk with him about love and sex.

(Note: The boom mic can be seen when Tommy leaves the diner. Actor Adam West portrayed Batman/Bruce Wayne in the TV series *Batman*.)

Episode 8 (1.8): "Big Daddy Dawson's Coming" (Original broadcast date: November 13, 1976)

Writers: Bruce Johnson and Arnold Kane

Director: Norman Abbott

Guest stars: Norman Alden and Patrick Cronin

Synopsis: Flo contemplates remarrying her first husband, Big Daddy Dawson, until she remembers why they got divorced in the first place.

(Note: The boom mic can be seen in Alice's apartment just before Big Daddy exits. Norman Alden played Frank Heflin in the TV series *Electra Woman and Dyna Girl*.)

Episode 9 (1.9): "Good Night, Sweet Vera" (Original broadcast date: November 20, 1976)

Writer: Simon Montner

Director: Norman Abbott

Guest star: Darrell Zwerling

Synopsis: Alice and Flo try to save Vera after she attempts to kill herself by overdosing on sleeping pills.

(Note: In this episode, the cash register has been moved to the opposite counter. The shadow of the boom mic can be seen reflecting off of the blinds in the front of the diner. Throughout the series, different street addresses for the diner are given. In this episode, Alice says that the diner is on Fourth Street.)

Episode 10 (1.10): "The Dilemma" (Original broadcast date: November 27, 1976)

Writer: Martin Donovan

Director: James Sheldon

Guest stars: Patrick Cronin and Paul Picerni

Synopsis: Alice's distant, wealthy friend, Vinnie, proposes marriage to her and an easy life. Alice reluctantly declines after concluding that love is more important than money.

Episode 11 (1.11): "Who Killed Bugs Bunny?" (Original broadcast date: December 4, 1976)

Writer: Lloyd J. Schwartz

Director: Bruce Bilson

Guest stars: Noble Willingham and Peter Zapp

Synopsis: Alice is reluctant to let Tommy go on a father-son weekend getaway with Mel when she learns that it's actually a hunting trip.

Episode 12 (1.12): "Mother-in-Law: Part 1" (Original broadcast date: December 11, 1976)

Writer: Martin Donovan

Director: William P. D'Angelo

Guest stars: Eileen Heckart and Clyde Kusatsu

Synopsis: Alice is overwhelmed with angst when her judgmental mother-in-law, Rose Hyatt, breaks up with her husband in New Jersey and decides to relocate to Phoenix.

(Note: Eileen Heckart played recurring roles in several TV series, including Jeanine in *Partners in Crime*, Emma Block in *Annie McGuire*,

Mother Emma Buchanan in *The 5 Mrs. Buchanans*, and Frances Wyle in *Murder One*.)

Episode 13 (1.13): "Mother-in-Law: Part 2" (Original broadcast date: December 18, 1976)

Writers: R. S. Allen, Bruce Johnson, and Arnold Kane

Director: William P. D'Angelo

Guest stars: Murray Hamilton, Eileen Heckart, and Noble Willingham

Synopsis: Alice helps Rose and her husband patch things up so they can resume their life together in New Jersey and give her some peace in the process.

Episode 14 (1.14): "Vera's Mortician" (Original broadcast date: December 25, 1976)

Writer: Bruce Kane

Director: Bill Hobin

Guest stars: John Fiedler, Burton Gilliam, and Tom Poston

Synopsis: Vera is elated by the prospect that the mortician she is dating wants to marry her. When Alice breaks the news to her that he is already married, Vera sorts through her feelings and accepts life without him.

(Note: The boom mic can be seen at the end of the first diner scene. Tom Poston was featured in many TV series, including as Cliff Murdock in *The Bob Newhart Show*, Mr. Bickley in *Mork & Mindy*, George Utley in *Newhart*, Floyd Norton in *Grace under Fire*, and the Clown in *Committed*.)

Episode 15 (1.15): "Mel's in Love" (Original broadcast date: January 15, 1977)

Writer: Gary David Goldberg

Director: Alan Rafkin

Guest stars: Maureen Arthur and Suze Lanier-Bramlett

Synopsis: Mel falls in love with a young, free-spirited woman who is twenty-five years his junior. Then she skips town and breaks his heart.

(Note: Suze Lanier-Bramlett played Miss Dazzle in *Electra Woman and Dina Girl*.)

Episode 16 (1.16): "The Accident" (Original broadcast date: January 22, 1977)

Writers: Harvey Bullock and Roy Kammerman

Director: Alan Rafkin

Guest stars: Hamilton Camp, Chi Chi Navarro, Raymond Singer, and Leonard Stone

Synopsis: Flo gets into an accident with Mel's car while he's out of town. She tries to get it fixed before he returns and discovers what happened.

Episode 17 (1.17): "The Failure" (Original broadcast date: January 29, 1977)

Writers: Art Baer and Ben Joelson

Director: William P. D'Angelo

Guest stars: Bernie Kopell, Lupe Ontiveros, and Henry Polk II

Synopsis: Alice tries to keep things from getting out of hand when a misguided young man holds up the diner.

(Note: Bernie Kopell played Jerry Bauman in the sitcom *That Girl*. He was best known for his role as Dr. Bricker on *The Love Boat*.)

Episode 18 (1.18): "The Hex" (Original broadcast date: February 5, 1977)
Writers: R. S. Allen and Arnold Kane

Director: Alan Rafkin

Guest stars: Kaye Ballard, Ron Carey, and Tom Mahoney

Synopsis: A shady medium puts a hex on Alice that appears to make her life fall apart. When she stops believing in its power, all is set right again in her life.

(Note: Kaye Ballard was a popular TV actress. Her notable roles included Kaye Buell in the sitcom *The Mothers-in-Law*, Angie Pallucci in *The Doris Day Show*, and Mrs. Treva Travalony in *What a Dummy*.)

Episode 19 (1.19): "The Pain of No Return" (Original broadcast date: February 12, 1977)
Writer: Rick Mittleman

Director: Alan Rafkin

Guest stars: Warren Berlinger, Arlene Golonka, and Tom Mahoney

Synopsis: Alice's financial future is jeopardized when an IRS agent informs her that she owes $2,000 for her deceased husband's unpaid taxes.

(Note: Before the tax agent leaves the diner in scene three, the edge of the set is visible when someone walks past it on the left of the screen.)

Episode 20 (1.20): "The Odd Couple" (Original broadcast date: February 26, 1977)
Writers: R. S. Allen, Harvey Bullock, Roy Kammerman, Arnold

Kane, Ellen Sherman and Diane Silver

Director: William P. D'Angelo

Guest stars: Tom Mahoney and Kenneth Mars

Synopsis: Alice lets Flo move in with her after Flo's trailer is stolen. They struggle to make the best of it even though each gets on the other's nerves.

Episode 21 (1.21): "A Night to Remember" (Original broadcast date: March 5, 1977)

Writers: R. S. Allen and Arnold Kane

Director: Alan Rafkin

Guest star: Tom Mahoney

Synopsis: Vera and Travis hit it off and decide to get married until Vera has second thoughts.

(Note: A crew member can be seen briefly in Alice's apartment when Vera waits for Travis.)

Episode 22 (1.22): "Mel's Cup" (Original broadcast date: March 12, 1977)

Writers: Harvey Bullock and Roy Kammerman

Director: Norman Abbott

Guest stars: Tom Mahoney and Billy Sands

Synopsis: Flo gives Mel's prize navy cup away only to discover that it has great sentimental value to him. She and Alice contemplate how to put it back in the diner without Mel's knowledge.

(Note: The boom mic is briefly seen when Alice approaches Mel in the diner's kitchen.)

Episode 23 (1.23): "The Bundle" (Original broadcast date: March 19, 1977)

Writers: Art Baer and Ben Joelson

Director: Norman Abbott

Guest stars: Florence Halop, Michael Keenan, and Tom Mahoney

Synopsis: When Flo finds a huge bag of money under a table in the diner, Alice urges her to try and locate its owner.

Episode 24 (1.24): "Mel's Happy Burger" (Original broadcast date: March 26, 1977)

Writer: Arnold Kane

Director: Burt Brinckerhoff

Guest stars: John Fiedler, Burton Gilliam, and Ronnie Schell

Synopsis: Alice and her coworkers shoot a TV commercial in an attempt to increase business at the diner.

(Note: The boom mic can be seen as Buford heads toward the door to leave the diner. It is also seen when Alice sings the TV commercial jingle in her apartment and at the end of the TV commercial shoot in the diner. In the last scene in Alice's apartment, a stain is visible near the neckline of Tommy's shirt. Although this was the last episode to air in season one, it was one of the first episodes shot.)

SEASON 2 (1977–1978)

Episode 25 (2.1): "The Second Time 'Round" (Original broadcast date: October 2, 1977)

Writer: Tom Whedon

Director: Kim Friedman

Guest stars: Lewis Arquette, MacIntyre Dixon, and Rod McCary

Synopsis: Flo's third husband, Langley Moss, informs her that their divorce was never finalized. Flo is excited by the prospect that they are still married but unhappy when she learns that Langley wants a divorce, so he can marry another woman.

Episode 26 (2.2): "The Indian Taker" (Original broadcast date: October 9, 1977)

Writer: Tom Whedon

Director: Marc Daniels

Guest stars: Don Chastain, Larry Hovis, and Victor Jory

Synopsis: When an aging Native American comes to the diner and insists that his people's ancient burial grounds are under the diner, Mel pays him $200 to reacquire the land, only to discover that the man is a fraud.

Episode 27 (2.3): "86 the Waitresses" (Original broadcast date: October 23, 1977)

Writer: Sybil Adelman

Director: Marc Daniels

Guest stars: Bill Fiore, Bob Harks, Dave Shelley, and J. S. "Joe" Young

Synopsis: When Mel hires a waiter at a high salary, the waitresses fight for equal pay.

(Note: The "change your order" plotline was previously used in the "Lucy Changes Her Mind" episode of *I Love Lucy*, which Madelyn Davis and Bob Carroll Jr. cowrote with Jess Oppenheimer.)

Episode 28 (2.4): "Alice by Moonlight" (Original broadcast date: October 30, 1977)

Writer: Tom Whedon

Director: Kim Friedman

Guest stars: Norman Alden, Morey Amsterdam, Duane R. Campbell, Patrick Cranshaw, Jane Dulo, Bernie Kuby, and Gloria LeRoy

Synopsis: Alice comes into work tired every morning after moonlighting as a singer at night. When Mel finds out, he fires her. Soon after, he realizes that he can't run the diner without her.

(Note: Linda Lavin sings "Embraceable You," "Get Happy," "But Not for Me," and "You Do Something to Me.")

Episode 29 (2.5): "Single Belles" (Original broadcast date: November 6, 1977)

Writer: Bruce Howard

Director: Kim Friedman

Guest stars: Victoria Carroll, Patrick Cranshaw, Robert Hogan, Jessamine Milner, Charles Thomas Murphy, Frank O'Brien, Christian Seaborn, Lynne Marie Stewart, John Welsh, and Marty Zagon

Synopsis: When Alice, Flo, and Vera discover that they are all dating the same man, they promptly break it off with him.

(Note: This episode marked Victoria Carroll's first appearance on *Alice*. In it, she plays the role of girl in the bar. In later episodes, Carroll returns as Mel's girlfriend, Marie.)

Episode 30 (2.6): "The Sixty Minutes Man" (Original broadcast date: November 13, 1977)

Writers: Warren S. Murray, George Tibbles, Tom Whedon

Director: Kim Friedman

Guest stars: Patrick Cranshaw, Michael V. Gazzo, Dave Ketchum, Bruce Kimmel, John Lawlor, and Bob McClurg

Synopsis: Alice sees a photo of a former gangster, Joe (Michael V. Gazzo), on the TV series *60 Minutes* and concludes that he's one of the diner's customers.

(Note: Linda Lavin and Michael V. Gazzo sing "Itsy Bitsy Spider.")

Episode 31 (2.7): "That Old Back Magic" (Original broadcast date: December 4, 1977)

Writers: Robert Fisher and Arthur Marx

Director: William Asher

Guest star: Edward Winter

Synopsis: Mel throws his back out during a get-together at Alice's apartment and has to stay until it mends.

(Note: This was the first episode that Arthur Marx, Groucho Marx's son, cowrote for the series.)

Episode 32 (2.8): "Love Is Sweeping the Counter" (Original broadcast date: December 11, 1977)

Writer: Arthur Rabin

Director: Kim Friedman

Guest star: Cliff A. Pellow

Synopsis: Flo and Mel strike up a passionate love affair, but Mel's feelings cool when Flo starts to run his life. He enlists Alice's help to break it off with Flo.

Beth Howland, Linda Lavin, Philip McKeon, Polly Holliday, and Vic Tayback in a scene from episode 33 (2.9), "A Semi-Merry Christmas"

Episode 33 (2.9): "A Semi-Merry Christmas" (Original broadcast date: December 18, 1977)

Writers: Bob Carroll Jr., Madelyn Davis, and Tom Whedon

Director: Marc Daniels

Guest stars: Patrick Cranshaw and Patrick Cronin

Synopsis: Mel offers to drive Tommy and the waitresses to Colorado Springs in a customer's rig so they can have a White Christmas. In the process, they get stuck on a desolate, snowed-out road. Some fancy CB talk attracts the attention of a tow truck that pulls them to safety.

(Note: Linda Lavin, Polly Holliday, Beth Howland, Vic Tayback, and Philip McKeon sing "Jingle Bells.")

Episode 34 (2.10): "Oh, George Burns!" (Original broadcast date: January 1, 1978)

Writers: Fred S. Fox and Seamon Jacobs

Director: Marc Daniels

Guest stars: George Burns and Duane R. Campbell

Synopsis: When actor George Burns stops in at the diner after playing God in the film *Oh, God!*, Vera thinks he really is God. Alice and George try to convince her that he's not.

(Note: Linda Lavin and George Burns sing "By the Light of the Silvery Moon.")

Episode 35 (2.11): "The Eyes of Texas" (Original broadcast date: January 8, 1978)

Writers: Robert Fisher and Arthur Marx

Director: Kim Friedman

Guest stars: Ron Masak, Bob McClurg, and John Myhers

Synopsis: Flo reluctantly gets glasses after her eyesight begins to fail. When she's teased for it, she switches to contact lenses instead.

(Note: This is the first episode in which we see three doors in the hall of Alice's apartment that lead to the bedrooms and a bathroom.)

Episode 36 (2.12): "Love is A Free Throw" (Original broadcast date: January 15, 1978)

Writers: Robert Fisher and Arthur Marx

Director: Marc Daniels

Guest stars: Patrick Cranshaw, Brad Gorman, Marvin Kaplan, and Joe Silver

Synopsis: Alice fends off Tommy's high-school friend's advances when he develops a crush on her.

(Note: Linda Lavin sings part of the song "As Time Goes By" in this episode.)

Episode 37 (2.13): "Close Encounters of the Worst Kind" (Original broadcast date: January 22, 1978)
Writers: Robert Fisher and Arthur Marx

Director: William Asher

Guest stars: Boyd Bodwell, Charles Cyphers, Larry Hovis, and Barbara Sharma

Synopsis: Alice employs various psychological techniques that she has learned in her night school psychology course to help her coworkers trust each other again.

(Note: In act two of this episode, the actors walk around a cushion that has been placed on the floor behind Alice's sofa. It is ultimately used to ease Linda Lavin's backward fall to the floor.)

Episode 38 (2.14): "The Pharmacist" (Original broadcast date: January 29, 1978)
Writers: Chris Hayward and Michael Loman

Director: Noam Pitlik

Guest stars: Patrick Cranshaw, Bob Dishy, Gordon Hurst, Stack Pierce, and William Sherwood

Synopsis: A pharmacist threatens to end his life by taking a cyanide pill in the diner if the president of the United States doesn't return his call and agree to stop killing people by putting additives in their food. Alice admires his stand but encourages him to live, pointing out that he can accomplish more that way.

(Note: Chris Hayward produced this episode during the summer of 1977, prior to Madelyn Davis and Bob Carroll Jr.'s taking over production of the series. At one point in the episode, the clock on the diner wall reads 11:40. After Alice learns that the pill the pharmacist wants to take really is cyanide, the clock reads 11:30.)

Episode 39 (2.15): "Love Me, Love My Horse" (Original broadcast date: February 5, 1978)

Writer: Tom Whedon

Director: William Asher

Guest star: Burton Gilliam

Synopsis: When Flo's brother, Jimmy-Joe, falls in love with Alice and proposes marriage, it takes all Alice can muster, along with some help from Jimmy-Joe's horse, to get him to realize that they should just be friends.

Episode 40 (2.16): "Florence of Arabia" (Original broadcast date: February 19, 1978)

Writer: Tom Whedon

Director: Kim Friedman

Guest stars: Richard Libertini and George Loros

Synopsis: Flo plans to marry a man from the Middle East until Alice informs her that he currently has three other wives.

(Note: Chris Hayward produced this episode during the summer of 1977, prior to Madelyn Davis and Bob Carroll Jr.'s taking over production of the series. It is the first episode to feature the large Mel's Diner sign outside of the diner in the opening credits.)

Episode 41 (2.17): "The Cuban Connection" (Original broadcast date: February 26, 1978)

Writers: Robert Fisher and Arthur Marx

Director: William Asher

Guest stars: Desi Arnaz, Marvin Kaplan, and Janis Paige

Synopsis: After Alice's singing teacher breaks up with her husband, Paco, Paco makes advances toward Alice. She declines his interest and tries to help the couple sort through their differences and get back together again.

(Note: During the last scene in Alice's apartment, the wire that makes the sofa close can be seen hanging down from the ceiling.)

Vic Tayback, Polly Holliday, Beth Howland, Marvin Kaplan, and Patrick Cranshaw in a scene from episode 42 (2.18), "Mel's Big Five-O"

Episode 42 (2.18): "Mel's Big Five-O" (Original broadcast date: March 5, 1978)

Writer: Warren S. Murray

Director: William Asher

Guest stars: Patrick Cranshaw, Patrick Cronin, Marvin Kaplan, Bob McClurg, and Noble Willingham

Synopsis: Mel is disappointed to find that no one wants to throw him a party for his fiftieth birthday. He soon learns that things aren't always as they seem.

(Note: Linda Lavin and Polly Holliday sing an a cappella parody of "I've Been Working on the Railroad.")

Episode 43 (2.19): "Don't Lock Now" (Original broadcast date: March 12, 1978)

Writer: Tom Whedon

Director: William Asher

Guest stars: Bill McClean and Nedra Volz

Synopsis: Mel and the waitresses are surprised to learn that the sweet old lady who sells pies to the diner actually steals their ingredients from Mel's storeroom.

(Note: The top of the boom mic can be seen as Esther walks over to Alice to show her her son's letter.)

Episode 44 (2.20): "The Star in the Storeroom" (Original broadcast date: March 19, 1978)

Writers: Robert Fisher and Arthur Marx

Director: Marc Daniels

Guest stars: Graham Jarvis, Marvin Kaplan, and Jerry Reed

Synopsis: When Jerry Reed comes to the diner to give his childhood babysitter, Flo, and her coworkers tickets to his concert, a series of mishaps make it look doubtful that he'll make it to the show that night.

(Note: Linda Lavin sings an excerpt from the song "Zing! Went the Strings of My Heart" in this episode.)

Episode 45 (2.21): "Mel's Recession" (Original broadcast date: April 2, 1978)

Writers: Robert Fisher, Arthur Marx, and Tom Whedon

Director: William Asher

Guest star: Marvin Kaplan

Synopsis: Mel's accountant informs him that the diner lost money the previous year and that he needs to reduce expenses. Mel decides to let one of the waitresses go to make up for the deficit, which leaves them all vying to keep their jobs.

Episode 46 (2.22): "Earthquake" (Original broadcast date: April 9, 1978)

Writers: Chris Hayward and Gary Markowitz

Director: Noam Pitlik

Guest stars: J. J. Barry, Edward Binns, Ancel Cook, and Gordon Hurst

Synopsis: Alice, Vera, Flo, and Mel panic as they wait for a predicted earthquake to hit.

(Note: Chris Hayward produced this episode during the summer of 1977, prior to Madelyn Davis and Bob Carroll Jr.'s taking over production of the series.)

Episode 47 (2.23): "The Reporter" (Original broadcast date: February 12, 1978)

Writer: Michael Loman

Director: Dennis Steinmetz

Guest stars: Wil Albert, Robert Costanzo, Gene Crowley, Richard Erdman, and Eleanor Zee

Synopsis: Alice aids a reporter who comes to the diner concerned that the mafia is after him for writing an important story.

(Note: Vera wears glasses in this episode.)

Episode 48 (2.24): "The Bus" (Original broadcast date: March 26, 1978)

Writers: Chris Hayward and Eric Tarloff

Director: Noam Pitlik

Guest stars: Michael Alldredge, Rod Browning, Rod Colbin, Beatrice Colen, Joe George, Lee Kessler, James Lashly, Walter Mathews, Lupe Ontiveros, Allan Rich, Gay Rowan, Lila Teigh, and Pat Van Patten

Synopsis: Mel is excited when a tour bus stops at the diner and hopes it will become a regular occurrence. Meanwhile, Alice, Vera, and Flo are concerned about how they will manage to keep up with all the extra work.

(Note: Chris Hayward produced this episode during the summer of 1977, prior to Madelyn Davis and Bob Carroll Jr.'s taking over production of the series. It features new clips in the opening credits and a new rendition of the theme song, "There's a New Girl in Town," sung by Linda Lavin. It is the only episode in this season to feature this opening. The opening was used regularly during season three.)

Philip McKeon and Linda Lavin (as Sam Butler) in a scene from episode 49 (3.1), "Take Him, He's Yours"

SEASON 3 (1978–1979)

Episode 49 (3.1): "Take Him, He's Yours" (Original broadcast date: September 24, 1978)

Writers: Robert Fisher and Arthur Marx

Director: William Asher

Guest stars: Patrick Cronin, Marvin Kaplan, and Bob McClurg

Synopsis: Mel agrees to let Tommy stay with him when Tommy gets tired of Alice's rules. Mel soon finds that parenting isn't as easy as he thought it would be.

(Note: Starting with this episode, the diner's pay phone has been moved to the wall near the main entrance. Linda Lavin scats the theme song to the series during the closing credits.)

Episode 50 (3.2): "Car Wars" (Original broadcast date: October 1, 1978)

Writers: Robert Fisher and Arthur Marx

Director: William Asher

Guest stars: Patrick Cronin, Marvin Kaplan, and Bob McClurg

Synopsis: Mel sells the waitresses his old car but tries to buy it back on the sly when he hears that a dealer will pay him top dollar for it.

(Note: The boom mic is seen in the diner when Mel, Alice, Vera, and Flo shake hands in the alley. This episode features Linda Lavin singing the theme song over the closing credits.)

Episode 51 (3.3): "Citizen Mel" (Original broadcast date: October 8, 1978)

Writer: Charles Isaacs

Director: William Asher

Guest stars: Patrick Cronin, Marvin Kaplan, Bob McClurg, and William Pierson

Synopsis: Mel helps the police identify a local jewelry thief but fears for his life when the man is released due to insufficient evidence.

(Note: When Cecil rushes in with the newspaper, it appears to be nighttime outside; however, the next time the window is shown in the scene, it looks like it's daytime.)

Episode 52 (3.4): "Vera's Popcorn Romance" (Original broadcast date: October 15, 1978)

Writer: Tom Whedon

Director: William Asher

Guest stars: Johnnie Decker, Alan Haufrect, Marvin Kaplan, Barbara Minkus-Barron, and Steve Nevil

Synopsis: When Vera starts to date fellow cinephile Brian, her coworkers become concerned for her well-being and sneak into the theater to make sure he's worthy of her.

(Note: This episode features Linda Lavin singing a new version of the series theme song during the opening credits. The boom mic can be seen in the movie theater scene from below when the couple argues.)

Episode 53 (3.5): "Block Those Kicks" (Original broadcast date: October 22, 1978)

Writers: Robert Fisher and Arthur Marx

Director: William Asher

Guest stars: Marvin Kaplan, Bob McClurg, Tara Talboy, and Lou Tiano

Synopsis: Alice, Flo, and Vera agree to give up their vices to help Mel kick his betting habit, so he won't gamble away the diner.

(Note: When Flo turns on the burner on Alice's stove, there is no flame.)

Episode 54 (3.6): "What Happened to the Class of '78" (Original broadcast date: October 29, 1978)

Writer: Tom Whedon

Director: William Asher

Guest stars: Harvey J. Goldenberg and Lyman Ward

Synopsis: Alice offers to help Flo study when she goes to night school to get a GED, but Flo is distracted by invitations to socialize.

Episode 55 (3.7): "Better Never Than Late" (Original broadcast date: November 5, 1978)

Writer: Tom Whedon

Director: William Asher

Guest stars: Steve Franken, Marvin Kaplan, Dave Madden, and Jim Varney

Synopsis: A thief holds up the diner when Alice works a late shift alone one night.

(Note: David Madden begins a recurring role as a soccer coach in this episode. Jim Varney, who plays Flo's date, Milo, went on to star as the character Ernest P. Worrell in a series of TV commercials, popular comedy films, and the sitcom *Hey Vern, It's Ernest!*)

Episode 56 (3.8): "Mel's in the Family Way" (Original broadcast date: November 11, 1978)

Writer: Jerry Winnick

Director: William Asher

Guest stars: Shirley Mitchell, Michael Pataki, Steve Shaw, and Dave Shelley

Synopsis: After Mel reconnects with an old high-school friend and his family, he wishes he had a wife and kids of his own. He tries to turn Alice and Tommy into his surrogate family, but it doesn't work out.

(Note: Beginning with this episode, the closing credits feature an instrumental version of the series' theme song.)

Episode 57 (3.9): "Who Ordered the Hot Turkey?" (Original broadcast date: November 19, 1978)

Writer: Tom Whedon

Director: William Asher

Guest stars: Joyce Bulifant, Owen Bush, John Colton, James Cromwell, Corey Feldman, Peter Leeds, Nancy McKeon, and Derek Wells

Synopsis: After Alice convinces Mel to let her host a Thanksgiving dinner for orphans at the diner, Mel calls the local TV station and tries to turn the occasion into a publicity event to bring in more business.

(Note: Joyce Bulifant plays the TV news reporter in this episode. She went on to appear regularly in the spin-off series *Flo* as Flo's close friend Miriam Willoughby. This is the first of two episodes in which Philip McKeon's sister, Nancy, appears. Here she portrays one of the orphans and sits beside him during the Thanksgiving dinner scene. Actor Corey Feldman also plays an orphan in that scene.)

Episode 58 (3.10): "The Happy Hoofers" (Original broadcast date: November 28, 1978)

Writers: Robert Fisher and Arthur Marx

Director: William Asher

Guest stars: Duane R. Campbell and Bob McClurg

Synopsis: Alice takes a second job singing telegrams to earn extra money to start a college tuition fund for Tommy. When Mel finds out that she's moonlighting, he fires her.

(Note: Linda Lavin, Polly Holliday, and Beth Howland sing a telegram to the melody of "Swanee.")

Episode 59 (3.11): "A Slight Case of ESP" (Original broadcast date: December 3, 1978)

Writers: Alan Rose and Fred Rubin

Director: William Asher

Guest stars: Marvin Kaplan, Hazel Shermet, and Tom Williams

Synopsis: After Vera predicts several events that then occur in the diner, she begins to think she might have ESP.

Episode 60 (3.12): "The Principal of the Thing" (Original broadcast date: December 10, 1978)

Writers: Robert Fisher and Arthur Marx

Director: William Asher

Guest stars: Miriam Byrd-Nethery, Gary Collins, Lou Frizzell, and Joseph V. Perry

Synopsis: Alice starts to date Tommy's principal, Jim Thorton. Their relationship causes friction between her and Tommy, however, so she stops seeing him.

Episode 61 (3.13): "What're You Doing New Year's Eve?" (Original broadcast date: December 31, 1978)

Writers: Dawn Aldredge and Marion Freeman

Director: Marc Daniels

Guest stars: Victoria Carroll, Randy Doney, Alan Haufrect, Robert Hogan, Will Hunt, Michael Keenan, Ed Kenney, Ted Lehman, and Dave Madden

Synopsis: Flo doesn't have a date on New Year's Eve, so she agrees to work a late shift at the diner. It's an uneventful evening until her coworkers stop by and help her ring in the new year.

(Note: This is Victoria Carroll's first appearance as Mel's girlfriend, Marie. The cast sings "Auld Lang Syne.")

Episode 62 (3.14): "Sweet Charity" (Original broadcast date: January 14, 1979)

Writers: Robert Fisher and Arthur Marx

Director: William Asher

Guest stars: Michael Ballard, Victoria Carroll, Patrick Cronin, Alan Haufrect, Cliff A. Pellow, and Ron Rifkin

Synopsis: Alice's boyfriend, Eric, lets her invite her coworkers to join them at a celebrity charity ball. When they realize they can't bring dates, conflict ensues. Luckily, Eric makes arrangements so everyone can attend.

Episode 63 (3.15): "The Fourth Time Around" (Original broadcast date: January 21, 1979)

Writers: Robert Fisher and Arthur Marx

Director: William Asher

Guest stars: Roger Bowen, Carmine Caridi, Patrick Cronin, Lou Frizzell, Marvin Kaplan, Bob McClurg, and Dick Wilson

Synopsis: Mel's brother, Al, and Flo have a whirlwind romance that leads to their engagement. During the wedding ceremony, Flo realizes that she's not ready for another marriage. They call it off but decide to go on the honeymoon anyway.

(Note: Dick Wilson plays a drunk in this episode. He also played a drunk in the TV series *Bewitched*. For twenty-five years, he portrayed the role of Mr. Whipple in the Charmin bathroom tissue commercials. Linda Lavin and Dick Wilson sing "The Yellow Rose of Texas" at the wedding ceremony. The wedding party later reprises the song without the bride and groom.)

Episode 64 (3.16): "Tommy's First Love" (Original broadcast date: January 28, 1979)

Writers: Robert Fisher and Arthur Marx

Director: William Asher

Guest stars: Olivia Barash, Duane R. Campbell, Bruce Kirby, and Dave Madden

Synopsis: Tommy becomes tired of Alice's rules and runs away with his girlfriend. Flo and Earl eventually find the two gorging on food late one night at the diner and convince them to go back home.

(Note: Olivia Barash was featured in many TV shows including a two-part episode of *Little House on the Prairie* in which she played Sylvia. She portrayed Maxie in the musical TV series *Fame* as well. The boom mic can be seen in Alice's apartment when Alice sits on the sofa.)

Episode 65 (3.17): "Mel Grows Up" (Original broadcast date: February 5, 1979)

Writers: Robert Fisher and Arthur Marx

Director: William Asher

Guest stars: Duane R. Campbell, Robert Hogan, and Martha Raye

Alice . . .

Synopsis: Mel is afraid to confront his mother because of a childhood trauma. Alice encourages him to take a loving stand.

(Note: This is Martha Raye's first appearance on the show as Mel's mother, Carrie Sharples.)

Martha Raye and Vic Tayback in a scene from episode 65 (3.17), "Mel Grows Up"

Episode 66 (3.18): "Vera's Broken Heart" (Original broadcast date: February 18, 1979)

Writers: Robert Fisher, Arthur Marx, and Tom Whedon

Director: Lee Lochhead

Guest stars: Michael Ballard, Terry Bolo, Marvin Kaplan, Michael Keenan, and Dawson Mays

Synopsis: Vera is heartbroken when her boyfriend, Brian, breaks up with her and starts to date another woman.

(Note: The boom mic can be seen from above in Vera's apartment when Vera is sitting in a chair.)

Episode 67 (3.19): "Alice's Decision" (Original broadcast date: February 25, 1979)

Writers: Robert Fisher, Arthur Marx, and Tom Whedon

Director: Lee Lochhead

Guest stars: Marvin Kaplan, Karen Morrow, and Bobby Ramsen

Synopsis: Alice is hired to replace the lead singer in her friend's group, The Clef Dwellers, but is forced to back out when she develops a chronic case of the hiccups.

(Note: Beth Howland sings "I'm Looking Over a Four-Leaf Clover." Linda Lavin sings "It's Only a Paper Moon." Linda Lavin and Philip McKeon sing "Ain't We Got Fun.")

Episode 68 (3.20): "The Last Stow It: Part 1" (Original broadcast date: March 11, 1979)

Writers: Robert Fisher and Arthur Marx

Director: William Asher

Guest stars: Duane R. Campbell, Don Chastain, Hans Conried, Bob Hastings, Marvin Kaplan, and Dave Madden

Synopsis: Mel retires and sells the diner to his golf partner, Randolph Briggs. When Mel wants the diner back, Randolph refuses to sell and throws Mel, Alice, Flo, and Vera out.

(Note: This episode features opening credits and clips reprised from season 2.)

Episode 69 (3.21): "The Last Stow It: Part 2" (Original broadcast date: March 11, 1979)

Writers: Robert Fisher and Arthur Marx

Director: William Asher

Guest stars: Michael Ballard, Duane R. Campbell, Hans Conried, Patrick Cronin, Randy Doney, Bob Hastings, Marvin Kaplan, Ed Kenney, and John Welsh

Synopsis: Alice dons her Sam Butler persona in an attempt to strong-arm Randolph Briggs into selling the diner back to Mel.

(Note: After Randolph Briggs flees the diner, he can be seen standing on the street outside the window.)

Episode 70 (3.22): "If the Shoe Fits" (Original broadcast date: March 18, 1979)

Writers: Charles Isaacs and Tom Whedon

Director: Marc Daniels

Guest stars: Danny Goldman and Fred McCarren

Synopsis: When Alice falls in love with the director of a children's play in which she and Vera get cast, she worries that he is too young for her.

Episode 71 (3.23): "My Fair Vera" (Original broadcast date: March 25, 1979)

Writers: Robert Fisher and Arthur Marx

Director: William Asher

Guest stars: Larry Breeding, Duane R. Campbell, Don Chastain, Lew Horn, Bryan O'Byrne, and Bobby Ramsen

Synopsis: Positive newspaper reviews for Vera's performance in a recent children's play help her land a job in a local TV commercial.

(Note: The boom mic is seen twice during the TV commercial shoot. During the shoot, Beth Howland sings a jingle that uses the melody to "Turkey in the Straw." Linda Lavin sings excerpts from "Am I Blue?," "Someone to Watch over Me," and "Anything Goes.")

Episode 72 (3.24): "Flo Finds Her Father" (Original broadcast date: April 1, 1979)

Writers: Dawn Aldredge and Marion Freeman

Director: William Asher

Guest stars: Hamilton Camp, Marvin Kaplan, and Forrest Tucker

Synopsis: Flo's estranged father reenters her life after a thirty-year absence and tries to make amends for all the pain he has caused her.

(Note: Flo's father says that he left his wife and daughter, but he doesn't mention that he also has a son named Jimmy-Joe. That was established in episode 39 [2.15], "Love Me, Love My Horse.")

SEASON 4 (1979–1980)

Episode 73 (4.1): "Has Anyone Here Seen Telly?" (Original broadcast date: September 23, 1979)

Writers: Robert Fisher, Charles Isaacs, Arthur Marx, and Tom Whedon

Director: Marc Daniels

Guest stars: George Savalas, Telly Savalas, and Marvin Kaplan

Synopsis: None of Vera's coworkers believes her when she tells them that Telly Savalas stopped at the diner while they were away.

(Note: Prior to the opening credits, an announcer mentions that Telly Savalas will guest star in this episode. Linda Lavin and Telly Savalas sing a parody of the song "My Bonnie.")

Episode 74 (4.2): "Mona Lisa Alice" (Original broadcast date: September 30, 1979)

Writers: Charles Isaacs and Tom Whedon

Director: Marc Daniels

Guest stars: Raleigh Bond, Duane R. Campbell, Robert Hogan, Marvin Kaplan, Nancy Lenehan, Dave Madden, and Dick Miller

Synopsis: Tommy wants a new father, so he encourages Alice's boyfriend, Greg, to marry her.

(Note: Philip McKeon sings "La Vie en Rose" and plays the guitar in this episode.)

Episode 75 (4.3): "Mel Loves Marie" (Original broadcast date: October 7, 1979)

Writers: Robert Fisher and Arthur Marx

Life Behind the Counter in Mel's Greasy Spoon

Director: Marc Daniels

Guest stars: Duane R. Campbell, Ed Carroll, Victoria Carroll, and Dave Madden

Synopsis: When Mel and Marie get engaged, Earl encourages Mel to get a prenuptial agreement.

Beth Howland and Philip McKeon in a scene from episode 76 (4.4), "Vera Robs the Cradle"

Episode 76 (4.4): "Vera Robs the Cradle" (Original broadcast date: October 21, 1979)

Writers: Robert Fisher and Arthur Marx

Director: Marc Daniels

Guest stars: Michael Ballard, Howard Platt, and Annrae Walterhouse

Synopsis: After Tommy develops a crush on Vera, she struggles to find a way to tell him that she just wants to be friends.

(Note: Philip McKeon sings "As Time Goes By" in this episode.)

Episode 77 (4.5): "Flo's Chili Reception" (Original broadcast date: October 28, 1979)

Writers: Robert Fisher and Arthur Marx

Director: Marc Daniels

Guest stars: Michael Alldredge, Med Flory, Ted Gehring, Richard B. Shull, and Claude Stroud

Synopsis: Flo is insulted when Mel tells her that the owner of Barney's Burger Barn is dating her only so he can get her to tell him what Mel's chili recipe is.

Episode 78 (4.6): "Little Alice Bluenose" (Original broadcast date: November 4, 1979)

Writers: Charles Isaacs and Tom Whedon

Director: Marc Daniels

Guest stars: Susan Campbell, Alan Haufrect, Spencer Milligan, and Terry Wills

Synopsis: Alice is surprised to learn that her boyfriend is picking up extra cash by posing nude in Vera's night-school art class.

Episode 79 (4.7): "Carrie Sharples Strikes Again" (Original broadcast date: November 11, 1979)

Writers: Robert Fisher and Arthur Marx

Director: Lee Lochhead

Guest stars: Michael Ballard, Duane R. Campbell, Patrick Cronin, Ted Gehring, Marvin Kaplan, and Martha Raye

Synopsis: Carrie takes over as chef at the diner when Mel's back goes out. She is surprised to learn that he feels threatened by her culinary skills, which prevent him from returning to work.

(Note: The boom mic is visible during the scene in Mel's apartment.)

Episode 80 (4.8): "Mel's in the Kitchen with Dinah" (Original broadcast date: November 18, 1979)

Writers: Charles Isaacs and Tom Whedon

Director: Norman Abbott

Guest stars: Ancel Cook, Guich Koock, Pamela Myers, Ronnie Schell, and Dinah Shore

Synopsis: Mel is invited to cook his chili on Dinah Shore's TV show but refuses to tell the world what his secret ingredient is.

(Note: Prior to the opening credits, an announcer mentions that Dinah Shore will guest star in this episode. Linda Lavin and Dinah Shore sing "Please Don't Talk About Me When I'm Gone.")

Episode 81 (4.9): "Cabin Fever" (Original broadcast date: December 2, 1979)

Writers: Thad Mumford and Dan Wilcox

Director: Marc Daniels

Guest stars: Victoria Carroll, Patrick Cronin, and Ed Kenney

Synopsis: Mel, Marie, and the waitresses get stuck in a rundown cabin during a severe storm.

Episode 82 (4.10): "My Cousin, Art Carney" (Original broadcast date: December 9, 1979)

Writers: Robert Fisher, Charles Isaacs, Arthur Marx, and Tom Whedon

Director: Lee Lochhead

Guest stars: Art Carney, and Alan Oppenheimer

Synopsis: Vera asks her distant relative, Art Carney, to partner with Mel and sell his chili commercially. In the process, Vera gives him 85 percent of the profits, leaving Mel with practically nothing.

(Note: Beth Howland sings "Brother, Can You Spare a Dime?" Art Carney and Linda Lavin sing a commercial jingle about chili.)

Episode 83 (4.11): "Mel, the Magi" (Original broadcast date: December 23, 1979)

Writers: Mark Egan and Mark Solomon

Director: Marc Daniels

Guest stars: Michael Alldredge, Ancel Cook, Randy Doney, Ted Gehring, Will Hunt, Marvin Kaplan, Ed Kenney, and Jack Kruschen

Synopsis: Alice and each of her coworkers secretly pawn one of their prized possessions to buy someone else a Christmas gift. When Mel discovers what they've done, he makes sure that everyone gets what they want for the holiday.

(Note: The cast sings "Deck the Halls" and "Silent Night." This episode was inspired by O. Henry's short story *The Gift of the Magi* [1905].)

Episode 84 (4.12): "Good Buddy Flo" (Original broadcast date: January 6, 1980)

Writers: Linda Morris and Vic Rauseo

Director: Marc Daniels

Guest stars: Sherry Jackson, Marvin Kaplan, and Michael MacRae

Synopsis: Flo tries to impress her trucker boyfriend, Sy, by telling him that she knows how to drive a truck. After he leaves, Flo asks Alice to teach her how to drive Sy's truck. The lesson leads to disastrous results.

(Note: The boom mic can be seen in the diner when Mel shakes Sy's hand. When the truck crashes through the front of the diner, the "closed" sign drops to the floor. A few moments later, it can be seen stuck in the grill of the truck.)

Episode 85 (4.13): "Alice in TV Land" (Original broadcast date: January 13, 1980)

Writers: Charles Isaacs and Tom Whedon

Director: Norman Abbott

Guest stars: Eve Arden, Michael Alldredge, Raleigh Bond, Kimberley Dashiell, Christian Juttner, Ed Kenney, and Dave Madden

Synopsis: Tommy calls his mother a nag on a TV talk show, causing a rift between him and Alice. The show's host comes to the diner to try and mediate the situation.

(Note: Prior to the opening credits, an announcer mentions that Eve Arden will guest star in this episode. The boom mic can be seen in the diner's kitchen when Mel enters and chats with the waitresses. The hamburgers that Alice makes on her apartment stove are uncooked when she flips them in the pan.)

Episode 86 (4.14): "Alice Beats the Clock" (Original broadcast date: January 27, 1980)

Writer: Katherine Green

Director: Marc Daniels

Guest stars: Michael Alldredge, Michael Ballard, Duane R. Campbell, and Ted Gehring

Synopsis: Mel makes Alice, Flo, and Vera use a time clock in an attempt to save money. They go on strike after he refuses to pay them for coming in on a Sunday to organize the storeroom.

(Note: Linda Lavin, Polly Holliday, and Beth Howland sing the last few lines of the song "Look for the Union Label" in this episode. The boom mic can be seen when Tommy skates in the picket line outside the diner.)

Episode 87 (4.15): "Carrie's Wedding" (Original broadcast date: February 3, 1980)

Writers: Mark Egan and Mark Solomon

Director: Gary Shirnokawa

Guest stars: Duane R. Campbell, Ancel Cook, Marvin Kaplan, Phil Leeds, Martha Raye, Vernon Weddle, and Howard Witt

Synopsis: Carrie and her fiancé come to Phoenix to get married. Mel wants no part of it when he discovers that his mother's husband-to-be is younger than he is.

(Note: Martha Raye sings part of the song "Ah, Sweet Mystery of Life.")

Episode 88 (4.16): "My Funny Valentine Tux" (Original broadcast date: February 10, 1980)

Writers: Charles Isaacs and Tom Whedon

Director: Marc Daniels

Guest stars: Raleigh Bond, Kelly Parsons, Wayne Storm, and Terry Wills

Synopsis: Tommy sings on the street in an attempt to earn money to rent a tuxedo for a school dance. When that doesn't produce results, Alice, Flo, and Vera chip in to make him an outfit instead.

(Note: In this episode, Philip McKeon sings "Bye, Bye, Blackbird." Linda Lavin sings "Mountain Greenery.")

Episode 89 (4.17): "Auld Acquaintances Should Be Forgot" (Original broadcast date: February 17, 1980)
Writers: Robert Fisher and Arthur Marx

Director: Marc Daniels

Guest stars: Michael Alldredge, Eddie Barth, Duane R. Campbell, Ted Gehring, Marvin Kaplan, and Reva Rose

Synopsis: Mel's old navy buddy, Rocky, comes to town looking for solace after his wife leaves him, but no one can lift his spirits.

Episode 90 (4.18): "Flo's Farewell" (Original broadcast date: February 24, 1980)
Writers: Robert Fisher and Arthur Marx

Director: Marc Daniels

Guest stars: Michael Alldredge, Duane R. Campbell, Ted Gehring, and Marvin Kaplan

Synopsis: Flo contemplates leaving the diner and taking a head hostess job at a restaurant in Houston.

(Note: This is Polly Holliday's last episode.)

Alice . . .

Diane Ladd in a scene from episode 91 (4.19), "For Whom the Belle Toils"

Episode 91 (4.19): "For Whom the Belle Toils" (Original broadcast date: March 2, 1980)

Writers: Linda Morris and Vic Rauseo

Director: Marc Daniels

Guest stars: Victoria Carroll, Ted Gehring, Hugh Gillin, and Howard Mann

Synopsis: One of Mel's former waitresses, Belle Dupree, stops at the diner and discusses her songwriting pursuits in town. When they fall through, Mel agrees to rehire her as a waitress.

(Note: Diane Ladd sings "Uncle Bud." Linda Lavin sings a ballad and then a disco version of "Uncle Bud.")

Episode 92 (4.20): "One Too Many Girls" (Original broadcast date: March 9, 1980)

Writers: Robert Fisher and Arthur Marx

Director: Marc Daniels

Guest stars: Duane R. Campbell, Ted Gehring, Kip Gilman, Robert Hogan, and Marvin Kaplan

Synopsis: Belle's Southern charm gives her influence over Mel while on the job and influence over Alice's and Vera's boyfriends while socializing.

(Note: Various numbers for Alice's apartment are given throughout the run of the show. In this episode, she lives in apartment 108, which is printed on the outside of her door.)

Episode 93 (4.21): "Vera, the Vamp" (Original broadcast date: March 16, 1980)

Writers: Linda Morris and Vic Rauseo

Directors: Linda Lavin and Lee Lochhead

Guest stars: Raleigh Bond, Duane R. Campbell, Ted Gehring, Alan Haufrect, Marvin Kaplan, Howard Mann, and Mickey Morton

Synopsis: When Vera's boyfriend loses interest in her, Belle gives her a makeover to reinvigorate her appeal.

Episode 94 (4.22): "Profit Without Honor" (Original broadcast date: March 23, 1980)

Writers: Robert Fisher and Arthur Marx

Director: Lee Lochhead

Guest stars: Marvin Kaplan and Dave Madden

Synopsis: Mel agrees to give the waitresses a percentage of the profits but tries to renege on the deal when he hears a rumor that he could make big bucks by selling the diner.

(Note: When Mel attempts to block the storeroom door, the entire wall moves. When Henry enters through the back door, it appears as if there's a hallway outside instead of an alley.)

Episode 95 (4.23): "Cook's Tour" (Original broadcast date: March 30, 1980)

Writers: Linda Morris and Vic Rauseo

Directors: Linda Lavin and Lee Lochhead

Guest stars: Reb Brown, Marvin Kaplan, Pamela Myers, and Howard Platt

Synopsis: When Vera's new friend, Bobbi, develops a crush on Mel, Mel finds the attention challenging to deflect. The situation becomes more complicated when Bobbi's overprotective, musclebound brother enters the picture.

(Note: Pamela Myers sings "The Man I Love." The lens of one of the cameras is visible when Bobbi enters the diner while Mel is dressed like an old man.)

Episode 96 (4.24): "Here Comes Alice Cottontail" (Original broadcast date: April 6, 1980)

Writers: Robert Fisher and Arthur Marx

Director: Marc Daniels

Guest stars: John Crawford, Hector Elias, John Hawker, Howard Mann, Felice Schachter, and Christopher Tayback

Synopsis: When Alice refuses to let Tommy go on an unsupervised, weeklong vacation, Mel lets him stay at his apartment instead. Alice bets Mel that he'll kick Tommy out before the week is over.

(Note: Diane Ladd sings "Your Eyes Shine Like a Possum" and "Your Eyes Shine Like a Bunny." Linda Lavin sings "Bugs Bunny's Easter Song." Vic Tayback's son, Christopher Tayback, plays Jack in this episode.)

SEASON 5 (1980–1981)

Episode 97 (5.1): "Mel and the Green Machine" (Original broadcast date: November 2, 1980)

Writers: Linda Morris and Vic Rauseo

Director: Lee Lochhead

Guest stars: Duane R. Campbell, Raleigh Bond, John Harkins, Marvin Kaplan, Damu King, and George Wyner

Synopsis: An ATM malfunction nets Mel's a $24,675 bankroll. He intends to keep it until Alice reads in the newspaper that the bank is looking for the money.

(Note: Vic Tayback sings "You Do Something to Me.")

Episode 98 (5.2): "Dog Day Evening" (Original broadcast date: November 9, 1980)

Writer: George Bloom

Director: Marc Daniels

Guest stars: Warren Berlinger, Duane R. Campbell, Richard Jamison, and Douglas Robinson

Synopsis: After the diner's safe is stolen, Mel hires guard dogs to watch his business while it's closed.

(Note: After Mel gets off the phone, someone can be seen holding something outside the diner's front window.)

Episode 99 (5.3): "Hello Vegas, Goodbye Diner" (Original broadcast date: November 16, 1980)

Writers: Mark Egan and Mark Solomon

Director: Marc Daniels

Guest stars: Lou Criscuolo, Lou Richards, Michael Tucci, and Nedra Volz

Synopsis: Vera invites her coworkers to join her on a trip she has won to Las Vegas. When they arrive, Mel gambles away the diner in a casino.

(Note: Linda Lavin sings part of the song "On a Clear Day." This episode and episode 100 [5.4] "Too Many Robert Goulets," aired as part of a full hour of *Alice* on November 16, 1980.)

Episode 100 (5.4): "Too Many Robert Goulets" (Original broadcast date: November 16, 1980)

Writers: Linda Morris and Vic Rauseo

Life Behind the Counter in Mel's Greasy Spoon

Director: Marc Daniels

Guest stars: Michael Ballard, Lou Criscuolo, Robert Goulet, Kimiko Hiroshige, Nancy Lenehan, Rollin Moriyama, Michael Tucci, and Nedra Volz

Synopsis: The casino's owner agrees to give Mel the diner back if he can get Robert Goulet to perform at the casino that evening. When contact with Goulet appears to be impossible, Alice's coworkers talk her into impersonating him instead.

(Note: Linda Lavin and Robert Goulet sing "On a Clear Day.")

Beth Howland and Mildred Natwick in a scene from episode 101 (5.5), "Vera's Aunt Agatha"

Episode 101 (5.5): "Vera's Aunt Agatha" (Original broadcast date: November 23, 1980)

Writers: Robert Fisher and Arthur Marx

Director: Marc Daniels

Guest stars: Greta Blackburn, Ted Gehring, Marvin Kaplan, Mildred Natwick, and Curtis Taylor

Synopsis: When Vera's free-spirited aunt, Agatha, comes to visit, Vera quits her job and plans to travel the country with Agatha by motorcycle. All looks promising until fate steps in and puts a wrench in Vera's plan.

(Note: The lens of one of the cameras can be seen when Aunt Agatha leaves the storeroom after doing yoga.)

Episode 102 (5.6): "Tommy's T.K.O." (Original broadcast date: November 30, 1980)

Writers: Linda Morris and Vic Rauseo

Director: Marc Daniels

Guest stars: Richard Balin, Jody Arthur Balsam, Marvin Kaplan, Paul Smith, Susan Tolsky, and Vernon Weddle

Synopsis: Tommy fights a bully at school, but he soon realizes that the best approach to settle a dispute is to talk it out.

(Note: The boom mic can be seen when Mel teaches Tommy how to box in the storeroom.)

Episode 103 (5.7): "The New Improved Mel" (Original broadcast date: December 7, 1980)

Writers: Mark Egan and Mark Solomon

Director: Marc Daniels

Guest stars: Ted Gehring, Maurice Hill, Marvin Kaplan, Mickey Morton, and Shavar Ross

Synopsis: Mel realizes that no one showed for his navy buddy's funeral because he wasn't well liked. Mel doesn't want that to happen to him, so he turns over a new leaf and tries to be nice to everyone.

(Note: Vic Tayback sings part of the song "Get Happy.")

Episode 104 (5.8): "Carrie Sings the Blues" (Original broadcast date: December 21, 1980)
Writers: Mark Egan and Mark Solomon

Directors: Christine Ballard and Linda Lavin

Guest stars: Michael Alldredge, Marvin Kaplan, Dave Madden, Martha Raye, and Howard Witt

Synopsis: A distraught Carrie bakes up a storm at the diner after a breakup with her husband, Robby. Customers love her pies. Mel loves the increased profits and hides the fact that Robby has called to patch things up with her.

(Note: Martha Raye sings "Am I Blue?" Linda Lavin, Philip McKeon, and Martha Raye sing "By the Light of the Silvery Moon.")

Alice...

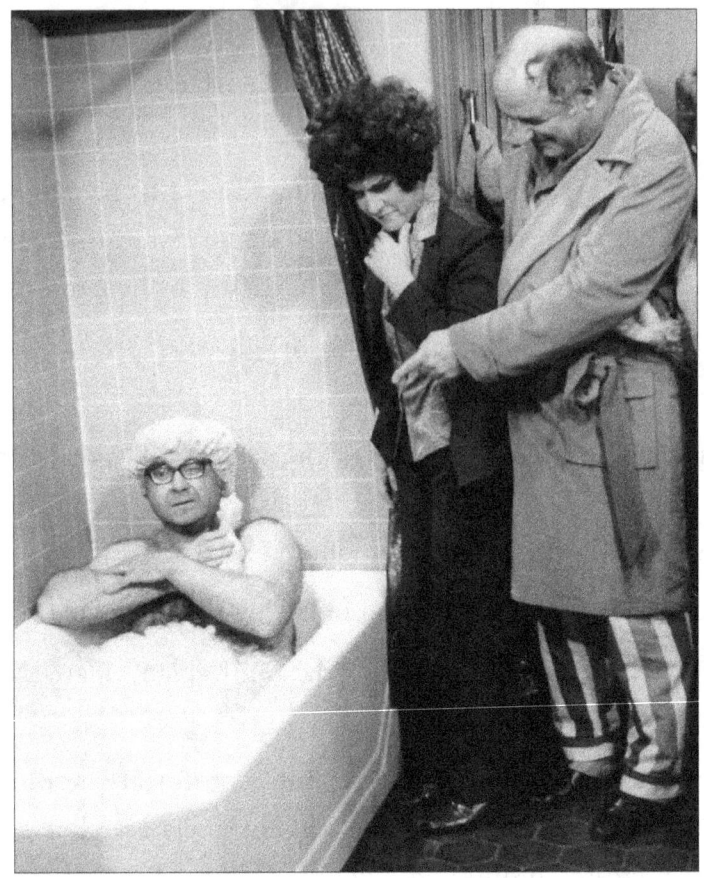

Marvin Kaplan, Ruth Buzzi, and Vic Tayback in a scene from episode 105 (5.9), "Henry's Bitter Half"

Episode 105 (5.9): "Henry's Bitter Half" (Original broadcast date: January 4, 1981)

Writers: Mark Egan and Mark Solomon

Director: Lee Lochhead

Guest stars: Ruth Buzzi, Duane R. Campbell, Marvin Kaplan, Zale Kessler, and Dave Madden

Synopsis: Henry and Chloe have a falling out on their twentieth wedding anniversary, prompting Henry to move out.

(Note: Vic Tayback sings a parody of the song "Rock-a-Bye, Baby." Diane Ladd sings "The Angels up in Heaven.")

Episode 106 (5.10): "Alice Locks Belle Out" (Original broadcast date: January 11, 1981)
Writers: Robert Fisher and Arthur Marx

Director: Nick Havinga

Guest star: John Sylvester White

Synopsis: Alice becomes the manager of her apartment building and is forced to lock Belle out of her unit when she cannot pay her rent on time.

(Note: Diane Ladd sings part of a song entitled "Friend." In this episode, Alice's apartment complex is called the Phoenix Palms, yet the signs in the season one and two opening credits call it the Desert Inn Apartments.)

Episode 107 (5.11): "Vera Goes Out on a Limb" (Original broadcast date: January 18, 1981)
Writers: Linda Morris and Vic Rauseo

Director: Marc Daniels

Guest stars: Ted Gehring, Marvin Kaplan, Ed Kenney, Tom Kindle, and Walter Olkewicz

Synopsis: Vera chains herself to a tree outside the diner to save it from being chopped down.

Episode 108 (5.12): "The Jerry Reed Fish Story" (Original broadcast date: February 1, 1981)

Writers: Robert Fisher and Arthur Marx

Director: Marc Daniels

Guest stars: Ted Gehring, Bob Gunter, and Jerry Reed

Synopsis: Jerry Reed is livid when he discovers that the waitresses cut up a prized fish he caught while on a trip with Mel.

(Note: Diane Ladd sings "Uncle Bud" with Linda Lavin and Beth Howland singing backup.)

Episode 109 (5.13): "Bye Birdie" (Original broadcast date: February 8, 1981)

Writer: George Bloom

Director: Marc Daniels

Guest stars: William Bogert, Lou Cutell, Marvin Kaplan, Dave Madden, Catherine Paolone, Douglas Robinson, and Tom Williams

Synopsis: Everyone at the diner believes that the stress from Mel's constant yelling killed Vera's new parrot. They soon discover that the pet store fraudulently sold her an old bird that was at death's door.

(Note: The boom mic can be seen overhead in the diner when Mel approaches the counter to hear Birdie say, "Stow it!" When Vera mentions where she purchased Birdie, her voice is dubbed to say, "Pet Care.")

Episode 110 (5.14): "Alice's Son, the Drop-Out" (Original broadcast date: February 15, 1981)

Writers: Robert Fisher and Arthur Marx

Director: Marc Daniels

Guest stars: Raleigh Bond, Marvin Kaplan, Tom Kindle, Dave Madden, Brien Varady, and Tom Williams

Synopsis: Alice takes over a few of Tommy's shifts singing at a local saloon to help him save for college. When Mel finds out that she's moonlighting, he fires her. Belle and Vera become Alice's backup singers to help her get her job at the diner back.

(Note: Linda Lavin sings "Too Marvelous for Words," which the full cast reprises. Linda Lavin, Diane Ladd, and Beth Howland sing "Don't Fence Me In.")

Episode 111 (5.15): "Carrie Chickens Out" (Original broadcast date: February 22, 1981)

Writers: Robert Fisher and Arthur Marx

Director: Marc Daniels

Guest stars: John Hawker, Marvin Kaplan, Jack Kruschen, Dave Madden, Martha Raye, and Douglas Robinson

Synopsis: Mel refuses to let Carrie cook in the diner when she comes for a visit, so she takes a job as cook at Benny's Beanery instead, which ultimately takes business away from the diner.

(Note: Dave Madden sings part of the song "Carry Me Back to Old Virginny." Martha Raye sings a takeoff of "Row, Row, Row Your Boat.")

Episode 112 (5.16): "Macho, Macho, Mel" (Original broadcast date: March 8, 1981)

Writers: Mark Egan and Mark Solomon

Director: Marc Daniels

Guest stars: Duane R. Campbell, Florence Halop, Marvin Kaplan, Dave Madden, Walter Robles, Andy Romano, and Paul Smith

Synopsis: After Mel is mugged, the diner falls victim to a series of robberies.

(Note: The boom mic can be seen overhead when the diner's cash register won't open.)

Episode 113 (5.17): "The Great Escape" (Original broadcast date: March 15, 1981)

Writers: Mark Egan, Linda Morris, Vic Rauseo, and Mark Solomon

Director: Marc Daniels

Guest stars: Robert Carnegie, Ted Gehring, Sham Haworth, Marvin Kaplan, and Douglas Robinson

Synopsis: As Belle leaves to embark on a singing career in Nashville, trucker Jolene Hunnicutt takes refuge from her business partner in the diner. A dish fight drives him away, but it forces Jolene to work as a waitress until she can repay Mel for the damage she's caused.

(Note: This episode is Diane Ladd's last. It is Celia Weston's first episode as Jolene Hunnicutt. When Alice answers the diner phone and talks with Belle, the wall shakes back and forth.)

Episode 114 (5.18): "Alice Strikes Up the Band" (Original broadcast date: March 29, 1981)

Writers: Mark Egan and Mark Solomon

Director: Marc Daniels

Guest stars: James T. Callahan, Duane R. Campbell, Ed E. Carroll, John Hawker, Howard Ray Huff, Marvin Kaplan, and Vern Rowe

Synopsis: Alice must choose between an exciting life singing on the road and working a stable job at the diner to give Tommy a consistent life while he's in high school.

(Note: Linda Lavin sings "Jeepers Creepers" as well as excerpts from the songs "Lucky Day," "With a Song in My Heart," "You're the Top," and "I've Got a Right to Sing the Blues." Beth Howland sings part of the song "Tea for Two" and "Shuffle off to Buffalo." Celia Weston sings "Rock-a My Soul.")

Linda Lavin in a scene from episode 114 (5.18), "Alice Strikes Up the Band"

Episode 115 (5.19): "Who's Kissing the Great Chef of Phoenix?" (Original broadcast date: April 5, 1981)

Writers: Robert Fisher and Arthur Marx

Director: Marc Daniels

Guest stars: Victoria Carroll, Ed Kenney, Bruce Morgan, and Walter Robles

Synopsis: After Mel and Vera break up with their dates, they go to the drive-in together to relieve their pain. During the movie, Mel kisses Vera. She begins to fall for him but then realizes that he only kissed her to make his former girlfriend jealous.

Episode 116 (5.20): "Baby Makes Five" (Original broadcast date: May 3, 1981)

Writers: Charles Isaacs and Tom Whedon

Directors: Christine Ballard and Linda Lavin

Guest stars: Irene Arranga, Nancy Jeris, Marvin Kaplan, John C. McLaughlin, James Murtaugh, Tom Taylor, and Tom Williams

Synopsis: Vera becomes a surrogate mother to a baby that she finds abandoned in a laundromat.

(Note: Linda Lavin sings "All through the Night." Vic Tayback sings a takeoff of "Twinkle, Twinkle, Little Star." Vic Tayback owned a horse named Paint Your Flag and asked the writers to include its name in this episode.)

SEASON 6 (1981–1982)

Vic Tayback and Beth Howland in a scene from episode 117 (6.1), "Bet a Million, Mel"

Episode 117 (6.1): "Bet a Million, Mel" (Original broadcast date: October 4, 1981)

Writers: Robert Fisher and Arthur Marx

Director: Nick Havinga

Guest stars: Hamilton Camp, Duane R. Campbell, Ted Gehring, and Marvin Kaplan

Synopsis: When the waitresses learn that Mel plans to use the diner as collateral for a $10,000 bet on a horserace, they tie him up before he can do so to save the diner and their jobs.

(Note: Vic Tayback's horse, Paint Your Flag, is mentioned in this episode.)

Episode 118 (6.2): "Guinness on Tap" (Original broadcast date: October 11, 1981)

Writers: Mark Egan and Mark Solomon

Director: Marc Daniels

Guest stars: David Ankrum, Dee Biederbeck, Duane R. Campbell, Marvin Kaplan, Donald O'Connor, Manuel Padilla Jr., Kathryn Reynolds, and Byron Webster

Synopsis: Mel capitalizes on Vera's desire to set a new world record for nonstop tap dancing by turning the event into a publicity stunt to increase business. When Vera becomes exhausted and thinks she can't go on, her favorite dancer, Donald O'Connor, stops by and encourages her on to set the record.

(Note: Linda Lavin sings "A Shine on Your Shoes.")

Episode 119 (6.3): "Comrade Mel" (Original broadcast date: October 18, 1981)

Writers: Prudence Fraser and Robert Sternin

Director: Marc Daniels

Guest stars: Marvin Kaplan, Robert Peirce, and Allan Rich

Synopsis: The Russian ballet's towel boy comes to the diner and decides to defect to the United States.

(Note: This episode was dedicated to A. J. "Pappy" Cunningham." Cunningham was the series' technical director from season 1 to season 6. He passed away not long after this episode was taped. Prudence Fraser, who cowrote the episode, cocreated the sitcom *The Nanny*, which starred Fran Drescher.)

Episode 120 (6.4): "Alice's Halloween Surprise" (Original broadcast date: October 24, 1981)
Writer: Gail Honigberg
Director: Marc Daniels
Guest stars: Phillip R. Allen, Nicki Armstrong, Jimmy Briscoe, Evan Cohen, Philip Gordon, Billy Jayne, Nancy McKeon, Dave Madden, Ty Mitchell, and Shavar Ross
Synopsis: Alice takes her new boyfriend's children out trick-or-treating and loses one of them in the process.

(Note: Philip McKeon's sister, Nancy, played a supporting role in this episode. Mistake: Alice says that one of the trick-or-treaters lives upstairs from her apartment. However, in episode 106 [5.10], "Alice Locks Belle Out," the exterior of Alice's apartment revealed it to have only one floor.)

Episode 121 (6.5): "Alice's Big Four-Oh!" (Original broadcast date: November 8, 1981)
Writers: Linda Morris and Vic Rauseo
Director: Marc Daniels

Guest stars: Will Hunt, Dave Madden, and Doris Roberts

Synopsis: Alice looks forward to celebrating her fortieth birthday until her mother comes to town and criticizes the life she leads.

(Note: The closing credits feature images of Alice's birthday party that are not a part of the actual episode.)

Episode 122 (6.6): "Mel's Cousin, Wendell" (Original broadcast date: November 15, 1981)

Writers: Mark Egan, Linda Morris, Vic Rauseo, and Mark Solomon

Director: Marc Daniels

Guest stars: Richard Jamison, Brian O'Brien, David Rounds, and June Whitley Taylor

Synopsis: Mel gives his awkward cousin, Wendell, some ill-conceived advice about women when he goes out with Vera.

(Note: When David Rounds, who plays Wendell, knocks into the counter towards the end of the episode, the entire counter unit slides along the floor. Celia Weston tries to steady it.)

Episode 123 (6.7): "Vera's Bouncing Check" (Original broadcast date: November 29, 1981)

Writers: Bob Brunner and Ken Hecht

Director: Marc Daniels

Guest stars: Duane R. Campbell, Marvin Kaplan, and Kip Niven

Synopsis: Mel is furious when Vera cashes a check for a friend, Steve Marsh, at the diner and it bounces.

Episode 124 (6.8): "After Mel's Gone" (Original broadcast date: December 6, 1981)

Writers: Bob Brunner and Ken Hecht

Director: Stockton Briggle

Guest stars: Hector Elias, Marvin Kaplan, Dave Madden, and Jerry Potter

Synopsis: When Mel tells his friends and coworkers what he plans to leave them in his will, they fight among themselves over their future inheritance. Mel is disheartened by the situation, so he drafts a new will and refuses to divulge its contents.

Episode 125 (6.9): "Mel's Christmas Carol" (Original broadcast date: December 20, 1981)

Writers: Linda Morris and Vic Rauseo

Director: Marc Daniels

Guest stars: Jack Gilford and Marvin Kaplan

Synopsis: After Mel turns Scrooge on Christmas Eve, the ghost of his former business partner, Jake Farley, stops by and encourages him to change his ways.

(Note: Linda Lavin, Marvin Kaplan, and Beth Howland sing a brief parody of "Deck the Halls." Later, Linda Lavin, Philip McKeon, Celia Weston, and Beth Howland sing the original version of the same song. Vic Tayback sings part of "Jingle Bells" as well as a parody of "Good King Wenceslas.")

Alice...

Episode 126 (6.10): "The Wild One" (Original broadcast date: December 27, 1981)

Writer: Michael Weinberger

Director: Marc Daniels

Guest stars: Marvin Kaplan, Jay Leno, Ron Palillo, and Susan Wolf

Synopsis: A biker insists that Alice become his girlfriend. When she refuses, he drags her off on his motorcycle. The situation worsens when the biker's former girlfriend shows up and sees Alice as her competition.

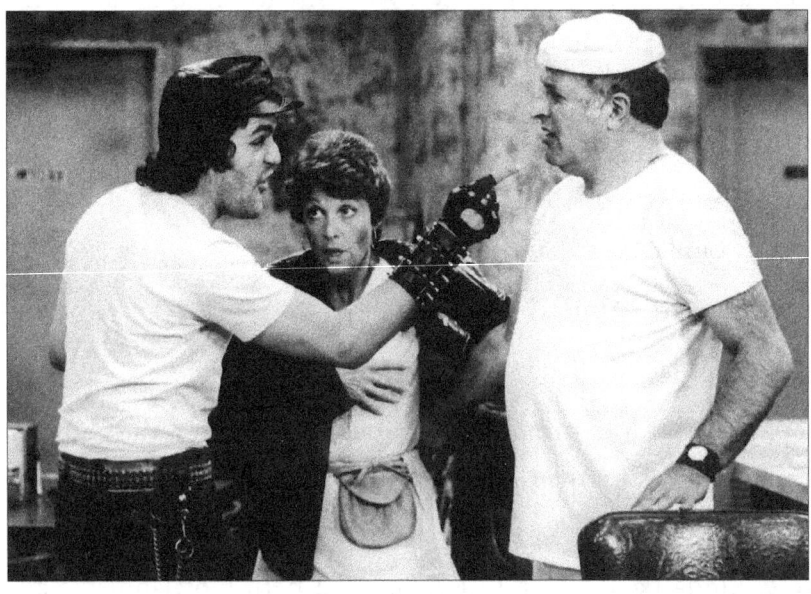

Jay Leno, Linda Lavin, and Vic Tayback in a scene from episode 126 (6.10), "The Wild One"

Episode 127 (6.11): "Alice Calls the Shots" (Original broadcast date: January 3, 1982)

Writer: Gail Honigberg

Director: Marc Daniels

Guest stars: Erin Blunt, David Bowe, Pete Leal, and Dave Madden

Synopsis: Alice grounds Tommy before an important basketball game because of his failing grades. Tommy's coach sneaks him off to the game anyway, but Tommy feels guilty for defying his mother's wishes.

Episode 128 (6.12): "Not with My Niece, You Don't" (Original broadcast date: January 17, 1982)

Writers: Chet Dowling and Sandy Krinski

Director: John Pasquin

Guest stars: Karlene Crockett, Marvin Kaplan, and Kim Richards

Synopsis: When Tommy dates Mel's niece, Alice and Mel worry that they're moving too fast. In the end, the relationship turns out to be rather innocent.

Marvin Kaplan, Beth Howland, Vic Tayback, and others in a scene from episode 129 (6.13), "Vera, Queen of the Soaps"

Episode 129 (6.13): "Vera, Queen of the Soaps" (Original broadcast date: January 31, 1982)

Writers: Mark Egan and Mark Solomon

Director: Marc Daniels

Guest stars: Jack Andreozzi, Susan Brecht, Jamie De Roy, Jerry Hausner, Marvin Kaplan, and Susan Tolsky

Synopsis: Vera becomes so obsessed with soap operas that she leaves the diner and takes a night job so she can stay home during the day and watch them.

Episode 130 (6.14): "Sharples vs. Sharples" (Original broadcast date: February 7, 1982)

Writers: Mark Egan and Mark Solomon

Director: Linda Day

Guest stars: Rose Arrick, Marvin Kaplan, Edie McClurg, Martha Raye, and Lou Richards

Synopsis: Mel has Carrie and the waitresses arrested when they go to his apartment to retrieve Carrie's cookbook manuscript, which he had stolen from her.

(Note: Linda Lavin, Beth Howland, Celia Weston, Martha Raye, Rose Arrick, and uncredited supporting cast members do a song-and-dance version of "The Lullaby of Broadway" while in jail. When the girls are released from their cell, the door is already open before the guard unlocks it. If you look closely during this scene, one of the cameras is visible on the right side of the screen.)

Episode 131 (6.15): "The Valentine's Day Massacre" (Original broadcast date: February 14, 1982)

Writers: Mark Egan and Mark Solomon

Director: John Pasquin

Guest stars: Phillip R. Allen, Pat Benson, Don Bovingloh, Victoria Carroll, Ron Kuhlman, Dave Madden, and Peter Scranton

Synopsis: When Alice, Vera, Jolene, Mel, and Earl break up with their Valentine's Day dates, Alice invites them to her apartment so they won't be alone.

(Note: Ron Kuhlman sings a telegram to the tune of "Jingle Bells.")

Episode 132 (6.16): "The Best Little Waitress in the World" (Original broadcast date: February 21, 1982)

Writers: Linda Morris and Vic Rauseo

Director: Mel Ferber

Guest stars: Arthur Abelson, Richard Andert, Beatrice Colen, Willie DeJean, Michael Goldfinger, Jerry Hausner, Marvin Kaplan, Steve Liebman, Justin Lord, Catherine Paolone, and Gary Spatz

Synopsis: Mel lets Vera take over the diner when he's away, but things snowball into a disaster that's beyond her control.

Episode 133 (6.17): "Alice and the Acorns" (Original broadcast date: March 7, 1982)

Writers: Mark Egan and Mark Solomon

Director: Marc Daniels

Guest stars: James T. Callahan, Duane R. Campbell, Marilyn Cooper, and Zale Kessler

Synopsis: Alice reconnects with a shy member of her high school singing group who comes to town; she lets her shine when they re-form the group and perform at Vinnie's House of Veal.

(Note: Linda Lavin, Beth Howland, Celia Weston, and Marilyn Cooper sing "At the Hop." Marilyn Cooper sings "It's All in the Game." Alice and the cast sing "At the Hop" over the closing credits.)

Episode 134 (6.18): "Jolene Hunnicutt, Dynamite Trucker"
(Original broadcast date: March 14, 1982)
Writers: Chet Dowling and Sandy Krinski

Director: Marc Daniels

Guest stars: Robert Carnegie, James Cavan, and Ted Gehring

Synopsis: Jolene, Vera, and Alice make a last-minute delivery for Jolene's exhausted former trucking partner so he can earn enough money to keep his truck from being repossessed.

(Note: Linda Lavin, Beth Howland, and Celia Weston sing part of the song "Ninety-Nine Bottles of Beer.")

Episode 135 (6.19): "Mel Wins by a Nose" (Original broadcast date: March 21, 1982)
Writers: Linda Morris and Vic Rauseo

Director: Marc Daniels

Guest stars: Joe Barrett, Dave Madden, Kenneth Mars, and Susan Tolsky

Synopsis: Mel contemplates getting a nose job. After seeing a specialist, he decides to keep it the way it is.

Episode 136 (6.20): "Give My Regrets to Broadway" (Original broadcast date: April 4, 1982)

Writer: Gail Honigberg

Director: John Pasquin

Guest stars: Robert Costanzo, Lisa Lindgren, Mario Roccuzzo, and Gail Strickland

Synopsis: During rehearsal for *Romeo and Juliet*, Tommy falls in love with acting and decides to go to New York to pursue it as a career. Alice is concerned because she wants him to finish his education first. In the end, Tommy befriends a female castmate and decides to attend college in Arizona to be near her instead.

(Note: Beth Howland and Celia Weston sing part of "Jeepers Creepers" in this episode.)

Episode 137 (6.21): "Vera's Reunion Romance" (Original broadcast date: April 11, 1982)

Writers: Mark Egan, Gail Honigberg, and Mark Solomon

Directors: Christine Ballard and Linda Lavin

Guest stars: Cisse Cameron, Rebecca Clemmons, Jane Dulo, Marvin Kaplan, Pamela Myers, Kip Niven, Robert Picardo, and Renny Temple

Synopsis: Vera attends her high school reunion and hits it off with her successful former classmate Steve Marsh. After a brief courtship, they get engaged. The more time they spend together, the more they realize they have little in common.

Episode 138 (6.22): "Monty Falls for Alice" (Original broadcast date: April 18, 1982)

Writers: Mark Egan, Linda Morris, Vic Rauseo, and Mark Solomon

Director: Marc Daniels

Guest stars: Duane R. Campbell, Marvin Kaplan, and George Wendt

Synopsis: A Las Vegas acquaintance of Alice's comes to Phoenix and falls in love with her. When she rejects him, he contemplates suicide.

(Note: George Wendt sings part of the song "You and the Night and the Music." Later in the episode, Beth Howland sings part of the song as well.)

Episode 139 (6.23): "Spell Mel's" (Original broadcast date: May 2, 1982)
Writers: Chet Dowling and Sandy Krinski

Director: Marc Daniels

Guest stars: Carl Ballantine, Marvin Kaplan, Jerry Potter, Douglas Robinson, and Hank Rolike

Synopsis: When the diner loses customers to a restaurant that offers a cash prize, Mel draws customers back by offering a larger prize. He is horrified to discover that the amount he offered is more than he can afford to pay.

Episode 140 (6.24): "My Mother the Landlord" (Original broadcast date: May 16, 1982)

Writers: Chet Dowling and Sandy Krinski

Director: Marc Daniels

Guest stars: Jack Andreozzi, Duane R. Campbell, Patrick Campbell, Susan Davis, Tony Longo, Martha Raye, and Tom Williams

Synopsis: When Mel's mother buys his apartment building and raises his rent, Mel refuses to pay the increase. Carrie considers evicting him but ultimately lets him stay on, rent free, as her apartment manager.

(Note: Linda Lavin, Beth Howland, Celia Weston, and Philip McKeon sing part of the song "Rock-a-Bye, Baby." Mistake: In this episode, Mel wants a copy of Carrie's cookbook, but she already sent him one in episode 130 [6.14], "Sharples vs. Sharples.")

SEASON 7 (1982–1983)

Episode 141 (7.1): "Sorry, Wrong Lips!" (Original broadcast date: October 6, 1982)

Writers: Howard Liebling and Lloyd Turner

Director: Mel Ferber

Guest stars: Elvia Allman, Bob Ari, Lucille Benson, Duane R. Campbell, Marvin Kaplan, Jerry Potter, and Debbie Reynolds

Synopsis: After reading a movie star's biography, Mel believes himself to be the young lover from Coney Island mentioned in her book. When the movie star stops by the diner, Mel realizes he was wrong.

(Note: Debbie Reynolds sings "You're the Top" in this episode.)

Alice...

Debbie Reynolds and Vic Tayback in a scene from episode 141 (7.1), "Sorry, Wrong Lips!"

Episode 142 (7.2): "Do You Take This Waitress?" (Original broadcast date: October 13, 1982)

Writer: Gail Honigberg

Directors: Christine Ballard and Linda Lavin

Guest stars: Marvin Kaplan, Tessa Richarde, and Jerry Stiller

Synopsis: Mel doesn't want to look like a failure with the ladies when his friend Gordy comes to town, so he makes a deal with Jolene to play his girlfriend.

Episode 143 (7.3): "The Secret of Mel's Diner" (Original broadcast date: October 20, 1982)

Writers: Chet Dowling and Sandy Krinski

Director: Marc Daniels

Guest star: Douglas Robinson

Synopsis: After reading a newspaper article, the waitresses and Mel suspect that the diner's former owner hid money somewhere in the building. Their search turns up a fortune, but a note that accompanies the money encourages them to donate it to a worthy cause.

(Note: Linda Lavin, Beth Howland, and Celia Weston sing "Tea for Two." Douglas Robinson reprises the song a few minutes later. Beth Howland and Vic Tayback sing a parody of "Twinkle, Twinkle, Little Star.")

Episode 144 (7.4): "Alice at the Palace" (Original broadcast date: October 27, 1982)

Writers: Mark Egan and Mark Solomon

Director: Marc Daniels

Guest stars: Lynn Eriks, Susan Carr George, Joel Grey, Marvin Kaplan, Michael Rupert, and Tom Williams

Synopsis: When the backer for a song-and-dance review that Alice is scheduled to appear in can't fund the show, Mel turns theater impresario and makes the headlining performer, Joel Grey, audition alongside a local singer of far lesser talent.

(Note: Linda Lavin sings parts of "I Happen to Like New York" and "Autumn in New York." She scats part of "Forty-Second Street" and then sings the song with Michael Rupert and a male chorus. Tom Williams and Vic Tayback sing a takeoff of "The Conga." Michael

Rupert and Vic Tayback sing a takeoff of "I Happen to Like New York." Tom Williams sings part of "Swanee"; Joel Grey sings the entire song. This is part one of a two-part episode. Both episodes were shot on the same night.)

Episode 145 (7.5): "Joel Grey Saves the Day" (Original broadcast date: November 3, 1982)

Writers: Mark Egan and Mark Solomon

Director: Marc Daniels

Guest stars: Ceil Cabot, Duane R. Campbell, Lynn Eriks, Susan Carr George, Joel Grey, Maurice Hill, Marvin Kaplan, Michael Rupert, and Tom Williams

Synopsis: Mel fires Joel Grey from the review and makes several tacky changes to the show. Alice, who finds them repulsive, refuses to perform until Mel forces her and the other waitresses to go on or face a permanent pay cut. Audience members wind up hating the show. As they are about to walk out, Joel Grey returns and saves the day.

(Note: Tom Williams sings part of "Swanee." Michael Rupert sings a takeoff of "The Conga." Linda Lavin sings part of "The Lullaby of Flagstaff." Joel Grey and Michael Rupert sing "I Happen to Like Arizona." Tom Williams sings part of the song "Phoenix." Linda Lavin, Beth Howland, Celia Weston, and Tom Williams sing "Two Tootsies from Tucson." Linda Lavin, Beth Howland, and Celia Weston sing "Ramona from Arizona." Linda Lavin, Joel Grey, and the rest of the cast sing a medley featuring "Manhattan," "New York, New York," "Forty-Second Street," and a reprise of "New York, New York." This is part two of a two-part episode.)

Episode 146 (7.6): "Alice's Turkey of a Thanksgiving" (Original broadcast date: November 10, 1982)

Writer: Gail Honigberg

Director: Mel Ferber

Guest stars: Robert Hogan and Doris Roberts

Synopsis: Alice's mother visits and plans to stay. Alice helps her realize that she'd be happier back in New Jersey with her memories and an occasional visit to Phoenix to see her family.

Episode 147 (7.7): "Carrie on the Rebound" (Original broadcast date: January 9, 1983)

Writers: Bob Bendetson and Howard Bendetson

Director: Marc Daniels

Guest stars: Charlie Callas, Duane R. Campbell, Lou Cutell, Dave Madden, Martha Raye, and Mykelti Williamson

Synopsis: Mel's mother, Carrie, comes to town after getting divorced and becomes infatuated with the high school basketball coach, Earl.

(Note: Martha Raye sings part of the song "La Cucaracha." The boom mic can be seen briefly in the first gymnasium scene.)

Episode 148 (7.8): "Jolene's Brother Jonas" (Original broadcast date: January 16, 1983)

Writers: David Silverman and Stephen Sustarsic

Director: John Pasquin

Guest stars: Marvin Kaplan and Guich Koock

Synopsis: Jolene's estranged brother gets Mel to invest $5,000 in a worm farm. He eventually returns the money to prove to Jolene that he's no longer a scammer.

Episode 149 (7.9): "Alice Sees the Light" (Original broadcast date: February 28, 1983)

Writers: Bob Bendetson and Howard Bendetson

Director: Marc Daniels

Guest stars: Elvia Allman, Lucille Benson, Duane R. Campbell, John Hawker, Marvin Kaplan, Tony Longo, James O'Sullivan, and Jerry Potter

Synopsis: Alice sees a UFO behind the diner one night. Word quickly spreads about the sighting. Mel uses the event to increase business at the diner.

Episode 150 (7.10): "Vera the Virtuoso" (Original broadcast date: March 7, 1983)

Writers: David Silverman and Stephen Sustarsic

Directors: Linda Lavin and John Pasquin

Guest stars: Frank Aletter, Marvin Kaplan, and Paul Sand

Synopsis: Vera fulfills her lifelong dream of taking cello lessons and performing with a string quartet.

(Note: Vera's teacher [Paul Sand] was Beth Howland's real-life friend. The closing credits feature the student quartet bowing to the audience while their recital music plays.)

Episode 151 (7.11): "Alice Faces the Music" (Original broadcast date: March 14, 1983)

Writers: David Silverman and Stephen Sustarsic

Directors: Marc Daniels and Vic Tayback

Guest stars: Wil Albert, Jack Andreozz, Marvin Kaplan, John McCook, Cliff Norton, Susan Tolsky, and Vernon Weddle

Synopsis: When the waitresses are selected as quiz show contestants, Alice pretends not to know an answer so their competitors can win and use the prize to visit their dying brother in Hawaii. After the show, Alice discovers that the brother is actually in excellent health. The opponents said he was ill in hope that Alice would throw the contest. Justice ultimately prevails when the competitors' victory is overturned.

(Note: Linda Lavin sings part of the song "Anything Goes." Marvin Kaplan sings part of "Tea for Two." Celia Weston and John McCook sing the beginning of "I Only Have Eyes for You." The boom mic can be seen twice during the quiz show scenes. Vic Tayback codirected this episode to increase his industry skills.)

Episode 152 (7.12): "Tommy, the Jailbird" (Original broadcast date: March 21, 1983)

Writers: David Silverman and Stephen Sustarsic

Director: Mel Ferber

Guest stars: Suzanne Adkinson, Thomas Byrd, Michael Crabtree, Tom Henschel, Marvin Kaplan, Dana Kimmell, Jennifer Richards, and Robert Picardo

Synopsis: Tommy's college friend Rudy encourages him to live each day like it's a party. When they wind up in jail after a food fight at the local pizza parlor, Tommy realizes that he's headed down the wrong path and needs to be more responsible.

(Note: This is Robert Picardo's second appearance in the series and the first time he plays a police officer. Beth Howland sings the song "Maroon and Gold.")

Episode 153 (7.13): "Jolene and the Night Watchman" (Original broadcast date: March 28, 1983)
Writers: Bob Bendetson and Howard Bendetson

Director: John Pasquin

Guest stars: Arthur Abelson, Tony Carroll, Donald Gibb, Daniel Greene, Tony Longo, John Lykes, Shane McCabe, and Pat Tanzillo

Synopsis: Jolene goes out with a night watchman who quickly becomes infatuated with her. She struggles to break it off with him and remain friends.

Episode 154 (7.14): "Mel's Dream Car" (Original broadcast date: April 11, 1983)
Writer: Barry Gold

Director: John Pasquin

Guest stars: Duane R. Campbell, Jim Jansen, Michael G. Kelley, Jim Knaub, Dave Madden, F. William Parker, and Cassandra Peterson

Synopsis: Mel gets a great deal on a red Porsche convertible. When Jolene parks it behind the diner and forgets to turn the alarm on, it gets stolen. By the time the police recover the car, all that's left is the frame.

Episode 155 (7.15): "Come Back Little Sharples" (Original broadcast date: April 17, 1983)

Writer: Gail Honigberg

Director: Mel Ferber

Guest stars: Duane R. Campbell, Victoria Carroll, Merie Earle, Marvin Kaplan, Douglas Robinson, and Martha Raye

Synopsis: Mel can't take life's pressures anymore, so he shuts himself up in his apartment. It takes a strong nudge from Grandma Sharples to make him rejoin life again.

(Note: In this episode, Carrie states that she wants grandchildren from Mel, but she doesn't mention that she already has a grandchild named Lisa. That was established in episode 128 [6.12] "Not with My Niece, You Don't." Vic Tayback sings part of "Tip-Toe Thru' the Tulips with Me." Martha Raye sings part of "Stout-Hearted Man.")

Episode 156 (7.16): "Vera the Torch" (Original broadcast date: April 24, 1983)

Writers: Mark Egan and Mark Solomon

Director: John Pasquin

Guest stars: Jane Bowers, Dave Madden, and Robert Picardo

Synopsis: When Vera's crabby new landlord, Mrs. Debbie Walden, demands she get rid of her pets, Vera wishes the worst on her. Soon after, Mrs. Walden's apartment burns down. Vera feels responsible for the fire and asks Mrs. Walden to move in with her until her apartment can be rebuilt. Mrs. Walden declines and reveals that her own carelessness caused the fire. She takes note of Vera's kindness, however, and lets her keep her pets.

(Note: Linda Lavin plays the role of Alice and Mrs. Debbie Walden in this episode. She sings part of the song "Puff, the Magic Dragon.")

Episode 157 (7.17): "The Grass Is Always Greener" (Original broadcast date: May 1, 1983)

Writers: Linda Morris and Vic Rauseo

Director: Marc Daniels

Guest stars: Richard Deacon, Joy Garrett, and Marvin Kaplan

Synopsis: When Mel tires of struggling to make ends meet at the diner, he sells the business to the waitresses and takes an office job. Before long, he discovers that he doesn't like taking orders from others. The waitresses realize that they make less money on their own than with Mel as their boss. All parties ultimately agree to undo their deal and sell the diner back to Mel.

Episode 158 (7.18): "Tommy Fouls Out" (Original broadcast date: May 15, 1983)

Writers: Michael Cassutt and Lew Levy

Director: Marc Daniels

Guest stars: Doug Cox, Meadowlark Lemon, and Dave Madden

Synopsis: The waitresses and Earl get tickets to Tommy's college basketball game only to discover that he plans to quit the sport because he feels he isn't a good player. When Alice's encouragement has no effect on Tommy, she asks Harlem Globetrotter Meadowlark Lemon to talk to him.

(Note: Linda Lavin, Vic Tayback, Beth Howland, and Celia Weston whistle part of "Sweet Georgia Brown." Later, Meadowlark Lemon and Linda Lavin whistle a reprise of the song.)

Episode 159 (7.19): "Vera on the Lam" (Original broadcast date: May 22, 1983)

Writer: Barry Gold

Director: Marc Daniels

Guest stars: Carol Arthur, Dave Madden, and F. William Parker

Synopsis: When Mel decides to have his insurance company bond the waitresses, Vera takes off in fear that her arrest during a peace protest in college might disqualify her and force her to lose her job. Alice, Tommy, Jolene, and Mel track her down and assure her that she has nothing to worry about. Her record was expunged long ago.

Episode 160 (7.20): "Mel's Cousin Wendy?" (Original broadcast date: May 29, 1983)

Writers: Linda Morris and Vic Rauseo

Director: John Pasquin

Guest stars: David Rounds and William G. Schilling

Synopsis: Mel's cousin Wendel agrees to "waitress" at Barney's Burger Barn in order to steal Barney's secret sauce recipe so Mel can make it at the diner and increase his profits.

Episode 161 (7.21): "Sweet Erasable Mel" (Original broadcast date: June 5, 1983)

Writer: Betty Yahr

Director: John Pasquin

Guest stars: Jack Andreozzi, Lou Cutell, Richard Moll, Howard Morton, Kip Niven, Mario Roccuzzo, and June Whitley Taylor

Synopsis: When Mel buys a computer to automate his business, Vera accidentally enters a command that transfers the diner's funds to another company.

(Note: Vic Tayback liked to incorporate aspects of his real life into the show when possible. Thom McAn and Buster Brown shoe boxes were used in this episode because Vic Tayback's son, Christopher, had worked a summer job selling shoes at Thom McAn. The boom mic can be seen at the top of the screen during the bank scene.)

Episode 162 (7.22): "Tommy Hyatt, Business Consultant" (Original broadcast date: June 12, 1983)

Writers: Bob Bendetson and Howard Bendetson

Director: Mel Ferber

Guest stars: Duane R. Campbell, Julius Carry, Phil Diskin, Douglas Robinson, Mark Sawyer, and Greg Zadikov

Synopsis: Tommy uses what he learned in his college marketing class to help Mel get the diner out of the red. Mel worries when his books continue to show a loss of profit. Tommy looks them over and finds an error. Once it's corrected, it's clear that the diner has made a lot of money.

Episode 163 (7.23): "Jolene Lets the Cat Out of the Bag" (Original broadcast date: September 18, 1983)

Writer: Gail Honigberg

Directors: Don Corvan and Linda Lavin

Guest stars: Dean Devlin, Marvin Kaplan, Helen Martin, and Doug Sheehan

Synopsis: When a series of burglaries in Jolene's apartment complex spook her, she invites her next-door neighbor over, hoping that the company will help to ease her fears. Jolene's neighbor turns out to be the thief and tries to rob her.

(Note: The main door to Jolene's apartment is unable to close fully once initially opened.)

SEASON 8 (1983–1984)

Episode 164 (8.1): "Mel Is Hogg-Tied" (Original broadcast date: October 1983)

Writers: Mark Egan and Mark Solomon

Director: John Pasquin

Guest stars: Sorrell Booke, Tony Longo, and Sonny Shroyer

Synopsis: An astute Southern businessman named Boss Hogg leases Mel's diner for a generous sum. What Mel doesn't realize is that the fine print grants Boss Hogg the right to purchase the diner for a single dollar whenever he chooses.

(Note: This crossover episode features the characters of Jefferson Davis "Boss" Hogg [Sorrell Booke] and Officer Enos Strate [Sonny Shroyer] from CBS's *The Dukes of Hazzard*.)

Episode 165 (8.2): "Vera's Secret Lover" (Original broadcast date: October 9, 1983)

Writer: Gail Honigberg

Director: Marc Daniels

Guest stars: Robert Costanzo, David Garrett, Marvin Kaplan, John McCook, Frank Nelson, Roger Rose, and Ian Wolfe

Alice...

Synopsis: Vera's secret admirer invites her to dinner. When they arrive at the restaurant, he winds up being too shy to disclose who he actually is. Vera discovers his real identity the next day and gently asks him out. He accepts.

Beth Howland and Celia Weston in a scene from episode 166 (8.3), "Jolene Gets Her Wings"

Episode 166 (8.3): "Jolene Gets Her Wings" (Original broadcast date: October 16, 1983)

Writers: Linda Morris and Vic Rauseo

Director: Marc Daniels

Guest stars: Raleigh Bond, Dick Gautier, Florence Halop, and Paul Rubinstein

Synopsis: Jolene graduates from flight attendant school and invites Alice, Vera, and Mel to join her on her first flight. Things go awry once they're in the air, leading Jolene to quit her new job and refocus on waitressing instead.

Episode 167 (8.4): "Alice's Blind Date" (Original broadcast date: October 23, 1983)

Writer: Bob Stevens

Director: Dolores Ferraro

Guest stars: Steven Barr, Dennis Holahan, Marvin Kaplan, and Richard Sanders

Synopsis: Alice dates a successful, blind businessman who helps her get in touch with her senses.

Episode 168 (8.5): "It Had to Be Mel" (Original broadcast date: October 30, 1983)

Writer: Lindsay Harrison

Director: Marc Daniels

Guest stars: Arthur Abelson, Marvin Kaplan, Jean Kasem, Florence Henderson, and Mark Sawyer

Synopsis: Mel plans to marry a well-known singer and move to California, until he realizes that they are from different worlds and not meant to be together.

(Note: Florence Henderson sings "I Got a Crush on You." Florence Henderson and Linda Lavin sing "I've Got Rhythm." Vic Tayback sings the beginning of "Dancing in the Dark." Celia Weston sings part of "Someone to Watch Over Me." Radio personality Casey Kasem's wife, Jean Kasem, plays Babette in this episode. This is the first time Alice's apartment is shown to have a patio.)

Episode 169 (8.6): "The Over-the-Hill Girls" (Original broadcast date: November 6, 1983)

Writers: Mark Egan and Mark Solomon

Director: Tom Trbovich

Guest stars: Joel Brooks, Marvin Kaplan, and Martha Raye

Synopsis: Alice helps Carrie fulfill her lifelong dream of becoming a singer.

(Note: Vic Tayback does not appear in this episode. Martha Raye sings "Embraceable You." Martha Raye and Linda Lavin sing a disco medley of "Little Old Lady" and "Da Ya Think I'm Sexy?" The boom mic can be seen briefly in the diner scene with Tommy.)

Episode 170 (8.7): "Vera Gets Engaged" (Original broadcast date: November 20, 1983)

Writers: Bob Bendetson and Howard Bendetson

Director: Marc Daniels

Guest stars: David Bond, Marvin Kaplan, Charles Levin, Robert Picardo, and Todd Susman

Synopsis: Vera's whirlwind romance with police officer Elliot Novak quickly leads to marriage. During the rehearsal, the absent-minded reverend mistakenly joins Vera and Mel in matrimony when Elliot is late. Vera is distraught by the situation and unsure what to do.

(Note: This is part one of a two-part episode. Linda Lavin, Vic Tayback, and Celia Weston scat sing "Here Comes the Bride.")

Promotional photo of Beth Howland and Charles Levin from episode 171 (8.8), "Vera's Wedding"

Episode 171 (8.8): "Vera's Wedding" (Original broadcast date: November 20, 1983)

Writers: Mark Egan, Gail Honigberg, and Mark Solomon

Director: Marc Daniels

Guest stars: David Bond, Duane R. Campbell, Marvin Kaplan, Charles Levin, Dave Madden, and Robert Picardo

Synopsis: The absent-minded reverend annuls Vera and Mel's marriage before officiating the ceremony for Vera and Elliot.

(Note: This is part two of a two-part episode. Linda Lavin sings Cole Porter's "True Love.")

Episode 172 (8.9): "The Robot Wore Pink" (Original broadcast date: December 18, 1983)

Writer: Peter Noah

Director: Marc Daniels

Guest stars: Andrea Aal, Jack Andreozzi, Lucille Benson, Conrad Dunn, Mitchel Evans, Bob Frank, Danny Goldman, Marvin Kaplan, June Whitley Taylor, and Marsha Warner

Synopsis: Alice quits due to poor treatment at work; a female robot replaces her. Vera and Jolene leave soon after. Mel is content having a robot for a waitress until it goes haywire and breaks down, at which point he desperately wants to rehire the waitresses.

Episode 173 (8.10): "Tis the Season to Be Jealous" (Original broadcast date: December 25, 1983)

Writers: Bob Bendetson and Howard Bendetson

Directors: Don Corvan and Linda Lavin

Guest stars: Candace Cameron Bure, Charles Levin, Howard Morton, Kip Niven, Robert Picardo, Luis Daniel Ponce, Venus DeMilo Thomas, Jennifer Ursitti, and Susan Wolf

Synopsis: Elliot becomes jealous when he spies an old beau of Vera's kissing her at the mall.

Episode 174 (8.11): "Tommy Goes Overboard" (Original broadcast date: January 1, 1984)
Writers: Nick Gore and Jerry Jacobius

Director: Oz Scott

Guest stars: Donnelly Rhodes and Isabel West

Synopsis: Mel's old navy buddy prompts Tommy to quit college and join the service. Tommy eagerly complies, only to realize he should have remained in school.

(Note: The boom mic can be seen over Tommy's head during the first scene in the diner.)

Episode 175 (8.12): "Vera, the Horse Thief" (Original broadcast date: January 8, 1984)
Writers: Bob Bendetson and Howard Bendetson

Director: John Pasquin

Guest stars: Duane R. Campbell, Robert Englund, Doris Hess, Jim Lefebvre, Tommy Madden, Robert Picardo, and Ernie Sabella

Synopsis: After seeing a miniature horse abused at the circus, Vera hides it in the diner and refuses to return it until the circus assures her that the horse's trainer will be fired.

Alice . . .

(Note: Robert Englund went on to play Freddy Krueger in the *A Nightmare on Elm Street* [1984] film series. Continuity error: From the diner, a sink is visible through the door of the ladies' room. However, when Vera is actually in the ladies' room, the room is configured differently.)

Episode 176 (8.13): "Jolene Throws a Curve" (Original broadcast date: January 15, 1984)

Writers: Sid Dorfman and Harvey Weitzman

Director: Marc Daniels

Guest stars: Jack Andreozzi, Duane R. Campbell, John Bedford Lloyd, Dave Madden, Mario Roccuzzo, Leonard Stone, and Dino M. Zaffina

Synopsis: Mel's Diner sponsors a softball team to beat Larry's Deli's team. All looks hopeless until the diner's star pitcher, Jolene, overcomes her anxiety and turns things around.

Episode 177 (8.14): "Lies My Mother Told Me" (Original broadcast date: January 29, 1984)

Writers: Sid Dorfman and Harvey Weitzman

Director: Marc Daniels

Guest stars: Joey D'Auria, Bob Gunter, Dave Madden, and Martha Raye

Synopsis: Carrie attempts to make up for treating Mel poorly in the past by showering him with gifts and telling him the truth about his childhood dog. Mel is hurt that she lied but ultimately forgives her.

(Note: The boom mic can be seen over Carrie's head when she is sitting at the table in the first scene. Vic Tayback plays a barely recognizable version of "Oh Susanna" on harmonica. Martha Raye plays "Taps" on harmonica. This is the first episode to feature a sign outside Mel's apartment door directing people to the pool or spa.)

Episode 178 (8.15): "Alice and the Devoted Dentist" (Original broadcast date: February 12, 1984)
Writer: Duncan Scott McGibbon

Director: Marc Daniels

Guest stars: James Coco, Dave Madden, and Pamela Myers

Synopsis: Alice's dentist grows fond of her. Upon learning that he plans to leave his wife, Alice encourages him to reevaluate the situation.

(Note: Linda Lavin and James Coco sing part of "'S Wonderful.")

Episode 179 (8.16): "Alice's Hot Air Romance" (Original broadcast date: March 4, 1984)
Writer: Michael Cassutt

Director: Marc Daniels

Guest stars: Arthur Abelson, Jed Allan, Peter Leeds, Charles Levin, and Tom Williams

Synopsis: Mel's self-centered friend Zack tries to entice Alice to go out with him by offering her a hot air balloon ride. However, she isn't interested.

Alice . . .

Philip McKeon, Linda Lavin, Dave Madden, Celia Weston, Martha Raye, and Beth Howland in a scene from episode 180 (8.17), "Dollars to Donuts"

Episode 180 (8.17): "Dollars to Donuts" (Original broadcast date: March 11, 1984)

Writers: David Silverman and Stephen Sustarsic

Director: Oz Scott

Guest stars: Dave Madden, Martha Raye, Douglas Robinson, and Pat Tanzillo

Synopsis: Tommy uses a computer at college to predict winners at the racetrack. Alice is concerned that he is becoming a gambler. After he loses big, Tommy quits gambling and refocuses on school.

(Note: Vic Tayback does not appear in this episode. The boom mic can be seen briefly after Tommy leaves the diner. Martha Raye, Philip McKeon, and Dave Madden sing part of "We're in the Money.")

Episode 181 (8.18): "My Dinner with Debbie" (Original broadcast date: March 18, 1984)

Writers: Mark Egan and Mark Solomon

Director: Marc Daniels

Guest star: Charles Levin

Synopsis: When Mel suspects that Vera's landlord, Mrs. Walden, is falling in love with him, he insists that Alice tell her he doesn't feel similarly about her. Mrs. Walden confesses that she isn't in love with Mel. She just loves when people appreciate her cooking.

(Note: Linda Lavin plays both Alice and Mrs. Debbie Walden in this episode. At one point, both characters are featured in the same scene.)

Episode 182 (8.19): "Vera's Fine Feathered Friends" (Original broadcast date: March 25, 1984)

Writers: David Silverman and Stephen Sustarsic

Director: Marc Daniels

Guest stars: Andrea Aal, Richard Kuss, Charles Levin, and Dave Madden

Synopsis: Mel blames a power outage at the diner on some pesky birds that Vera is feeding on the roof. She tries to save them from Mel's wrath but falls in the process and winds up hospitalized. Soon after, it is revealed that faulty wiring caused the power outage, not the birds.

Episode 183 (8.20): "Jolene Is Stuck on Mel" (Original broadcast date: April 1, 1984)

Writer: Gail Honigberg

Directors: Don Corvan and Linda Lavin

Guest stars: Alice Cadogan, Gail Hyatt, Charles Levin, Jeffrey Lippa, John McCook, Dick Sargent, Jean Smart, and Bunny Summers

Synopsis: As Jolene wavers on marrying and moving away with her fiancé, a mishap gets her glued to Mel. It takes an emergency room trip to get them unstuck and give Jolene the strength to break it off with her fiancé.

(Note: Dick Sargent played Darren in the sitcom *Bewitched*.)

Episode 184 (8.21): "Don't Play It Again, Elliot" (Original broadcast date: April 15, 1984)
Writer: Larry Balmagia

Directors: Marc Daniels and Nancy Walker

Guest stars: Hamilton Camp, Charles Levin, Tony Longo, and John Lykes

Synopsis: Elliot's obsessive piano playing drives a wedge between him and Vera. To help her, Vera's friends quietly remove the piano, but that only causes more problems. Elliot and Vera eventually reconcile, and the piano is mysteriously returned.

(Note: Linda Lavin, Vic Tayback, Celia Weston, Philip McKeon, Beth Howland, and Charles Levin sing part of "Don't Fence Me In." Charles Levin sings part of "Ninety-Nine Bottles of Beer." Linda Lavin, Vic Tayback, Celia Weston, Beth Howland, Tony Longo, John Lykes, and Charles Levin sing part of "I've Got Rhythm.")

Episode 185 (8.22): "Mel Spins His Wheels" (Original broadcast date: May 13, 1984)
Writers: Richard Marcus and Michael Poryes

Director: Marc Daniels

Guest stars: Frances Bay, Bartine Burkett, Hugh Farrington, Marvin Kaplan, Jeffrey Lippa, Douglas Robinson, Frank Schuller, and Leonard Stone

Synopsis: Mel gains insight into the plight of the handicapped after an accident leaves him wheelchair-bound.

(Note: The men's room door in the diner was made smaller for this episode so that wheelchairs couldn't fit through it. During the series, different street addresses for the diner are given. In this episode, the diner is said to be at 2128 Bush Highway; in at least two other episodes, the diner's location is said to be 1130 Bush Highway. In episode 9 [1.9], "Good Night, Sweet Vera," Alice says that the diner is on Fourth Street. The real Mel's Diner is located at 1747 Grand Avenue.)

Episode 186 (8.23): "Be It Ever So Crowded" (Original broadcast date: May 20, 1984)

Writers: David Silverman and Stephen Sustarsic

Director: Marc Daniels

Guest stars: Jack Andreozzi, David Bond, and Douglas Robinson

Synopsis: Vera and Elliot buy their first home and discover that they inherited the absent-minded reverend, who married them, as a tenant. They struggle to ask him to move.

SEASON 9 (1984–1985)

Episode 187 (9.1): "Romancing Mr. Stone" (Original broadcast date: October 14, 1984)

Writers: Cindy Begel and Lesa Kite

Director: Marc Daniels

Guest stars: Angela Aames, Michael Durrell, Martin Ferrero, and Denise Loveday

Synopsis: Vera and Jolene secretly place a personal ad in the newspaper to help Alice find a mate. When responses pour in, Alice reluctantly agrees to go out with the best-sounding responders, but each man she meets turns out to be an oddball.

(Note: Starting with this episode, Charles Levin became a regular member of the cast, and his name appeared in the opening credits.)

Episode 188 (9.2): "Space Sharples" (Original broadcast date: October 1984)

Writers: Bob Bendetson and Howard Bendetson

Director: Marc Daniels

Guest stars: Steve Begel, John Bloom, Hayley Carr, Lucy Lee Flippin, Dan Gilvezan, Loretta Greenwood, Larry Flash Jenkins, Marvin Kaplan, Don Keefer, Kenneth Lloyd, and Howard Morton

Synopsis: Mel overtakes a bank robber and comes to believe that he has crime-fighting powers. A few days later, a bully shows up and proves him wrong.

(Note: Lucy Lee Flippin played Eliza Jane Wilder in the drama series *Little House on the Prairie*. She was also a regular cast member in *Flo*.)

Episode 189 (9.3): "Big Bad Mel" (Original broadcast date: November 4, 1984)

Writers: David Silverman and Stephen Sustarsic

Director: Marc Daniels

Guest stars: Brice Beckham, Hayley Carr, Doug Cox, Lou Cutell, Charles Hyman, Rue McClanahan, Randal Patrick, Jonathan Prince, and Fred D. Scott

Synopsis: When parking becomes an issue at the diner, Mel buys the school next door and plans to turn it into a parking lot. The nursery school teacher, Alice, Vera, and Jolene encourage him to reconsider and let the school stay open instead.

(Note: Linda Lavin sings a takeoff of "My Bonnie" with nursery school children. Rue McClanahan was part of the main cast in the sitcoms *Maude* and *The Golden Girls*.)

Episode 190 (9.4): "Houseful of Hunnicutts" (Original broadcast date: November 18, 1984)

Writers: Lisa A. Bannick and Jack Carrerow

Director: Don Corvan

Guest stars: Duane R. Campbell, Robin Eurich, Trevor Henley, Natalie Masters, Steve McGriff, Kent Perkins, Gregory Walcott, and Grant Wilson

Synopsis: Jolene's family visits and expects her to wait on them hand and foot.

(Note: Linda Lavin sings part of "Home, Sweet Home." Duane R. Campbell, Trevor Henley, Kent Perkins, Grant Wilson, Robin Eurich, and Steve McGriff sing backup. Gregory Walcott sings a brief reprise of "Home, Sweet Home" later in the episode.)

Alice...

Beth Howland, Philip McKeon, and Celia Weston in a scene from episode 191 (9.5), "Tommy's Lost Weekend"

Episode 191 (9.5): "Tommy's Lost Weekend" (Original broadcast date: November 25, 1984)

Writers: Bob Bendetson, Howard Bendetson, and Arnold Schmidt

Director: Marc Daniels

Guest stars: Michael Durrell and Marvin Kaplan

Synopsis: When Tommy's newfound party lifestyle leads him to drink daily, Alice helps him realize he has a drinking problem.

(Note: The boom mic can be seen in the diner when Henry and Mel are near the pay phone.)

Episode 192 (9.6): "Undercover Mel" (Original broadcast date: December 1984)

Writers: Linda Morris and Vic Rauseo

Director: Marc Daniels

Guest stars: Jack Andreozzi, Aaron Fletcher, Paul Mantee, Mike Muscat, Robert Picardo, and Johnny Silver

Synopsis: Mel goes undercover to help Elliott and his partner Maxwell nab a group of cattle rustlers.

(Note: Robert Picardo sings part of "Swanee.")

Episode 193 (9.7): "Footloose Mel" (Original broadcast date: December 23, 1984)

Writers: Bob Bendetson and Howard Bendetson

Director: Lee Shallat Chemel

Guest stars: Fred Berry, Jason Desilva, Hugo Huizar, Kenneth Kimmins, Donovan Leitch Jr., Andy Levine, Richard Minchenberg, Daniells Silva, Jonathan Prince Steven, and Leonard Stone

Synopsis: To help pick up business, Mel agrees to have the Boys Alternative Dance Symposium (B.A.D.S.) perform in the diner during an arts festival. When the boys arrive, he mistakes them for hoodlums and throws them out. After realizing his error, he gives them a heartfelt apology and gets them to return to the diner to perform.

(Note: The B.A.D.S. make up a song that teases the character Danny. Film equipment can be seen briefly on the right side of the screen when Mel and Danny are outside talking with the B.A.D.S. Fred Berry, who played Bobo in this episode, was known for his role as Rerun in the sitcom *What's Happening?* In addition to being an actor,

Berry was a member of the Lockers, a street dance troupe formed by Toni Basil and Don Campbell.)

Episode 194 (9.8): "Vera's Anniversary Blues" (Original broadcast date: January 8, 1985)

Writers: Lisa A. Bannick and Jack Carrerow

Director: Don Corvan

Guest stars: John George Campbell, Richard W. Cox, Reid Cruickshanks, Dave Madden, Bill Maher, Barry Pearl, Douglas Robinson, Steve Tolman, Billy Vera, and Curry Worsham

Synopsis: Vera and Elliot plan to celebrate their anniversary by recreating the magic of the day they first met, but mounting obstacles prevent them from doing so. Nevertheless, they wind up connecting in a meaningful way.

(Note: Billy Vera sings the beginning of "What Now, My Love?" Barry Pearl sings part of "The Man I Love." The Indian River Boys [John George Campbell, Stephen Tolman, Rick Cox, and Curry Worsham] sing "Love's Old Sweet Song" and "I Love You Truly." Bill Maher makes his TV debut as Officer Gary Conroy.)

Episode 195 (9.9): "Kiss the Grill Goodbye" (Original broadcast date: January 15, 1985)

Writers: Cindy Begel and Lesa Kite

Director: Nancy Walker

Guest stars: Janet Carroll, Dick Gautier, Maurice Hill, Marvin Kaplan, Dave Madden, Douglas Robinson, Armin Shimerman, June Whitley Taylor, and Marsha Warner

Synopsis: Jolene's jokes about the diner during an appearance on TV hurt business so much that Mel has to close down. Jolene feels awful about the situation and enlists Alice and Vera's help to encourage the diner's regular patrons to return so the diner can reopen.

Episode 196 (9.10): "Vera, the Nightbird" (Original broadcast date: January 22, 1985)

Writers: Linda Morris and Vic Rauseo

Director: Don Corvan

Guest stars: Ralph Bruneau, Duane R. Campbell, Michael Crabtree, Dave Madden, and Stephen Tobolowsky

Synopsis: Vera's sultry voice attracts a good deal of admirers when she MC's at a radio station.

Episode 197 (9.11): "Alice Doesn't Work Here Anymore: Part 1" (Original broadcast date: January 29, 1985)

Writers: David Silverman and Stephen Sustarsic

Director: Don Corvan

Guest stars: Kelly Ann Conn, Michael Durrell, Mickey Jones, Paige Matthews, Michael McManus, Kip Niven, Christine Scott, and Joe Unger

Synopsis: Alice falls in love with a country singer named Travis Marsh. He offers her a job performing with him on the road. When Alice wavers on what to do, Travis invites her onto his tour bus and kidnaps her.

(Note: In the series, Travis Marsh was Steve Marsh's cousin. Both roles were played by Kip Niven. Mickey Jones, who plays Buford in this episode, had a recurring role in *Flo*. Linda Lavin sings "Just One of Those Things." Linda Lavin and Kip Niven sing part of "[Your Love Keeps Lifting Me] Higher and Higher.")

Episode 198 (9.12): Alice Doesn't Work Here Anymore: Part 2 (Original broadcast date: February 5, 1985)

Writers: Bob Bendetson, Howard Bendetson, Mark Egan, and Mark Solomon

Director: Don Corvan

Guest stars: Gregg Berger, Clinton Derricks-Carroll, Michael Durrell, Mickey Jones, Michael McManus, and Kip Niven

Synopsis: Alice agrees to give life on the road with Travis a twenty-four-hour trial run. In the end, the police pull the bus over, and Alice decides to return to the diner.

(Note: Kip Niven sings "Sweet Harmony," an original song written for the show. Later, Linda Lavin and Kip Niven sing part of the same tune.)

Episode 199 (9.13): "The Night They Raided Debbie's" (Original broadcast date: February 6, 1985)

Writers: Mark Egan and Mark Solomon

Director: Nancy Walker

Guest stars: Mary Grace Canfield, Dan Frischman, and Margaret Wheeler

Synopsis: When Vera and Elliot decide to rent out a room in their house, Vera's old landlord pushes her way into becoming their tenant. Before long, she drives them crazy. They ultimately encourage her to move out.

(Note: Linda Lavin reprises her role as Mrs. Walden in this episode.

During the first scene, in which Mel and Vera discuss a typo on the diner's new menu, Charles Levin can be seen standing outside the front door, awaiting his cue to enter.)

Episode 200 (9.14): "One on One" (Original broadcast date: March 5, 1985)
Writers: Linda Morris and Vic Rauseo

Director: Don Corvan

Guest stars: Danny Goldman, Michael Goodwin, Bob Gunter, Christopher Templeton, and Dino M. Zaffina

Synopsis: Mel coaches Jolene so she can audition for the women's professional basketball team in Phoenix. Because of their sessions' intensity, they develop a newfound affection for one another. When Jolene doesn't make the team, she and Mel realize they don't have much in common and decide to end the romantic aspect of their relationship.

Episode 201 (9.15): "Vera's Grounded Gumshoe" (Original broadcast date: March 12, 1985)
Writers: Cindy Begel and Lesa Kite

Director: Marc Daniels

Guest stars: Michael Alldredge, Duane R. Campbell, Jamie De Roy, Ian Fried, Kim Hamilton, and Jeffrey Lampert

Synopsis: Elliot loses confidence in himself as a police officer when he accidentally gets shot with his own gun at a crime scene. It takes stopping a robbery at the diner for him to regain his courage and sense of purpose.

Episode 202 (9.16): "Th-th-th-that's All Folks" (Original broadcast date: March 19, 1985)

Writers: Bob Carroll Jr. and Madelyn Davis

Director: Marc Daniels

Guest stars: Duane R. Campbell, Marvin Kaplan, Dave Madden, and Douglas Robinson

Synopsis: Mel sells the diner and gives the waitresses a surprise gift as they part ways.

(Note: The closing credits feature memorable images from the series and end with a clip of Alice in a bunny costume saying, "That's all folks!")

CHAPTER 11:

Alice—Fan Quiz

Season 1

1. What line of dialogue from the feature film *Alice Doesn't Live Here Anymore* is also spoken in the *Alice* pilot?

2. According to Flo, what is the subtle, ladylike approach to getting a man to notice you?
   a. Whisper in his ear.
   b. Drop your house key in his lap.
   c. Shake your patoot and then smile at him over your shoulder.

3. What sport does Mel like to play?

4. How does Flo stop an obscene phone caller from contacting her?

5. What famous person in the world of *Alice* comes to the diner for an important visit?
   a. The mayor
   b. Muhammad Ali
   c. A renowned critic from *The Phoenix Times* called Mr. James

Alice...

6. Flo frequently wears earrings shaped like _____ at work.

7. In season one, what does Tommy want to be when he grows up?

8. True or false: Vera takes a course in shorthand so she can write down orders faster.

9. Burton Gilliam played Buford Baker in *Alice* episodes 14 (1.14), "Vera's Mortician," and 24 (1.24), "Mel's Happy Burger." What role did he play later in *Alice* and in the series *Flo*?

10. _____ is Flo's favorite type of dance to do at the VFW Hall.

Season 2

1. What are the names of Vera's goldfish?
    a. Hansel and Gretel
    b. Abbott and Costello
    c. Starsky and Hutch

2. How does Mel describe the diner?

3. What is Flo's third husband's name?

4. True or false: Mel was seventeen when he left home.

5. What is one of Tommy's favorite TV shows?

6. Mel fought in _____.

Life Behind the Counter in Mel's Greasy Spoon

7. What is the name of the Middle Eastern man Flo becomes engaged to?

8. In episode 45 (2.21), "Mel's Recession," what high-paying job does Vera win by drawing straws with her colleagues?
   a. A waitress in a sandwich shop
   b. Playing Bugs Bunny at an amusement park
   c. Senior taste-tester at a vegetarian food company

9. _____ is the first name of Alice's favorite uncle.

10. In episode 46 (2.22), "Earthquake," who has taken money out of the tip jar for the past six months without telling anyone?

Linda Lavin (as Sam Butler) in a scene from episode 49 (3.1), "Take Him, He's Yours"

Season 3

1. What type of earrings does Belle wear?

2. What does Belle wear that the character Flo also wears in *Alice Doesn't Live Here Anymore*?

3. True or false: Tommy studies the guitar and then the cymbals during this season.

4. _____ are pictured on the diner's wallpaper.

5. Who was the bully in Mel's high school class?
    a. Sister Josephine
    b. Mel
    c. The gym teacher

6. Who was Mel's best friend in high school?

7. True or false: In high school, Vera was voted "nicest legs."

8. What celebrity does Flo look forward to seeing at the Golden Circle Charity Ball?

9. According to Flo, how long has she been dating?
    a. Since the day she was born
    b. Since she was four years old
    c. Ever since she learned how to boogie

10. In what role was Vera cast in her first-grade play?

Season 4

1. In the opening credits, Tommy is seen in a bathtub with other cast members. Who is in the bathtub in the actual episode this clip comes from?

2. How is Vera related to Art Carney?
   a. He is her long-lost father.
   b. Through a relative in Ireland
   c. Vera's Aunt Agatha has recently married him.

3. What play is Tommy cast in during this season?

Beth Howland, Vic Tayback, and Linda Lavin in a scene from episode 85 (4.13), "Alice in TV Land"

4. In episode 73 (4.1), "Has Anyone Here Seen Telly?," Telly Savalas says that _____ was Greek applause.

5. True or false: Mel suspects Barney Curkwood, the owner of Barney's Burger Barn, of wanting to steal his chili recipe.

6. Who takes over as waitress after Flo leaves?
    a. Mel's girlfriend, Marie
    b. Mel's mother, Carrie
    c. A sanitation worker who comes to the diner for a bite to eat

7. Why does Belle initially come to Phoenix?

8. Belle is from _____.

9. What does Belle get to keep the creeps away from her at bars?

10. What does Mel have cases of and uses in most of the recipes he makes at the diner?

Season 5
1. What does Belle's little voice call her?
    a. Loretta Lynn
    b. Honey lamb
    c. Isabel

Life Behind the Counter in Mel's Greasy Spoon

2. What leads Mel to have a cast put on his foot?

3. What is Vera's Aunt Agatha's secret to keeping healthy?

4. True or false: Belle lives three blocks away from Alice.

5. Alice's alter ego, _____, shows up when Alice needs some muscle in a challenging situation.

6. Why does Mel's mother take a job at Benny's Beanery?

7. How does Mel wind up locked in a dumpster?

8. True or false: Jolene is a truck driver before she becomes a waitress at Mel's Diner.

9. Why does Belle quit her job at the diner?
    a. To become a backup singer in her cousin's country-western band in Nashville
    b. She won the lottery and doesn't need to work anymore.
    c. To open a restaurant featuring singing waitresses in Las Vegas

10. Vera finds a _____ at the laundromat while doing her laundry.

Season 6

1. What do Jolene Hunnicutt and Samantha Stephens from *Bewitched* have in common?

Alice . . .

2. What does Vera make in her first ceramics class?

3. True or false: When Carrie bakes pies at the diner, Mel's customers stay away in droves.

4. Who inspires Vera to study tap dance?
   a. Michael Jackson
   b. Donald O'Connor
   c. Ruby Keeler

Nancy McKeon, Billy Jacobi, and Linda Lavin in a scene from episode 120 (6.4), "Alice's Halloween Surprise"

5. What companion does Mel keep by his side in his recliner in his apartment?

6. True or false: When Mel writes his will, he leaves the diner to Marie.

7. Tommy attends _____ High School.

8. What is Vera's CB name?

9. During high school, Vera was a member of _____.

10. What does Mel do at the banquet at his high school reunion?

Season 7

1. What happens as a result of Henry's playing the lead role in his high school's production of the musical *No, No, Nanette*?

2. Why does Carrie divorce Robby?
    a. He has become a better cook than Carrie, making her jealous.
    b. He has cheated on her.
    c. She cannot deal with his excessive gambling any longer.

5. Why does Jolene hold a grudge against her brother Jonas?

6. True or false: Henry's lifelong dream is to be the first person to install telephones on the moon.

7. How is Mel able to purchase a Porsche for only $20.00?

8. What woman does Mel fear?

Alice ...

9. What is the name of Earl's ex-wife?
   a. Margie
   b. Madelyn
   c. Marcia

10. Why does Vera name her new cat Mel?

11. Earl attends law school for _____.

12. What movie poster does Vera have in the bathroom of her apartment?

Season 8

1. Who does Jolene discover she is related to?
   a. Robert Redford
   b. Boss Hogg
   c. Florence Jean Castleberry

2. What is Tommy's major in college?

3. The first words that Henry's infant twins say are_____.

4. Why does Mel let Jolene moonlight as a stewardess?

5. True or false: In high school, Alice was voted most likely to succeed.

6. How much schooling has Carrie had?

7. How do Vera and Elliot meet?

Life Behind the Counter in Mel's Greasy Spoon

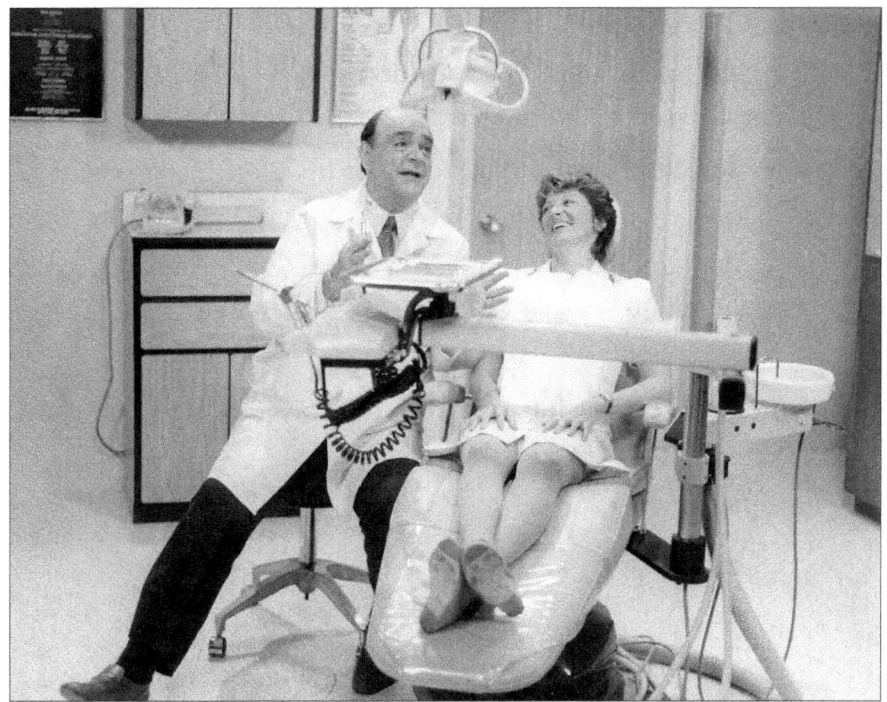

James Coco and Linda Lavin in a scene from episode 178 (8.15), "Alice and the Devoted Dentist"

8. What does Vera do while playing in a game on Mel's softball team?
   a. Beats up the umpire
   b. Hits a home run
   c. Skins her knee

9. Mel's dentist's phone number is _____.

10. What happens when Earl plays hooky from coaching basketball practice?

Season 9

1. What do Jolene and Vera do behind Alice's back?

2. Who do Alice, Jolene, and Vera dress up as for Halloween?
   a. The Three Stooges
   b. Alvin and the Chipmunks
   c. The Marx Brothers

3. True or false: The fraternity brothers give Tommy a mohawk haircut.

4. Elliot's career goal is to _____.

5. In episode 192 (9.6), "Undercover Mel," what do the meat thieves do with Mel when they discover he is a spy?

6. How many serious girlfriends has Mel had in the past year?

7. Vera's other identity is _____.

8. How does Elliot become a good dancer?

9. When Vera and Elliot have to rent out a room in their house to make ends meet, who is their renter?
   a. Vera's old landlord, Debbie Walden
   b. Johnny Cash
   c. A member of the Hell's Angels

10. What does Mel give each of the waitresses as a gift before the diner is shut down and sold?

CHAPTER 12:

Creating the Spin-off TV Series Flo

DURING THE FIRST SEASON of *Alice*, producers approached Polly Holliday about creating a new series centered on her character, Flo. Holliday was thrilled about the idea. They put her under option and gave her a wide degree of creative control in developing the show. Her initial concept was to have Flo return home to Cowtown, Texas, where she would marry a local politician who would soon become governor. Each episode would focus on Flo's new life as first lady of Texas and her humorous exploits as an outsider among the state capital's elite.

Network executive Alan Shayne didn't think Holliday's concept robust enough to sustain a series, so he brought in three writers to help her develop a new concept. Holliday loved working with the writers. She found it a continuation of the puzzle-solving technique she used to develop her character on *Alice*, except now she could create an entire story world.

The writers helped Holliday revamp her initial idea into a premise that focused on Flo returning to her hometown and turning an old saloon into a popular new tavern called Flo's Yellow Rose. She would move her mobile home into her mother's backyard and live out of it. The government aspect that was a focal point of Holliday's original idea was channeled into one character, a banker, Farley Waters, who would hold the mortgage on Flo's business and run for public office. He and Flo would usually be at odds. Studio executives found the new concept engaging. Everyone agreed that the show should be called *Flo*. All they needed was the right time to move the program into production.

By the time the fourth season of *Alice* began, a renewed interest in TV shows featuring the American South had emerged. Series such as *Dallas* and *The Dukes of Hazzard* were extremely popular. This fact, coupled with a growing fan base for Holliday's character on *Alice*, convinced CBS that the time was ripe to move forward with *Flo*. With that, Holliday completed her work on *Alice* and prepared to begin production for her new show.

Holliday was involved in all aspects of production and credited as a creative consultant on *Flo*. She cast the series with theater actors because they had extensive experience working before live audiences. Lucy Lee Flippin (Fran) and Leo Burmester (Randy) had performed with Holliday in regional theater. Joyce Bulifant (Miriam) and Geoffrey Lewis (Earl) had theater experience and worked with Holliday in episodes of *Alice*. The remaining members of the main cast—Jim Baker (Farley), Sudie Bond (Mama), and Stephen Keep Mills (Les)—had backgrounds in theater as well.

During rehearsals, Holliday occasionally guided the cast on how to best deliver their lines. In keeping with theatrical practice, she had signs posted backstage stating that visitors were prohibited there starting thirty minutes prior to taping. That way, the cast and crew could use the time to make final preparations. In postproduction, Holliday reviewed footage and suggested changes as needed. Her input strengthened the overall quality of the show.

Flo premiered on March 24, 1980. It was the most watched program of the week. The first season, which consisted of six episodes, wound up being one of the highest-rated new shows and finished in the top ten in the Nielsen ratings. The network took note of this and promptly gave a "green light" for another season.

As season two moved into production, Holliday and her creative team decided that each new episode would highlight a different character in the main cast. One episode would explore Flo's close friend Miriam's domestic situation. Other episodes would focus on piano player Les's private life, bar patron Randy Stumphill and his secret desire to become a singer, Fran's business affairs, and Earl's connection to his ranch and animals.

Flo and her family were an essential part of the series. Holliday reasoned that since Flo's father had run out on the family, she had been left without a male role model in her life. She married three times because she was constantly looking for a surrogate father but could never find one. During season two, Holliday requested that a special two-part episode be written to explore Flo's background.

That episode, entitled "A Castleberry Thanksgiving," centers on a Thanksgiving dinner at Flo's mother's house during which the entire family, including their estranged father, Jarvis, convenes for the first time in years. It is a tense situation in which the family struggles to work through their differences and find peace and appreciation for one another. Life will never be as it was before Flo's father abandoned the family, but their reunion partly fills the void that his departure left in Flo and her siblings' lives.

By the end of season two, ratings had declined. The network decided to cancel the series. Despite this, Holliday was nominated for a Primetime Emmy Award for Outstanding Lead Actress in a Comedy

Alice . . .

Series and a Golden Globe Award for Best Performance by an Actress in a Television Series—Comedy or Musical. Geoffrey Lewis, who played the bartender, Earl, was nominated for a Golden Globe Award for Best Supporting Actor in a Series, Miniseries or Motion Picture Made for Television as well.

CHAPTER 13:

The Cast of Flo

Polly Holliday *(Flo)*
See page 83.

Geoffrey Lewis *(Earl)*
Geoffrey Lewis was born in 1935 in Plainfield, New Jersey. His family moved to California when he was ten years old. In high school, Lewis studied drama and starred in one-person shows that he wrote himself. After graduating, he moved to New York and trained as an actor at the Neighborhood Playhouse. The skills he learned there helped him get cast in several off-Broadway and regional theater productions.

In 1963, Lewis made his first film appearance as "the man in the park" in *The Fat Black Pussycat*. In 1973, he married Glenis Batley. That same year he began to work with Clint Eastwood in a host of films, the first of which was *Thunderbolt and Lightfoot* (1974). Lewis's marriage to Batley was tenuous and ended in divorce in 1975.

Lewis soon met and married Tracy Darroll. While they were married, he appeared in episodes of many TV series, among them *Alice*, *Lou Grant*, and *Mork & Mindy*. In 1980, he was cast in a main role in *Flo*. Lewis received a Golden Globe nomination for his work in the series. He went on to have recurring parts in *Falcon Crest* and *Gun Shy*.

Alice...

Geoffrey Lewis

By 1984, Lewis's relationship with Darroll had become strained and they divorced. A few months later, he cofounded Celestial Navigations, a company that recorded original stories enhanced by electronic accompaniment. Lewis received a Drama-Logue Award for his performance with the company. Over the next twenty years, Celestial Navigations produced eight albums of stories.

In 1991, Lewis married cellist Paula Hochhalter. He continued to act in guest roles on shows such as *Walker, Texas Ranger*, after which he was cast in a leading role in the action series *Land's End*. *Midnight in the Garden of Good and Evil* (1997) marked Lewis's final film collaboration with Eastwood.

In 2006, the California Independent Film Festival Slate Awards selected Lewis as best actor for his performance in the short film

Old Man Music (2005). Between his three marriages, Lewis collectively fathered ten children. He dedicated his life to his family and his work. He died of a heart attack on April 7, 2015.

Sudie Bond

Sudie Bond *(Mama)*

Born in Kentucky in 1928, Sudie Bond originally trained to become a dancer and choreographer. She married Cornelius "Neil" Massini Noland. They had a son. In 1951, Bond made her acting debut as Millie Young in the TV series *Love of Life*. The next year she entered the New York theater world, playing Olga in the revival of the comedy *Tovarich* (1936). Many comedic roles in Broadway shows followed, including in *The Waltz of the Toreadors* (1957), *The Egg* (1962),

Harold (1962), and *The Impossible Years* (1965). This last show was written by Robert Fisher and Arthur Marx, who would later write for *Alice*.

In 1970, Bond played Clara in the Broadway revival of Noël Coward's *Hay Fever* (1925). After that, Bond portrayed the school principal, Miss Lynch, in the popular Broadway musical *Grease* (1972). She then appeared in recurring roles in the TV series *The New Temperatures Rising Show* and *Mary Hartman, Mary Hartman*.

In 1980, Bond was hired as a main cast member on *Flo*. When the show ended, she returned to Broadway and performed the part of Juanita in *Come Back to the 5 & Dime Jimmy Dean, Jimmy Dean* (1982). She reprised the role in the feature film version of the play, which was released in 1983.

In her final screen appearance, Bond portrayed a cleaning lady in the comedy *Johnny Dangerously* (1984). Later that year, she was cast in the part of Betty Meeks in *The Foreigner* (1984) at the Astor Place Theater in New York. During the show's run, she died of complications related to asthma. Bond was posthumously nominated for a Drama Desk Award for Outstanding Featured Actress in a Play for her performance.

Jim B. Baker *(Farley)*

Jim B. Baker was born in 1941 in Great Falls, Montana. He grew up a few miles away in Conrad, Montana. He was quite mischievous as a child. His parents sent him to military school to instill some discipline in him. Baker was expelled after three years due to his unruly behavior. Nevertheless, he managed to graduate from high school a year later.

While attending the University of Montana in the early 1960s, Baker became interested in acting. He performed with the Oregon

Shakespeare Festival and the Bigfork Playhouse each summer. After college, he enlisted in the army and served a tour of duty in the Vietnam War. Upon returning home, Baker focused on his acting career. In 1971, he became a member of the Milwaukee Repertory Theater. During his time in Wisconsin, he met and married his wife, Mary Eichholz.

Jim B. Baker

In 1978, Baker was cast as a soccer coach in the film *Manny's Orphans*. Soon after, he joined the main cast of the sitcom *Flo*. More roles followed, including guest appearances in series such as *Private Benjamin*, *Open All Night*, *Simon & Simon*, and *Silver Spoons*.

In 1986, Baker began an eight-year association with the Denver Center Theater. He favored serious roles, especially those in plays written by Arthur Miller. In 1995, Baker reconnected with the Milwaukee Repertory Theater. He remained with that theater until 2006, when a back injury during rehearsal for *King Lear* made performing difficult. Baker retired the following year to his childhood town of Conrad, where he led a quiet life with his wife until his death in 2014.

Lucy Lee Flippin *(Fran)*

Lucy Lee Flippin was born in Philadelphia in 1943. She made her first appearance onstage as Gabriel in her church's Christmas pageant. She got the part because she was taller than everyone else. Flippin excelled at ice skating and was active in the competitive side of the sport for a few years. After high school, she pursued a bachelor of science degree in speech at Northwestern University. During her studies, she took classes in performance and film production with the intent of working as a movie or TV editor once she graduated.

In 1965, Flippin completed her degree at Northwestern University and decided to focus on her ability as a performer instead of working behind the camera. Soon, she was hired to be a skater in the ice show *Holiday on Ice*. It was exciting work, but daily performances with eight costume changes per show exhausted her. She left the production after a year and moved to New York City, where she began looking for work as an actor. It took her five years of doing odd jobs before she could make a living acting in TV commercials.

In 1971, Flippin was cast as the obscene caller in the film *The Telephone Book*. Additional roles in New York followed and ultimately led her to Hollywood to meet with an agent. The agent told Flippin that it was the age of beauty in film and TV and she would never be cast in Hollywood. He recommended she give up acting and get married instead.

Lucy Lee Flippin

Flippin ignored the agent's advice and returned to New York. Not long after, she began getting cast in stage plays, including being featured with Richard Gere in *A Midsummer Night's Dream* at Lincoln Center. In 1974, she made her Broadway debut understudying the roles of Beauty Lady, Lavoris, and Mother in *Mert & Phil*. During this time, she turned her hand to playwriting and had three of her plays produced in New York.

In 1975, Flippin met and married actor Tom Tarpey. They reevaluated their careers and decided to relocate to Los Angeles. Soon after their move, Flippin got a part on *The Bob Newhart Show*. She was then cast in two Woody Allen movies: *The Front* (1976) and *Annie Hall* (1977). In 1978, Flippin and Tarpey had a son. Tarpey found it increasingly difficult to get work as an actor in California. This strained their marriage and eventually led them to divorce.

Around that time, Flippin realized that she wasn't getting as many parts as she had a few years ago either. She decided to get a shag haircut and darken her hair. Once she made these changes, acting roles arrived more steadily. She was cast in a guest part in the sitcom *The Ropers*. That was followed by work in several made-for-TV movies.

In 1979, Flippin was featured in a recurring role as Eliza Jane Wilder in the popular TV series *Little House on the Prairie*. In 1980, her agent asked whether she'd be interested in joining her fellow client Polly Holliday in the main cast of *Flo*. Flippin accepted. Her agent asked *Little House* producer Michael Landon to write her out of the series. A few months later, Flippin began playing the title character's sister, Fran, in *Flo*.

When *Flo* ended after two seasons, Flippin moved on to a memorable role as the dance conservatory secretary in the blockbuster film *Flashdance* (1983). She then returned to her part as Eliza Jane in *Little House*. Since then, Flippin has appeared in many TV shows, including in a recurring role in the sitcom *The Last Precinct*. She has also been featured on *The Munsters Today, Beverly Hills, 90210, ER*, and *Still Standing*.

Joyce Bulifant *(Miriam)*

Joyce Bulifant was born in 1937 in Newport News, Virginia. She attended high school at the Solebury School in New Hope, Pennsylvania, where she met actress Helen Hayes's son, James MacArthur. They graduated in 1955, got married, had two children, and then pursued acting careers together.

One of Bulifant's first TV roles was as a dancer on *Arthur Murray's Dance Party*. In 1959 she made her Broadway debut as Nancy in the comedy *Tall Story*. Two years later, she appeared in an episode of *Play of the Week* entitled "Therese Raquin." Supporting parts in shows followed, including in *My Three Sons* and *McHale's Navy*. In 1962, she received a Theatre World Award for her performance in the play *Take Her, She's Mine* (1961).

Joyce Bulifant

In 1964, Bulifant was cast as Mary in the TV series *Tom, Dick and Mary*. After the series ended, she returned to Broadway where she appeared in the comedy *The Paisley Convertible* (1967). By that point, her relationship with MacArthur had become strained, and they divorced. Despite her personal challenges, Bulifant forged forward with her career and was featured in recurring roles in the series *Dr. Kildare* and *The Bill Cosby Show*.

In 1969, she was selected to play Carol Brady in the popular sitcom *The Brady Bunch*. However, producers decided to recast the role before the series went into production. Not long afterward, Bulifant married actor Edward Mallory. They had one child.

In the 1970s, she became a fixture of daytime television and appeared in 182 episodes of *The Match Game*. She was also seen on *The $10,000 Pyramid* and several other game shows. Though her career was blossoming, her marriage to Mallory was not. They divorced in 1974.

In 1976, Bulifant was hired for a main role in the series *Big John, Little John*. Later that year, she married TV and film producer William Asher. She went on to appear in episodes of *Three's Company*, *Alice*, and the miniseries *Little Women*. In 1980, Bulifant landed a featured part in the comedy film *Airplane!* A few months later, she became a member of the ensemble cast of *Flo*.

In 1985 Bulifant wrote and produced the hour-long video *Gifts of Greatness*, which dramatized how historical figures, including Thomas Edison and Albert Einstein, overcame dyslexia. Bulifant had conquered the disorder herself, which inspired her to work on the project to help others afflicted with it.

In 1993, she and Asher divorced. Soon after, Bulifant was cast to play the mother of her real-life son John Asher's character, Gary Wallace, in the sitcom *Weird Science*. Bulifant acted sporadically in television roles after that. In 2000, she married Glade Bruce Hansen. Their brief union ended in divorce in 2001. The following year she married writer Roger Perry. They remained together until his death in 2018.

Leo Burmester

Leo Burmester *(Randy)*

Leo Burmester was born in 1944 in Louisville, Kentucky. He majored in biology at Western Kentucky University but eventually transferred to the theater department, where he earned a bachelor of arts degree in drama. In 1972, he got a master of fine arts degree in drama from the University of Denver and then worked briefly as a teacher before pursuing a career in acting.

In the mid-1970s, Burmester performed in the plays *Lone Star* (1975) and *Getting Out* (1978) at the Actors Theatre of Louisville. He was in the casts of both shows when they opened in New York. Burmester made his first film appearance in *Cruising* (1980). This was followed by a main role in *Flo* and supporting parts in other TV series, including *Private Benjamin*, *Nurse*, and *One Life to Live*.

In 1981, Burmester married Lauren Aimee Cookson. They had two children. Two years later, he originated the role of Thénardier in the Broadway production of *Les Misérables* (1987). After his run in the show ended, he returned to TV, where he played Officer Red Tollin in the series *True Blue* and Officer Bill Ruskin in the show *Arresting Behavior*. By then, Burmester's relationship with Cookson had deteriorated, and they divorced.

In 1996, he went to New York to perform in the Broadway run of Sam Shepard's drama *Buried Child* (1978). He won a New York Fanny award in 1998 for Best Supporting Actor for his role in Eugene O'Neill's *Ah, Wilderness!* (1933). He went on to appear in more New York productions including *The Civil War* (1999) and Harry Connick Jr.'s musical *Thou Shalt Not* (2001).

In 2003, Burmester was cast in the Broadway musical *Urban Cowboy*. The same year, he married his third wife, actress Lora Lee Ecobelli. They recorded an album of original folk and blues songs entitled *Blue Horse* (2004) and gave concerts in the New York area. During the aftermath of Hurricane Katrina, they produced a benefit concert to help victims of the natural disaster. Burmester died on June 28, 2007, after a brief illness.

Stephen Keep Mills *(Les)*

Stephen Keep Mills was born in 1947 in Camden, South Carolina. He graduated from the Yale School of Drama in 1969 with a master of fine arts degree in Drama/Theatre Arts and Stage Craft. For two seasons, he acted with the Guthrie Theatre Company. Mills went on to perform with regional theaters throughout the US and Canada. In 1977, he made his Broadway debut in the drama *The Shadow Box*.

In 1978, Mills moved to Los Angeles to pursue a career as a TV actor. He appeared in guest roles in series including *Lou Grant*, *Eight is Enough*, *The Love Boat*, *Dallas*, *The Incredible Hulk*, and *A Rumor of War*. In 1980, he became a part of the ensemble cast of *Flo*. A steady stream of guest appearances in made-for-TV movies and television series followed.

Stephen Keep Mills

During the Fall of 1983, Mills was cast in the New York production of Václav Havel's *A Private View* (1978). He was nominated for a Drama Desk Award for his work in the production. By 1985, he had started to write and produce his own scripts. He also got married.

In 1990, Mills and his wife had a son. Mills was then nominated for an Ovation award for his play *A Christmas Carol: The Ghost Story of Christmas*. He directed the show in association with Deaf West Theatre, where it was performed in American Sign Language. In

2003, Mills produced a film adaptation of his play *Hotel Lobby*. His short film *A Cigar at the Beach* (2006) screened at 166 film festivals worldwide and won forty-seven awards. His next short film, *Liminal* (2009), screened at eighty-four festivals and received thirty awards. He continues to write and produce films to this day.

The cast of the TV series *Flo*. Front row, left to right: Geoffrey Lewis, Polly Holliday, Joyce Bulifant, and Sudie Bond. Back row, left to right: Stephen Keep Mills, Lucy Lee Flippin, Jim B. Baker, and Leo Burmester.

CHAPTER 14:

The Characters in Flo

Florence Jean Castleberry
See page 111.

Earl Tucker
Earl is the bartender at Flo's Yellow Rose. He was born on his family's farm and delivered by a veterinarian who was there to examine the family's livestock. In his younger days, he worked on the rodeo circuit and briefly dated a female cowgirl named B. J. (Billie June).

He likes to pepper his daily speech with Spanish words even though his pronunciation of them is poor. In addition to bartending, Earl brands cattle at The Roundup. He also co-owns a ranch. His business partner named it Casa de Huevos because he thought it meant "House of Dreams"; it actually means "House of Eggs." After his partner died, Earl decided to run the ranch on his own. He won his horse, Beauty, in a poker game. When Beauty gives birth to a new filly, Earl names her Flo because Flo helps birth her. His dog, Bob, has full rein over his living room couch.

Alice . . .

Mama *(Velma Castleberry)*

Mama is a homemaker who has spent her entire life in Cowtown. She and Flo's father, Jarvis, had a strained relationship. Mama loves him even though he cheated on her and abandoned the family twenty-five years ago. For her, their relationship has been characterized by pain. Nevertheless, she manages to come to terms with her feelings towards him when they are reunited briefly one Thanksgiving. Mama occasionally quotes Bible passages to keep Flo in line. She eventually starts dating a man named Harold who lives in a retirement home.

Farley Waters

Farley is a local banker. He talks Flo into purchasing a bar from him. She renovates it and renames it Flo's Yellow Rose. He holds the mortgage on the building and accepts free beer in lieu of charging Flo late fees when she needs extra time to make monthly payments. In general, Farley isn't well liked in town. Even so, he is elected to the town's zoning commission.

Fran *(Flo's sister)*

Fran is Flo's younger sister. Socially awkward and extremely proper, she lives at home with her mother and conducts eye examinations at the DMV. Fran is engaged to Wendell Tubs for twelve years until he breaks her heart and elopes with an exotic dancer.

Fran doesn't have much recollection of her father, since he abandoned the family when she was young. Her most cherished memory of him involves a day when she stayed home sick from school. He sat by her bedside and read her the book *Mr. Hippity Hop Goes to the Fair*. She has never forgotten the connection they shared that day and holds onto the book because it means so much to her.

At one point, Fran is overlooked for promotion at the DMV. She is so upset that she quits her job. Flo hires her at the Yellow Rose in an attempt to lift her spirits. As soon as Fran starts working there, however, she takes over and tries to reorganize Flo's business. That makes things tense between the sisters. Flo eventually helps Fran realize that she belongs at the DMV because, overall, she was happy there. Fran agrees and manages to regain her old job.

After Farley is elected to the town's zoning commission, Fran becomes the commission's administrative assistant and watches over its activities with an eagle eye.

Miriam Willoughby

Miriam is Flo's lifelong friend. Flo taught her how to wear her first bra and how to stuff it with Kleenex. During high school, they loved eating brownies and drinking beer together. Miriam is thrilled when Flo returns home and opens the Yellow Rose. Flo remembers how Miriam aced algebra in school and promptly hires her as the bar's bookkeeper. Miriam also works there as a waitress.

She is married and has children. Her husband, Hollis, is a telephone lineman. Miriam works as a crossing guard on Wednesdays. She takes her role as wife and mother seriously. When Flo raffles off her extra ticket to Disney World, Miriam's name is drawn. It is the first time she has ever won anything.

Randy Stumphill

A twenty-one-year-old mechanic, Randy works at the local filling station, which his father owns. He is a regular customer at the Yellow Rose and knows the staff well. Though his dream is to become a singer, his father doesn't support his ambition. At one point, Randy quits his job and seeks to break into the singing profession. His father sees him perform and takes note of his potential. He encourages

Randy to return to his job and work up a solid act before venturing out again. Randy agrees to do so.

Les Kincaid

Les is the Yellow Rose's laid-back, cigarette-smoking piano player. When he was growing up, his father took up residence in New York City, while his mother lived in Southampton, Long Island. Despite his parents' distant relationship, they cared about him and encouraged him to study to become a classic pianist. He abided by their wishes—though he longed to play the blues.

As an adult, Les moved to New Orleans to pursue his musical ambitions. While there, he fell in love with a woman who broke his heart. He fled to Europe to escape the pain and eventually found his way to Cowtown. He set up a new life there and lived alone in a small apartment. His total assets consist of a Liberty dime collection worth about nine dollars and several thousand cigarette coupons. He enjoys telling the Yellow Rose's patrons and employees obscure facts about the world.

CHAPTER 15:

The World in Flo

FLO IS SET IN Florence Jean Castleberry's hometown of Cowtown, Texas. Cowtown was founded by Ed Whitlock when he mistakenly drove three thousand head of longhorn cattle south rather than north along the Chisholm Trail. He brought them to Oakland, Texas, which because of his error became the state's new livestock terminal. At that point, it was renamed Cowtown.

The following list of memorable business establishments in the TV series *Flo* defines the town in which the characters live.

Al's World of Weenies
A fast-food restaurant

Brenda's Beauty Nook
A beauty parlor that Flo goes to

The Cowtown Arms
An upscale hotel

Cowtown Auto
The town's main car repair shop, owned and operated by Randy Stumphill's father

Alice...

Cowtown Clarion-Bugle
A local newspaper

Cowtown Garden Club
An organization for garden enthusiasts

Cowtown Little Theatre
A community theater

Cowtown Taxi
The local cab company

Department of Motor Vehicles
A state agency where Flo's sister, Fran, works giving eye tests

Dial-a-Granny
An organization that enables children who don't have grandmothers to have one on a temporary basis

Flo's Yellow Rose
A roadhouse run by Florence Jean Castleberry

The Golden Rattler
A saloon

The Gospel Mission
A volunteer organization that assists the community

Hotel Lorado
An older hotel in town

The Local Order of the Lonestar
A private social club. Flo is the first woman invited to become a member.

Longhorn Lager
The company that supplies beer to Flo's Yellow Rose

KCAL
One of two radio stations in town

KKOW
The second of two radio stations in town

Myrtle Hill Senior Citizens Home
An assisted-living facility for older adults

Parker Chicken Packing Plant
A business that prepares chickens for consumer sale

Pedell's Grocery Store
A supermarket

Roaring Tornado Saloon
A local bar

Shopping for Shut-Ins
A volunteer organization that helps the less fortunate

The Silver Saddle Roadhouse
A bar cum restaurant that competes with Flo's Yellow Rose

Alice . . .

Sparky Light Bulb Company
The local electric company

Tubbs' Feed and Grain
A farm supply business owned by Fran's fiancé, Wendell

Waters' Press
A publishing company created by Farley Waters

CHAPTER 16:

Flo—Episode Log

SEASON 1 (1980)

Episode 1 (1.1): "Homecoming" (Original broadcast date: March 24, 1980)

Writers: Dick Clair and Jenna McMahon

Director: Marc Daniels

Guest stars: James Cromwell, George "Buck" Flower, David Hollander, Gordon Hurst, Mickey Jones, and Terry Wills

Synopsis: Flo stops off in Cowtown, Texas, to visit family on her way to a hostess job in Houston. While there, she decides to buy a run-down roadhouse and be her own boss. It takes more work and money than she anticipates to get the business in order. But with help from friends and family, she is able to do it.

(Note: The opening scene of this episode is the only time during the series when a real exterior shot was used. The rest of the series was shot on a soundstage. The opening credits in this episode run over the first scene. Stephen Keep Mills plays "The Yellow Road of Texas" on the piano.)

Alice...

Polly Holliday, Stephen Keep Mills, and Jim B. Baker in a scene from episode 1 (1.1), "Homecoming"

Episode 2 (1.2): "Showdown at the Yellow Rose" (Original broadcast date: March 31, 1980)

Writer: Stephen A. Miller

Director: Marc Daniels

Guest stars: Ben Davidson, George "Buck" Flower, Gordon Hurst, Mickey Jones, and Terry Wills

Synopsis: Joe Shaw comes to town to even a score with Earl for stealing his girlfriend during their rodeo days. Everyone in the bar except Earl and Flo eagerly awaits their fight.

Episode 3 (1.3): "Happy Birthday, Mama" (Original broadcast date: April 7, 1980)

Writers: Tom Biener, George Geiger, and Ron Landry

Director: Marc Daniels

Guest stars: George "Buck" Flower, Gordon Hurst, Henry Jones, Mickey Jones, Georgia Schmidt, Amzie Strickland, and Terry Wills

Synopsis: Flo and Fran prepare a surprise birthday party for Mama at the Yellow Rose, which is made all the merrier when Mama's boyfriend, Harold, leaves the retirement home he lives at and joins the festivities.

(Note: Leo Burmester sings "Baby Face." Joyce Bulifant sings "Aloha 'Oe." Stephen Keep Mills plays "The Stripper," "Aloha 'Oe," and "Peachtree Special" on the piano.)

Episode 4 (1.4): "Take My Sister, Please" (Original broadcast date: April 14, 1980)

Writers: Bob Illes and James R. Stein

Director: Marc Daniels

Guest stars: James Cromwell, Kathy McCullen, and Terry Wills

Synopsis: Fran quits her DMV job after being passed over for a promotion. Flo hires her at the Yellow Rose, hoping to pick up her spirits. It doesn't take long before Fran's micromanagement drives everyone crazy. Flo eventually fires her and helps her understand that quitting the DMV was a mistake and she needs to get her old job back.

(Note: Geoffrey Lewis, Stephen Keep Mills, and Joyce Bulifant sing "For She's a Jolly Good Fellow." Stephen Keep Mills plays "As Time Goes By" on the piano.)

Alice...

Episode 5 (1.5): "The Hero of Flo's Yellow Rose" (Original broadcast date: April 21, 1980)

Writers: Bob Illes and James R. Stein

Director: Marc Daniels

Guest stars: Robert Englund, Hap Lawrence, and Marty Zagon

Synopsis: Flo's friend Charlie Mayfield comes to town and asks Flo to marry him. She struggles with the situation but ultimately decides that remaining single is the best option.

(Note: Stephen Keep Mills plays "Secret Love" and "The Yellow Rose of Texas" on the piano.)

Lucy Lee Flippin, Sudie Bond, and Polly Holliday in a scene from episode 6 (1.6), "The Reunion"

Episode 6 (1.6): "The Reunion" (Original broadcast date: April 28, 1980)

Writer: Rick Orloff

Director: Marc Daniels

Guest star: Arlen Dean Snyder

Synopsis: When Farley chokes on his food at the Yellow Rose, Les performs the Heimlich maneuver and saves his life. Les is branded a hero for the act but doesn't take well to the praise.

SEASON 2 (1980–1981)

Episode 7 (2.1): "The Enemy Below" (Original broadcast date: October 27, 1980)

Writers: Tom Biener, George Geiger, and Ron Landry

Director: Marc Daniels

Guest stars: Robert Hastings and Mickey Jones

Synopsis: When a skunk is found living underneath the Yellow Rose, customers leave in droves. Flo tries everything she can to get the skunk to leave so her customers will return.

Episode 8 (2.2): "Farley, the People's Choice" (Original broadcast date: November 3, 1980)

Writer: Stephen A. Miller

Director: Dick Martin

Guest stars: Randall Carver, Rod Colbin, John Fujioka, Denise Gallup, Dian Gallup, and Edmund Stoiber

Synopsis: Flo unwittingly helps bolster Farley's public image when he runs for Cowtown zoning commissioner. Her support enables Farley to be elected.

(Note: Supporting cast members sing "The Battle Hymn of the Republic.")

Episode 9 (2.3): "Bull is Back in Town" (Original broadcast date: November 17, 1980)
Writers: Tom Biener, George Geiger, and Ron Landry

Director: Bob LaHendro

Guest stars: G. W. Bailey, George "Buck" Flower, Gordon Hurst, and Lou Richards

Synopsis: A crazed recluse named Bull develops an interest in Flo and asks her to marry him. Flo struggles to get out of the situation without hurting his feelings.

(Note: G. W. Bailey sings "Oh Susanna," which Stephen Keep Mills later plays on the piano.)

Episode 10 (2.4): "A Castleberry Thanksgiving: Part 1" (Original broadcast date: November 24, 1980)
Writers: Bob Illes and James R. Stein

Director: Dick Martin

Guest stars: Robert Ayers, G. W. Bailey, Christi Dobkin, Kaela Dobkin, Kristy Dobkin, Burton Gilliam, Jerry Hardin, David Hollander, Sharon Spelman, and Forrest Tucker

Synopsis: Flo reunites the Castleberry family for their first Thanksgiving dinner in years. All discuss the pain their estranged father, Jarvis, created when he abandoned them as kids. He then shows up, leaving everyone speechless.

(Note: The boom mic can be seen when Flo's brothers roughhouse in the backyard before dinner. G. W. Bailey would reprise the role of Flo's brother Lonny in episode 21 [2.15], "Welcome to the Club." He also played Bull in episode 9 [2.3] "Bull is Back in Town." Polly Holliday sings "We Gather Together.")

Forrest Tucker and Polly Holliday in a scene from episode 11 (2.5), "A Castleberry Thanksgiving: Part 2"

Episode 11 (2.5): "A Castleberry Thanksgiving: Part 2" (Original broadcast date: November 24, 1980)

Writers: Bob Illes and James R. Stein

Director: Dick Martin

Guest stars: Robert Ayers, G. W. Bailey, Christi Dobkin, Kaela Dobkin, Kristy Dobkin, Burton Gilliam, Jerry Hardin, David Hollander, Sharon Spelman, and Forrest Tucker

Synopsis: Jarvis struggles to work through his differences with the family.

(Note: The end credits in this episode feature a hand placing Polaroid photos from the Castleberry's Thanksgiving dinner on top of one another.)

Episode 12 (2.6): "Willoughby vs. Willoughby" (Original broadcast date: December 1, 1980)

Writer: Phillip Harrison Hahn

Director: Lee Lochhead

Guest stars: George "Buck" Flower, Gordon Hurst, Donegan Smith, and John Welsh

Synopsis: Flo gives her extra Disney World ticket to Miriam, causing a rift between Miriam and her husband, Hollis, who doesn't want to be away from her. Flo solves the problem by giving her ticket to Hollis so the couple can go together.

Episode 13 (2.7): "So Long, Shorty" (Original broadcast date: December 8, 1980)

Writers: Bob Illes and James R. Stein

Director: Bob LaHendro

Guest stars: Dolores Albin, Alan Oppenheimer, Woodrow Parfrey, and Richard Stahl

Synopsis: Flo honors a former Yellow Rose patron, Shorty, by hosting his funeral and a tribute to his life and love for Cowtown at the Yellow Rose.

(Note: Stephen Keep Mills and Leo Burmester sing a modified version of "Quando, Quando, Quando." They also play "The Yellow Rose of Texas" on the piano and guitar.)

Episode 14 (2.8): "Deserted Islands" (Original broadcast date: December 15, 1980)

Writers: Tom Biener, George Geiger, and Ron Landry

Director: Nick Havinga

Guest stars: Kenn Chertok, Jay Garner, Walter Janovitz, George Lindsay, Jim Weston, and Kai Wulff

Synopsis: Randy quits his job at the garage and camps out at the Yellow Rose after his father dismisses his desire to become a singer. Flo manages to bring father and son together to talk out the situation. In the end, Randy resumes his job and decides to pursue a singing career on the side.

(Note: Leo Burmester sings part of "Don't Fence Me in," "Home on the Range," "$100 Woman with a Two-Bit Heart," and "The Streets of Laredo," and a takeoff on the song "Kind Hearted Woman Blues.")

Episode 15 (2.9): "The Miracle of Casa de Huevos" (Original broadcast date: December 22, 1980)

Writers: Tom Biener, George Geiger, and Ron Landry

Director: Marc Daniels

Synopsis: On Christmas Eve, Flo, Les, and Earl get trapped in Earl's barn during a storm and help his horse give birth.

(Note: Polly Holliday sings "Jingle Bells" and "Silent Night." Stephen Keep Mills sings part of "O Christmas Tree.")

Sudie Bond and Polly Holliday in a scene from episode 16 (2.10), "The Grey Escape"

Episode 16 (2.10): "The Grey Escape" (Original broadcast date: January 5, 1981)

Writer: Phillip Harrison Hahn

Director: Marc Daniels

Guest stars: Greg Finley, Henry Jones, Mickey Jones, Rose Michtom, Ann Nelson, Leonard Stone, and Ian Wolfe

Synopsis: Flo and Fran overload their mother with volunteer work to make her feel useful—only to learn she was content with her laid-back life at home.

Episode 17 (2.11): "Pretty Baby" (Original broadcast date: January 12, 1981)

Writer: Coslough Johnson

Director: Marc Daniels

Guest stars: Ted Ashford, Rick Hill, Archie Mulligan, and Rebecca Reynolds

Synopsis: Flo becomes a temporary mother to a baby named Little Beaver but soon finds that parenting cramps her easygoing style.

Episode 18 (2.12): "Not with My Sister, You Don't" (Original broadcast date: January 26, 1981)

Writers: Bob Illes and James R. Stein

Director: Tony Mordente

Guest stars: Henry Jones, Donegan Smith, and Terry Wills

Synopsis: Flo throws Fran a party to cheer her up after her fiancé of twelve years leaves her for another woman. The festive atmosphere gives Fran a new lease on life and helps her start dating again.

(Note: Lucy Lee Flippin sings part of "Someone to Watch Over Me." Stephen Keep Mills plays part of "As Time Goes By" on the piano.)

Episode 19 (2.13): "The Price of Avocados: Part 1" (Original broadcast date: February 7, 1981)

Writers: Tom Biener, George Geiger, and Ron Landry

Director: Bob LaHendro

Guest stars: George "Buck" Flower, Gordon Hurst, Mickey Jones, and Michael Keenan

Synopsis: Flo discovers that she won't be able to pay the Yellow Rose's mortgage unless a risky investment she made comes through. Farley threatens to take her trailer as collateral if she doesn't pay the mortgage by the deadline. As time runs out, Flo's trailer goes missing.

Episode 20 (2.14): "The Price of Avocados: Part 2" (Original broadcast date: February 14, 1981)

Writers: Tom Biener, George Geiger, and Ron Landry

Director: Bob LaHendro

Guest star: Michael Keenan

Synopsis: Farley and the police have a standoff with Flo after they discover her trailer in Earl's barn. Flo's investment comes through in the nick of time.

Episode 21 (2.15): "Welcome to the Club" (Original broadcast date: February 21, 1981)

Writers: Bob Illes and James R. Stein

Director: Wes Kenney

Guest stars: Ted Ashford, Barbara Babcock, G. W. Bailey, Linden Chiles, Mickey Jones, Rock Mackenzie, and Tom Rayhall

Synopsis: Flo fights to save the Yellow Rose when a women's morality group tries to shut it down.

(Note: G. W. Bailey reprises his role as Flo's brother Lonnie in this episode.)

Episode 22 (2.16): "Gunsmoke at the Yellow Rose" (Original broadcast date: February 28, 1981)

Writer: John Boni

Director: Bob LaHendro

Guest stars: Ted Ashford, George "Buck" Flower, Gordon Hurst, and Mickey Jones

Synopsis: In this comedic tribute to *Gunsmoke*, Flo daydreams about what life would be like for women in the Yellow Rose back in the Old West.

(Note: The act one credits are written in Branding Iron Regular, a font reminiscent of a typeface used in the days of the Old West.)

Episode 23 (2.17): "What Are Friends For?" (Original broadcast date: March 14, 1981)

Writers: Bob Illes and James R. Stein

Director: Bob LaHendro

Guest stars: Dan McBride and Vic Tayback

Synopsis: Flo's former boss, Mel Sharples, makes a surprise visit and helps Flo through a financial slump at the Yellow Rose.

Episode 24 (2.18): "Just What the Doctor Ordered" (Original broadcast date: March 21, 1981)

Writer: Phillip Harrison Hahn

Director: Bob LaHendro

Guest stars: Cal Bartlett, K. Callan, Stephen Johnson, and Ann Walker

Synopsis: Flo seeks to set the record straight when a newspaper article claims she's older than she actually is.

Episode 25 (2.19): "Footsie" (Original broadcast date: April 4, 1981)

Writer: David G. B. Brown

Director: Bob LaHendro

Guest stars: Joanna Cassidy and Ralph Strait

Synopsis: Flo and Earl's old female rodeo buddy, B. J., vie for Earl's attention while he recuperates from an injury at work.

Episode 26 (2.20): "You Gotta Have Hoyt" (Original broadcast date: April 11, 1981)

Writer: Phillip Harrison Hahn

Director: Bob LaHendro

Guest stars: Hoyt Axton, George "Buck" Flower, Gordon Hurst, and Mickey Jones

Synopsis: Hoyt Axton and his band help Flo end a brawl that erupts among the patrons of the Yellow Rose.

(Note: Hoyt Axton sings the series theme song, "Flo's Yellow Rose," in this episode. He also sings a song called "Torpedo.")

Episode 27 (2.21): "Flo's Encounter of the Third Kind" (Original broadcast date: April 18, 1981)

Writer: Michael Weinberger

Director: Bob LaHendro

Guest stars: Herbert L. Becker and James Staley

Synopsis: Flo is spooked after seeing a flying saucer. No one believes her, so she sets out to prove what she saw.

Episode 28 (2.22) "No Men's Land" (Original broadcast date: June 23, 1981)

Writer: John Boni

Director: Bob LaHendro

Guest stars: Kenn Chertok, Jay Garner, Walter Janovitz, George Lindsay, Jim Weston, and Kai Wulff

Synopsis: Randy's father, Buddy, wants to charge Flo rent after he learns that the Yellow Rose encroaches on his property. When things turn ugly, Flo gets Buddy's attorney to confirm that she has a right to use that section of his property free of charge.

(Note: Starting with this episode, the signs on the bathroom doors in Flo's Yellow Rose are reversed. One scene briefly features German dialogue subtitled in English. Stephen Keep Mills plays "America the Beautiful" on the piano.)

Episode 29 (2.23) "The Daynce" (Original broadcast date: June 30, 1981)

Writers: Tom Biener, George Geiger, and Ron Landry

Director: Bob LaHendro

Guest stars: Rod Colbin, Gracia Lee, Jerry Prell, Herb Voland, and Dixie K. Wade

Synopsis: Earl reluctantly agrees to accompany Flo to her induction ceremony when she becomes the first woman admitted to an exclusive club.

CHAPTER 17:

Flo–Fan Quiz

1. What does Flo mortgage to buy the Yellow Rose?
    a. Her grits
    b. Her trailer
    c. Her gold rings

2. What is Flo's CB name?

3. How is Hoyt Axton connected to the series?

4. True or false: Earl's dog's name is Bob.

5. What is Flo's mother's favorite movie?
    a. *Mame*
    b. *Smokey and the Bandit*
    c. *The Nutty Professor*

6. What is the name of the nail polish that Flo wears?

7. Why does Joe Shaw hold a grudge against Earl?

8. The call letters of Cowtown's radio station are _____.

Alice...

Joyce Bulifant and Polly Holliday in a scene from episode 4 (1.4), "Take My Sister, Please"

9. What is Randy's father's business named?

10. True or false: Fran quits her job at the DMV after fourteen years because she gets engaged to a millionaire.

11. What is the content of Farley's letter to his opponent when he wins the race to become zoning commissioner?

12. True or false: Bull is a retired matador.

13. How does Flo win two tickets to Disney World?

Polly Holliday and Joanna Cassidy in a scene from episode 25 (2.19), "Footsie"

14. What are the ashtrays shaped like in the Yellow Rose?
    a. Spittoons
    b. Stetson hats
    c. Horse saddles

15. What labels are posted on the bathroom doors in the Yellow Rose?

16. The perfume Flo wears is called _____.

17. What do sailors talk Flo into?

18. What is Fran's favorite game?
    a. Hopscotch
    b. Post Office
    c. Charades

19. In what does Flo invest all of the Yellow Rose's money?

20. How does Earl injure his foot?
    a. By falling off a ladder at the Yellow Rose while installing a smoke detector
    b. During a bronco-busting contest
    c. He never injured his foot.

CHAPTER 18:

More about Alice Doesn't Live Here Anymore, Alice, and Flo

The History of the "Real" Mel's Diner

The Mel's Diner sign featured in *Alice*'s opening credits came from an actual diner on Phoenix's Grand Avenue; it is still in operation today. That diner opened in the 1950s and hasn't changed much since. It was originally called Lester's Diner. Outside the building was a large sign with the restaurant's name on it and a fourteen-ounce coffee cup with flashing lights around it to advertise that the diner served coffee.

In 1970, Lester Bammesberger sold the business to a couple that renamed it Glenn's Diner. They, in turn, sold it to Christine Harris, who renamed it Chris' Diner. While Harris owned it, a producer for *Alice* contacted her and asked whether CBS could change the name on the sign from Chris to Mel and film it for use in the show. Harris agreed.

In 1978, Harris sold the diner. The new owner didn't like the flashing lights around the sign's coffee cup and let them all burn out. In 1992, the diner was sold and renamed Pat's Family Restaurant. In 2003, John Stivaktakis became the owner and renamed it John's Diner. He had the sign repainted and eventually passed the business along to his nephew, Emmanouil (Mano), and his wife, Christina, when they immigrated to the US from Greece.

Mel's Diner as it looked in January 2019 (*Photo provided by Steve Halvorsen.*)

Once the Stivaktakises realized the diner's pop history, they renamed it Mel's Diner. It attracted visitors from around the world. According to a piece from 2016 that aired on the public radio station KJZZ in Phoenix, Arizona, tourists stop by on an ongoing basis and ask Christina Stivaktakis whether she is Alice. Others imitate Florence Jean Castleberry and tell Christina to "Kiss my grits!" Once a woman called the diner and asked to talk with Mel. Christina told her that she had the wrong number, but the woman was insistent that Mel had to be there. Visitors have called Mano "Mel" sometimes as well. He enjoys being connected to entertainment history. He says that Mel yelled while working in the kitchen and he does too so that people can understand what he's saying.

As a tribute to the TV series and its fans, waitresses at the diner now dress in pink uniforms reminiscent of those worn in the show. The Stivaktakises have decorated the walls with photos and newspaper clippings about the series. The diner menu includes cast photos and refers to the "world famous" Mel's Diner. In addition, the restaurant contains a case of *Alice* memorabilia, including an original script from the series.

How an *Alice* Enthusiast Met the Cast and Supported the Show

Alice enthusiast David Barry Plunkett started watching the series early in the first season. He was a teenager at the time. Plunkett was initially drawn to the program because the environment in Mel's Diner shared some characteristics with the supermarket his father owned. Soon after being introduced to the series, Plunkett began compiling a scrapbook about the show. It contained articles, photos, letters, autographs, and more. He brought the book with him when his family vacationed in California. Their trip included attending a taping of an *Alice* episode. Plunkett showed his scrapbook to fellow audience members during their five-hour wait for studio admission. While he was in line, the cast learned about his book. A member of the production team approached him and asked whether he'd like to meet Linda Lavin. Moments later, Plunkett was escorted backstage and introduced to her. She looked through his scrapbook and thanked him for his support of the series.

Alice...

David Barry Plunkett with his *Alice* scrapbook

The following year, Plunkett and his family again vacationed in California and attended another taping of the sitcom. Before the show, they dined at El Chiquito Mexican Restaurant, which was located across the street from the studio that *Alice* taped in. Their waitress noticed Plunkett's scrapbook and mentioned that the cast usually hung out at the restaurant after each taping. Plunkett and his family returned to El Chiquito after the show. Plunkett was able to meet Vic Tayback, Linda Lavin, Celia Weston, and Philip McKeon at that point. Many of them looked through his scrapbook and signed it. Tayback invited him to attend rehearsal for an episode that was being taped the following week. Unfortunately, because the family's vacation didn't extend that long, Plunkett couldn't attend the rehearsal. But the invitation meant a lot to him and was a great example of Tayback's kindness. Since then, Plunkett has maintained his scrapbook and been a major advocate for the series, helping to bring fans together through the various online platforms he runs, including the website alicesitcom.blogspot.com.

Life Behind the Counter in Mel's Greasy Spoon

Warner Brothers Studio where *Alice* was taped *(Photo provided by David Barry Plunkett.)*

Alice the TV Series Reboot

In 2018, a reboot of the sitcom *Alice* went into development. The initial concept for the new series centered on Alice Hyatt, a Long Island housewife who leaves her unfaithful husband and drives across the country to Arizona with her teenage son, Tommy. She finds a job at a diner there and sets up a life in which her boss and coworkers become her new family. Liz Astrof, the coexecutive producer of the TV show *2 Broke Girls*, and Diablo Cody, series creator of *Our Mississippi*, wrote the pilot script for the show. The project didn't advance beyond that initial stage. Hope for a future reboot of the series remains.

Broadcast Information

Alice (primetime broadcast schedule on CBS)
August 1976: Mondays 9:30–10:00 p.m.
September–October 1976: Wednesdays 9:30–10:00 p.m.
November 1976–September 1977: Saturdays 9:30–10:00 p.m.
October 1977–October 1978: Sundays 9:30–10:00 p.m.
October 1978–February 1979: Sundays 8:30–9:00 p.m.
March 1979–September 1982: Sundays 9:00–9:30 p.m.
October–November 1982: Wednesdays 9:00–9:30 p.m.
March–April 1983: Mondays 9:00–9:30 p.m.
April–May 1983: Sundays 9:30–10:00 p.m.
June 1983–January 1984: Sundays 8:00–8:30 p.m.
January–December 1984: Sundays 9:30–10:00 p.m.
January–July 1985: Tuesdays 8:30–9:00 p.m.

Flo (primetime broadcast schedule on CBS)
March–April 1980: Mondays 9:30–10:00 p.m.
July 1980–January 1981: Mondays 8:00–8:30 p.m.
February 1981: Saturdays 9:00–9:30 p.m.
March–May 1981: Saturdays 8:30–9:00 p.m.
June–July 1981: Tuesdays 8:30–9:00 p.m.

Websites
https://alicesitcom.blogspot.com
(a fan site for the *Alice* TV series run by David Barry Plunkett)

https://www.alicehyatt.com
(a fan site for the *Alice* TV series run by Sue Glover)

https://www.facebook.com/groups/AliceTVTrivia
(a Facebook page dedicated to trivia about the *Alice* TV series run by David Barry Plunkett)

https://www.facebook.com/groups/ALICECastNews
(a Facebook page dedicated to news about former cast members of the *Alice* TV series run by David Barry Plunkett)

https://www.facebook.com/groups/VicLivesOn
(a Facebook page dedicated to the memory of Vic Tayback run by David Barry Plunkett)

https://www.facebook.com/AliceTVShow
(a Facebook page dedicated to the *Alice* TV series)

https://www.facebook.com/groups/AliceTVShowFanClub
(a Facebook page dedicated to the *Alice* TV series)

https://www.facebook.com/AliceTvSeries
(a Facebook page dedicated to the *Alice* TV series)

DVD/Streaming Releases

The complete series of *Alice* and the spin-off series *Flo* has been released on DVD. Both programs are available through iTunes and Amazon Prime Video. As of the printing of this book, both programs are available through iTunes and Amazon Prime Video.

Select Sound Recordings Featuring Actors from *Alice*

A Good House for a Killing. Released in 2011. Audio drama produced by California Artists Radio Theatre. (Features Marvin Kaplan in a lead role)

A Midsummer Night's Dream. Released in 2011. Audio drama produced by California Artists Radio Theatre. (Features Marvin Kaplan in a lead role)

Adventures in Odyssey—Album 08: Beyond Expectations. Released in 2005. Produced by Focus on the Family. (Features Dave Madden in the role of Bernard Walton)

Adventures in Odyssey—Album 09: Just in Time. Released in 2005. Produced by Focus on the Family. (Features Dave Madden in the role of Bernard Walton)

Adventures in Odyssey—Album 10: Other Times, Other Places. Released in 2005. Produced by Focus on the Family. (Features Dave Madden in the role of Bernard Walton)

Alice in Wonderland. Released in 2011. Audio drama produced by California Artists Radio Theatre. (Features Marvin Kaplan in a lead role)

Blue Horse by Lora Lee and Leo Burmester. Released in 2004 through CD Baby. (Features fourteen songs sung by Leo Burmester and his wife, Lora Lee Ecobelli)

Celestial Navigations. Released in 1988. Produced by Geoff Levin Music. (Features Geoffrey Lewis in spoken word performance)

Celestial Navigations, Chapter II. Released in 1988. Produced by Geoff Levin Music. (Features Geoffrey Lewis in spoken word performance)

Celestial Navigations, Chapter III: Ice. Released in 1992. Produced by Geoff Levin Music. (Features Geoffrey Lewis in spoken word performance)

Celestial Navigations, Chapter IV: Road Train. Released in 1995. Produced by Geoff Levin Music. (Features Geoffrey Lewis in spoken word performance)

Celestial Navigations, Chapter V: The Connection. Released in 2005. Produced by Geoff Levin Music. (Features Geoffrey Lewis in spoken word performance)

Celestial Navigations, Chapter VI: The Space Race. Released in 2006. Produced by Geoff Levin Music. (Features Geoffrey Lewis in spoken word performance)

Celestial Navigations, Chapter VII: Special Edition. Released in 2007. Produced by Geoff Levin Music. (Features Geoffrey Lewis in spoken word performance)

The Christmas Pearl. Written by Dorothea Benton Frank. Audiobook version narrated by Celia Weston. Released on October 23, 2007. Published by HarperAudio.

Contact. Written by Carl Sagan. Audiobook narrated by Jodie Foster. Released on February 11, 2004. Published by Simon & Schuster Audio.

The Fisherman and His Wife. Written by the Brothers Grimm, Eric Metaxas (adapter). Audiobook narrated by Jodie Foster. Released on October 27, 2016. Published by Rabbit Ears Entertainment LLC.

I Love You, Ronnie: The Letters of Ronald Reagan to Nancy Reagan. Written by Nancy Reagan. Audiobook narrated by Leo Burmester and Allison Daughtery. Released on March 29, 2016. Published by Random House Audio.

I Send a Voice. Written by Evelyn Eaton. Audiobook narrated by Ellen Burstyn. Released on November 11, 2017. Published by Phoenix Books.

Jataka Tales. Written by Noor Inayat Khan. Audiobook narrated by Ellen Burstyn. Released on December 6, 2016. Published by Phoenix Books.

Janis Joplin—Rock of Ages by Geoffrey Giuliano. Audiobook narrated by Kris Kristofferson. Released on March 16, 2018. Published by Icon Audio Arts.

Jesus Was a Capricorn by Kris Kristofferson. Released in 1972 by Monument Records.

Jewel written by Bret Lott. Audiobook version narrated by Celia Weston. Released on May 4, 2012. Published by Simon & Schuster Audio.

Joy to the World. Released in 2011. Audio drama produced by California Artists Radio Theatre. (Features Marvin Kaplan in a lead role)

Lessons in Becoming Myself by Ellen Burstyn. Audiobook narrated by Ellen Burstyn. Released on October 13, 2006. Published by Penguin Audio.

The Man with Bogart's Face. Released in 2011. Audio drama produced by California Artists Radio Theatre. (Features Marvin Kaplan in a lead role)

Mary and the Fairy. Released in 2011. Audio drama produced by California Artists Radio Theatre. (Features Marvin Kaplan in a lead role)

My Client Curley. Released in 2011. Audio drama produced by California Artists Radio Theatre. (Features Marvin Kaplan in a lead role)

No End Save Victory Vol. 1: Perspectives on World War II. Written by Stephen E. Ambrose, Caleb Carr, William Manchester, et al. Audiobook narrated by Leo Burmester. Released on January 11, 2002. Published by HighBridge, a division of Recorded Books.

Norman Corwin's 100th Birthday Tribute. Released in 2011. Audio drama produced by California Artists Radio Theatre. (Features Marvin Kaplan in a lead role)

On the Occasion of My Last Afternoon. Written by Kay Gibbons. Audiobook version narrated by Polly Holliday. Released on May 11, 2000. Published by Simon & Schuster Audio.

Our Lady of the Freedoms. Released in 2011. Audio drama produced by California Artists Radio Theatre. (Features Marvin Kaplan in a lead role)

The Plot to Overthrow Christmas. Released in 2011. Audio drama produced by California Artists Radio Theatre. (Features Marvin Kaplan in a lead role)

Possibilities by Linda Lavin. Released on November 1, 2011, by Ghostlight Records. (Features twelve new recordings of songs Linda Lavin sang throughout her career)

The Strange Affliction. Released in 2011. Audio drama produced by California Artists Radio Theatre. (Features Marvin Kaplan in a lead role)

Vocal & Big Band Jazz by Martha Raye. Released on May 1, 2012, by Stardust Records.

The Wheel of Life: A Memoir of Living and Dying. Written by Elisabeth Kübler-Ross. Audiobook narrated by Ellen Burstyn. Released on November 4, 2014. Published by Simon & Schuster Audio.

The Wonderful Wizard of Oz. Released in 2011. Audio drama produced by California Artists Radio Theatre. (Features Marvin Kaplan in a lead role)

CHAPTER 19:

Fan Quiz Answer Guide

Alice Doesn't Live Here Anymore

1. b. Mel and Ruby's Café

2. The opening sequence in Kansas from the film *The Wizard of Oz*

3. Coca-Cola

4. He dies in a motor vehicle accident while on the job.

5. c. Ellen Burstyn. She practiced for several months prior to the start of production.

6. He fills bullet cases with powder.

7. False. It is in Tucson, Arizona.

8. She lives on the property right next to the café.

9. Alice meets David at Mel and Ruby's Café on her first day of work. He is one of her customers.

10. The tattoo on Mel's right arm says "Dee Dee." His left arm has a rectangle tattoo on it.

11. Yes, Mel also employs a janitor and a short-order cook in the restaurant.

12. a. Al

13. Tommy is eleven at the start of the film. He turns twelve as the story progresses.

14. The picture features images of JFK, the Statue of Liberty, Robert Kennedy, and the American flag.

15. Mel's Famous BBQ

Alice the TV Series

Season 1

1. In the feature film, Alice tells Tommy, "Shall I open a vain and sign it in blood?" In the pilot episode of *Alice,* Tommy says, "Do you want me to slit open a vain and sign it in blood?"

2. b. Drop your house key in his lap

3. Bowling

4. She marries him.

5. c. A renowned critic from *The Phoenix Times* called Mr. James

6. A pair of green dice

7. Quarterback for the Rams

8. True

9. Flo's younger brother, Jimmy-Joe Castleberry

10. The jitterbug

Season 2

1. c. Starsky and Hutch

2. As an elegant bistro with continental cuisine

3. Langley Moss

4. False. He was 33.

5. *Charlie's Angels*

6. World War II

7. Abdul Ben Ishmal

8. a. A waitress in a sandwich shop. She doesn't realize, however, that the waitresses are required to work topless.

9. Fred

10. Vera. She uses the money to open a savings account for the girls. They get 6 percent interest and have saved $72.13 until that point thanks to her.

Alice . . .

Vic Tayback and Philip McKeon in a scene from episode 49 (3.1), "Take Him, He's Yours"

Season 3

1. Belle's earrings are made from a group of bells.

2. A cross pendent on a chain

3. True

4. Cowboys on bucking horses

5. b. Mel

6. Bob. He went on to become a successful plumber.

7. False. She was voted "Miss Congeniality."

8. Roy Clark

9. b. Flo has dated since she was four years old.

10. A cloud

Season 4

1. Mel's girlfriend, Marie

2. b. Through a relative in Ireland. Carney is Vera's sixth cousin on her father's side of the family.

3. *King Lear*. He misses the performance, though, because he gets locked in the diner.

4. Breaking a dish when you see something you like

5. True

6. a. Mel's girlfriend, Marie. She quits after a few days.

7. To try to sell her song "Uncle Bud" to the country singer Wailin' Tammy Hawkins

8. Mississippi

9. A wedding band to wear on her finger

10. Liquid lard

Alice...

Linda Lavin, Vic Tayback, Beth Howland, and Diane Ladd in a scene from episode 97 (5.1), "Mel and the Green Machine"

Season 5

1. c. Isabel

2. Mel flirts with a lady in the bank line, and her husband drops a bowling ball on his foot.

3. Not paying attention to how old you are

4. False. Belle lives in the apartment next to Alice's.

5. Sam Butler

6. She starts working at Benny's Beanery because Mel refuses to let her work at the diner.

7. An elderly woman pushes him into the dumpster after she mugs him.

8. True

9. a. Belle quits to accept an offer to be a backup singer in her cousin's country-western band in Nashville.

10. A baby

Season 6

1. Their favorite saying was "Oh, my stars!"

2. A ceramic anteater. It was supposed to be an elephant, but that didn't work out, so she turned it into an anteater.

3. False. When Carrie bakes pies at the diner, Mel doubles his profits.

4. b. Donald O'Connor

5. A teddy bear

6. False. Mel leaves the diner to Tommy.

7. Hidden Valley

8. Gearshift Gorman

9. The pep club

10. He and friends moon the vice-principal

Alice...

Linda Lavin and Doris Roberts in a scene from episode 121 (6.5), "Alice's Big Four-Oh!"

Season 7

1. The director of personnel for the Phoenix phone company sees him perform and hires him to work at the phone company.

2. c. She cannot deal with his excessive gambling any longer.

3. He is a con man and cons people all the time.

4. True

5. He meets a divorcée who sells the car to him cheap to get back at her ex-husband.

6. Grandma Sharples. She can swing a mean cane.

7. a. Margie

8. Vera names her new cat Mel because he is fat and loves to prowl the streets at night.

9. Almost four months

10. A framed poster of Mae West in *Every Day's A Holiday* (1937)

Season 8

1. b. Boss Hogg. Jolene's Granny Gums's maiden name is Hogg.

2. Business

3. Ma Bell

4. She promises to get him a discount on airfare.

5. False. Alice was voted "cutest knees."

6. She went through the fifth grade.

7. They meet when Elliot comes to the diner to give Vera a ticket for jaywalking.

8. b. Hits a home run

9. 555-OUCH

10. The team fills his sneakers with peanut butter.

Alice . . .

Season 9

1. They place a personals ad so Alice can find a boyfriend.

2. c. The Marx Brothers

3. True

4. To be promoted to detective

5. They put him on a meat hanger in the freezer next to sides of beef.

6. Thirty

7. The Nightbird, a sultry radio DJ

8. He spends three months undercover at an Arthur Murray dance studio.

9. a. Vera's old landlord, Debbie Walden

10. A check for $5,000 from the profits of the sale of the diner

Flo the TV Series

1. b. Her trailer

2. Hot Cargo

3. He sings the theme song during the opening credits and appears as himself in episode 26 (2.20), "You Gotta Have Hoyt."

4. True

5. c. *The Nutty Professor*

6. Jungle Fire

Life Behind the Counter in Mel's Greasy Spoon

7. Joe Shaw holds a grudge against Earl because seventeen years ago, Earl stole his girlfriend.

8. KKOW

9. Cowtown Auto

10. False. Fran quits her job because someone else gets the promotion that was meant for her.

11. Ha. Ha. Ha. Ha. Ha.

12. False. Bull is a crazy miner who comes out of the woodwork once a year to whoop it up and have a drink at the saloon.

13. By selling thirty-one kegs of her distributor's beer at the Yellow Rose—the most of any establishment in their contest

14. b. Stetson hats

15. Dudes and Darlin's

16. Midnight Massacre

17. Getting a tattoo

18. c. Charades

19. Avocados, hoping for a 200 percent return on her investment

20. a. By falling off a ladder at the Yellow Rose while installing a smoke detector

Further Reading

Alice Doesn't Live Here Anymore: A Novel by Robert Getchell. Published by Warner Books. 1975.

The Complete Directory to Prime Time Network and Cable TV Shows, 1946–Present by Tim Brooks and Earle Marsh. 9th edition. Published by Ballantine Books, 2007.

"In the American Grain: An Interview with Robert Getchell" by Richard Thompson. Published in *Sight & Sound*. 1976.

Laughing with Lucy: My Life with America's Leading Lady of Comedy by Madelyn Pugh Davis with Bob Carroll Jr. Published by Emmis Books. 2005.

Lessons in Becoming Myself by Ellen Burstyn. Published by Riverhead Books. 2006.

Martin Scorsese: Interviews by Peter Brunette. Published by University Press of Mississippi. 1999.

My Four Hollywood Husbands by Joyce Bulifant. Published by Tilton Bass Publishing. 2017.

Recipes for Busy People. Edited by Silvia Schur. Published by Warner Books. 1980.

Reuben on Wry: The Memoirs of Dave Madden by Dave Madden. Published by BookSurge Publishing. 2007.

Spiraling through the School of Life: A Mental, Physical, and Spiritual Discovery by Diane Ladd. Published by Hay House Inc. 2006.

"Something's Always Cooking at Mel's Diner" by Barbra Zuanich. Published in the *Los Angeles Herald Examiner*. 12/12/1976.

Index

$10,000 Pyramid, The 266
$100 Woman with a Two-Bit Heart (song) 289
2 Broke Girls 305
20th Century Fox 99
5 Mrs. Buchanans, The 144
60 Minutes 151
"86 the Waitresses" 149
967-Evil II 90
9JKL 80

Aal, Andrea 224, 229
Aames, Angela 232
Abbott, Bud 242
Abbott, Norman 142, 147-148, 175, 177
ABC 17
Abelson, Arthur 203, 214, 222, 227
Academy Award (Oscar) 13-14, 16-17, 19, 28, 32, 35, 39-41, 83
"Accident, The" 145
Accused, The 32
Actors Studio 4, 16, 20, 30
Actors Theatre of Louisville 267
Adam's Rib 92
Adam-12 23
Adams, Lee 78
Adelman, Sybil 149
Adkinson, Suzanne 213
Adler, Stella 33
Adventures in Odyssey 98, 308
After Hours 40

"After Mel's Gone" 199
Age of Innocence, The 40
Ah, Sweet Mystery of Life (song) 178
Ah, Wilderness! 268
Ain't We Got Fun (song) 169
Airplane! 266
Alabama 55, 58
Albee, Edward 88
Albert, Wil 159, 213
Albin, Dolores 289
Albuquerque, New Mexico 44
Alden, Norman 142, 150
Aldredge, Dawn 165, 171
Aletter, Frank 212
Alexander, William 15
ALF 106
Ali, Muhammad 241
"Alice and the Acorns" 109, 203
"Alice and the Devoted Dentist" 227; photo 251
"Alice at the Palace" 209
"Alice Beats the Clock" 178
"Alice by Moonlight" 150
"Alice Calls the Shots" 200
Alice Doesn't Live Here Anymore ix-x, 1-6, 10, 12-13, 15, 17, 19, 21, 23-24, 26, 28, 30-31, 33, 35-36, 39, 43, 51, 53, 58, 78, 137, 241, 244, 301, 313; photo 3, 8, 10, 42
Alice Doesn't Live Here Anymore: A Novel 325

Alice...

"Alice Doesn't Work Here Anymore: Part 1" 237
"Alice Doesn't Work Here Anymore: Part 2" 238
"Alice Faces the Music" 213
"Alice Gets a Pass" 59, 137-138
"Alice in TV Land" 177; photo 245
Alice in Wonderland 93, 96, 308
"Alice Locks Belle Out" 189, 197
"Alice Sees the Light" 212
"Alice Strikes Up the Band" 192; photo 193
Alice viii-x, 19, 22, 24, 36, 53, 56-58, 60-67, 71-72, 77-79, 83-84, 86, 88-90, 93, 96, 98, 100-102, 104-106, 109, 123, 137, 141, 150, 184, 241-242, 253-254, 257, 260, 266, 301, 303-307, 314; photo 59, 73, 108
"Alice's Big Four-Oh!" 197; photo 320
"Alice's Blind Date" 221
"Alice's Decision" 169
"Alice's Halloween Surprise" 197; photo 248
"Alice's Hot Air Romance" 227
"Alice's Son, the Drop-Out" 190
"Alice's Turkey of a Thanksgiving" 211
All My Children 46
All over Town 84
All the President's Men 84
All through the Night (song) 194
Allan, Jed 227
Alldredge, Michael 159, 174, 176-179, 187, 239
Allen, Gracie 63
Allen, Phillip R. 197, 203
Allen, R. S. 141, 144, 146-147
Allen, Steve 101, 103
Allen, Woody 24, 88, 90, 264
Allman, Elvia 207, 212
Aloha Oe (song) 283
Alsberg, Arthur 106
Alvin and the Chipmunks 252
Alzheimer's disease 96
Am I Blue? (song) 171, 187

Amazing Stories 90
Amazon Prime Video x, 307
Ambrose, Stephen E. 310
America the Beautiful (song) 295
American Film Institute 39
American Horror Story 88
American Sign Language 269
Amerika 26
Amsterdam, Morey 150
...And Justice for All 28
Andert, Richard 203
Andreozzi, Jack 202, 206, 213, 217, 224, 226, 231, 235
Angels in the Outfield 93
Angels up in Heaven, The (song) 189
Ankrum, David 196
Annie Hall 90, 264
Annie McGuire 143
Anxton, Hoyt 294, 297
Anything Goes (song) 171, 213
Apocalypse Now 34
Arden, Eve 177
Ari, Bob 207
Arizona 11, 45, 135, 205, 305
Arizona State University 111
Armstrong, Nicki 197
Arnaz, Desi 156
Arnold, Alvena Louis 98
Arquette, Lewis 149
Arranga, Irene 194
Arresting Behavior 268
Arrick, Rose 202
Art of Love, The 99
Arthur Marx's Groucho: A Photographic Journey 105
Arthur Murray's Dance Party 265
Arthur, Carol 217
Arthur, Maureen 145
As Time Goes By (song) 154, 174, 283, 292
As Told by Ginger 83
Ash, Paul 93
Asher, John 266
Asher, William 151, 154-158, 160-

167, 169-171, 266
Ashford, Ted 291, 293
Asolo Repertory Theater 84
Astor Place Theatre 260
Astrof, Liz viii, 305
At the Hop (song) 204
"Auld Acquaintances Should be Forgot" 179
Auld Lang Syne (song) 166
Autumn in New York (song) 209
Aviator, The 41
Ayers, Robert 286, 288

Babcock, Barbara 293
Baby Dance, The 32
Baby Face (song) 283
"Baby Makes Five" 194
Bachelor Father 106
Bad (song) 40
Bad Afternoon for a Piece of Cake, A 20
Bad News Bears in Breaking Training, The 24
Bad News Bears, The 24
Baer, Art 139, 145, 148
Bailey, G. W. 286-288, 293
Baker, Jim B. 254, 260-262; photo 261, 272, 282
Bakunas, Steve 79
Balin, Richard 186
Ball, Lucille 61, 68, 101-105
Ballantine Books 325
Ballard, Christine 187, 194, 205, 208
Ballard, Kaye 146
Ballard, Michael 166, 169-170, 174-175, 178, 185
Ballatine, Carl 206
Balmagia, Larry 230
Balsam, Jody Arthur 186
Bammesberger, Lester 301
Band, The 39
Bannick, Lisa A. 233, 236
Barash, Olivia 167
Barnaby Jones 23
Barney Miller 54, 98

Barr, Steven 221
Barrett, Joe 204
Barrett, Rachel D. viii
Barrie, David 48
Barry, J. J. 158
Barth, Eddie 179
Bartlett, Cal 294
Basil, Toni 236
Batley, Glenis 257
Battle Hymn of the Republic, The (song) 286
Bauman, Jerry 146
Bay, Frances 231
"Be It Ever So Crowded" 231
BearManor Media viii
Becker 93
Becker, Herbert L. 295
Beckham, Brice 233
Beer, Frances Mavia 25
Begel, Cindy 232, 236, 239
Begley, Edward Thomas 95-96
Behave Yourself 93
Bel Air, California 103
Bell, Michael 100
Ben Stiller Show, The 98
Bendetson, Bob 211-212, 214, 218, 222, 224-225, 232, 234-235, 238
Bendetson, Howard 211-212, 214, 218, 222, 224-225, 232, 234-235, 238
Bendixsen, Mia 7, 23; photo 23
Benson, Lucille 207, 212, 224
Benson, Pat 203
Berger, Gregg 238
Berghof, Herbert 88
Bergman, Alan 56
Bergman, Marilyn 56
Berlinger, Warren 146, 184
Bernard, Cydney 32
Bernly, Judy 29
Berry, Fred 235
Best Friend from Heaven 27
Besson, Luc 37
Best Friends 29

"Best Little Waitress in the World, The" 203
"Bet a Million, Mel" 195; photo 195
"Better Never Than Late" 163
Between the Lines 90
Between the Raindrops (song) 80
Beverly Hills, 90210 264
Bewitched 21, 167, 230, 247
Biederbeck, Dee 196
Biener, Tom 283, 285-286, 289-290, 292, 295
"Big Bad Mel" 233
Big Broadcast of 1937, The 94
"Big Daddy Dawson's Coming" 142
Big John, Little John 266
Big Shave, The 38
Big-block comedy 65
Bigfork Playhouse 261
Bill Cosby Show, The 266
Billingsley, Jennifer 139
Bilson, Bruce 141, 143
Biltmore Hotel, The 129
Binns, Edward 158
Birdland 80
Birth control ix
Blackburn, Greta 186
"Block Those Kicks" 162
Block, Emma 143
Blondie in the Dough 105
Blondie movie series 105
Bloom, George 184, 190
Bloom, John 232
Blue Horse 268, 308
Blunt, Erin 200
Boardwalk Empire 41
Bob & Carol & Ted & Alice 31
Bob Newhart Show, The 23, 141, 144, 263
Bodwell, Boyd 154
Bogart, Humphrey 114
Bogert, Paul 137
Bogert, William 190
Bolo, Terry 169
Bonaduce, Danny 98
Bond, David 223-224, 231
Bond, Raleigh 172, 177, 179, 181, 183, 191, 221
Bond, Sudie 254, 259-260; photo 259, 272, 284, 290
Boni, John 293, 295
Bonnie and Clyde 82
Book of Daniel, The 17
Booke, Sorrell 219
BookSurge Publishing 325
Boom mic 140-142, 144, 147-148, 157, 161-162, 167, 169, 171, 175, 177-178, 186, 190, 192, 211, 213, 218, 222, 225-226, 228, 234, 287
Boston, Massachusetts 77, 113
Bound for Glory 35
Bovingloh, Don 203
Bowe, David 200
Bowen, Roger 166
Bowers, Jane 215
Bowling Green State University Library vii
Boxcar Bertha 3, 38
Boy From, The (song) 80
Boy Meets World 98
Boys Alternative Dance Symposium (B.A.D.S.) 235
Bracco, Lorraine 34-35
Brady Bunch, The 266
Branding Iron Regular 293
Brave One, The 33
Brecht, Susan 202
Breeding, Larry 171
Brennan, Eileen 86
Brennan, Laraine Marie 37-38
Bride Screamed Murder, The 48
Briggle, Stockton 199
Brinckerhoff, Burt 148
Briscoe, Jimmy 197
British Academy of Film and Television Arts (BAFTA) Award 13-14, 17, 19, 35, 41
Broadway 15, 17-18, 78-80, 82, 86, 88-89, 91, 94, 96, 99, 105-106, 202, 205, 259-260, 263, 265, 268
Broadway Bound 79

Brody, Adrien 90
Brookline, Massachusetts 80
Brooklyn, New York 20, 33, 92, 115-116, 120
Brooklyn Bridge 56
Brooklyn College 92
Brooks, Joel 222
Brooks, Tim 325
Brother Can You Spare a Dime? (song) 176
Brothers Grimm 309
Brown, David G. B. 294
Brown, Reb 182
Browning, Rod 159
Brownsville, Texas 25
Bruneau, Ralph 237
Brunette, Peter 325
Brunner, Bob 198-199
Buell, Kaye 146
Bugaloos, The 96
Bugs Bunny's Easter Song (song)183
Bulifant, Joyce viii, x, 164, 254, 264-266, 283, 325; photo 265, 272, 298
"Bull is Back in Town" 286-287
Bullock, Harvey 141, 145-147
"Bundle, The" 148
Buono, Victor 141
Burbank, California 60, 137
Bure, Candace Cameron 225
Buried Child 268
Burkett, Bartine 231
Burmester, Leo 254, 267-268, 283, 289, 308-310; photo 267, 272
Burns, George 64, 153
Burstyn, Ellen 2, 4-6, 8-12, 15, 17, 51, 53, 309-311, 313, 325; photo 3, 8, 16, 42
Burstyn, Jefferson 5
Burstyn, Neil 16
"Bus, The" 159
Bush, Billy Green 4, 27-28; photo 3, 27
Bush, Owen 164
Bush, William Warren 27

Busy People's Recipe Contest Cook-Off 22
But Not for Me (song) 150
Butte, Montana 93
Buzzi, Ruth 188; photo 188
By the Light of the Silvery Moon (song) 153, 187
"Bye Birdie" 190
Bye Bye Birdie 82
Bye, Bye, Blackbird (song) 179
Bypass surgery 71
Byrd, Thomas 213
Byrd-Nethery, Miriam 165

"Cabin Fever" 68, 175
Cabot, Ceil 210
Cadogan, Alice 230
Caesar, Sid 21
Café Carlyle 80
Café Trocadero 94
Caffe Cino 33
Cagney & Lacey 30, 93
Calandro, Daniel vii
California 56, 82, 89, 94, 101, 103-104, 106, 222, 257, 264, 303-304
California Artists Radio Theatre 93, 307-308, 310-311
California Independent Film Festival Slate Awards 258
California State University 1, 35
"Call to Arms, A" 140
Callahan, James T. 192, 203
Callan, K. 294
Callas, Charlie 211
Calling All Stars 94
Camden, New Jersey 77
Camden, South Carolina 268
Cameron, Cisse 205
Cameron, Julia 39
Camp Runamuck 97
Camp, Hamilton 145, 171, 195, 230
Campbell, Carole Kay 27
Campbell, Don 236

Campbell, Duane R. 150, 153, 164, 167, 170-173, 175, 178-179, 181, 183-184, 188, 192, 195-196, 198, 203, 206-207, 210-212, 214-215, 218, 224-226, 233, 237, 239-240
Campbell, John George 236
Campbell, Patrick 206
Campbell, Susan 174
Canada 268
Cancer 83
Canfield, Mary Grace 238
Cannes Film Festival 13, 39
Cape Fear 40
Capital News 91
"Car Wars" 161; photo 66
Carey, Ron 146
Caridi, Carmine 166
Carlin, Elliot 141
Carnegie, Robert 192, 204
Carney, Art 116, 176, 245, 317
Carr, Caleb 310
Carr, Hayley 232-233
Carrerow, Jack 233, 236
"Carrie Chickens Out" 191
"Carrie on the Rebound" 211
"Carrie Sharples Strikes Again" 175
"Carrie Sings the Blues" 187
"Carrie's Wedding" 178
Carrol, Ed 173
Carroll Jr. Bob 61-66, 68-69, 71, 149, 101-106, 152, 155, 158-159, 240, 325; photo 62
Carroll Victoria 68, 99-100, 126, 150, 165-166, 173, 176, 180, 194, 203, 215; photo 99
Carroll, Ed E. 192
Carroll, Janet 236
Carroll, Tony 214
Carruthers, Ben 30
Carry Me Back to Morningside Heights 18
Carry Me Back to Old Virginy (song) 191
Carry, Julius 218
Cartier, Celeste 139

Carver, Randall 285
Cash, Johnny 25, 252
Casino 40
Cassidy, Joanna 294; photo 299
Cassutt, Michael 216, 227
Castleberry Thanksgiving: Part 1, A 255, 286
Castleberry Thanksgiving: Part 2, A 255, 288; photo 287
Cat on a Hot Tin Roof 86
Catalina Bar & Grill 80
Catholic 37, 39, 80, 115
Cavan, James 204
CBS ix, 19, 24, 53-54, 57, 62, 71, 78, 82, 84, 101, 103, 137, 219, 254, 301, 306
CD Baby 308
Celestial Navigations 258, 308-309
Charlie's Angels 111, 315
Chastain, Don 149, 170-171
Chemel, Lee Shallat 235
Chertok, Kenn 289, 295
Chesapeake Shores 20
Chevrolet 85
Chicago, IL 90, 116
Chicken Soup for the Soul 83
Childress, Alice 84
Chiles, Linden 293
Chili 22, 116, 120, 127, 141, 174-176, 246
Chinatown 19
CHiPs 90
Chisholm Trail 277
Chris' Diner 55, 301
Christmas Carol: The Ghost Story of Christmas, A 269
Christmas in Connecticut 26
Christmas Pearl, The 309
Christy, June 109
Chrysler 48
Cigar at the Beach, A 270
Cinematic Arts Library vii
Circle Theater 92
"Citizen Mel" 161

City of Angels 91
Civil Action, A 91
Civil War, The 268
Clair, Dick 281
Claremont, California 25
Clark, Roy 317
Cleghorne 107
Clemmons, Rebecca 205
Client, The 37, 86
Cline, Patsy 36
Clooney, Rosemary 109
"Close Encounters of the Worst Kind" 154
Coca-Cola 45, 313
Coco, James 227; photo 251
Cody, Diablo 305
Cohen, Evan 197
Colbin, Rod 159, 285, 296
Colen, Beatrice 159, 203
Collected Stories 80
College Holiday 94
College of William and Mary vii, 77
Collins, Gary 165
Color of Money, The 40
Colorado Springs, Colorado 152
Colton, John 164
Columbia Recording Studios 25
"Come Back Little Sharples" 215
Come Back to the 5 & Dime Jimmy Dean, Jimmy Dean 260
Commission on Working Women 61
Committed 144
Communism 33
Company 82
Company of Angels 20, 99
Complete Directory to Prime Time Network and Cable TV Shows, 1946-Present, The 325
"Comrade Mel" 196
Comstock Hotel, The 130
Condos, Melodye 95
Condos, Nick 95
Coney Island 115, 207
Conga, The (song) 209-210
Conn, Kelly Ann 237

Connick Jr., Harry 268
Conrad, Montana 260, 262
Conried, Hans 170; photo 124
Conroy, Gary 236
Contact 309
Cook, Ancel 158, 175-176, 178
"Cook's Tour" 182
Cookson, Lauren Aimee 268
Coolidge, Rita 25-26
Cooper, Darcy Jo 104
Cooper, Marilyn 203-204
Copacabana 17
Cop-Out 78
Coppola, Francis Ford 2, 33-34
Corvan, Don 218, 224, 229, 233, 236-239
Costanzo, Robert 159, 205, 219
Costello, Lou 242
Country Music Awards 25
Courtship of Eddie's Father, The 31
Coward, Noël 260
Cox, Doug 216, 233
Cox, Richard W. 236
Crabtree, Michael 213, 237
Cranshaw, Patrick 139, 141, 150-154, 157; photo 156
Crawford, Christina 36
Crawford, Joan 36, 183
Criscuolo, Lou 184-185
Crockett, Karlene 201
Cromwell, James 164, 281, 283
Cronin, Patrick 142-143, 152, 157, 160-161, 166, 170, 175-176
Crowley, Gene 159
Cruickshanks, Reid 236
Cruise, Tom 40
Cruising 267
"Cuban Connection, The" 156
Cunningham, A. J. "Pappy" 197
Curtin, Valerie 28-29; photo 29
Curtis, Tony 16
Cutell, Lou 190, 211, 217, 233
Cyphers, Charles 154

D'Angelo, William P. 143-145, 147
D'Auria, Joey 226
Da Ya Think I'm Sexy? (song) 222
Dalai Lama 40
Dallas 254, 269
Dancing in the Dark (song) 222
Daniels, Marc 64, 149, 152-153, 157, 165, 170, 172-181, 183-186, 189-192, 194, 196-200, 202-204, 206, 209-213, 216-217, 219, 221-222, 224, 226-227, 229-235, 239-240, 281-285, 290-291
Darkroom 56
Darroll, Tracy 257-258
Dashiell, Kimberley 177
Daughtery, Allison 309
Davidson, Ben 282
Davis, Madelyn (Pugh) 61-66, 68-69, 71, 101-106, 149, 152, 155, 158-159, 240, 325
Davis, Richard Merrill 102
Davis, Susan 206
Day, Linda 202
"Daynce, The" 295
Dayton, Ohio 79
De Fina, Barbara 40
De Niro, Robert 38
De Roy, Jamie 202, 239
Deacon, Richard 216
Deaf West Theatre 269
Dean Martin Show, The 45
Dean, Erica 15
Death Watch 34
Deck the Halls (song) 176, 199
Decker, Johnnie 162
DeHetre, Katherine 91
DeJean, Willie 203
Denver Center Theater 262
Department of Motor Vehicles (DMV) 274-275, 278, 283, 298
Dern, Bruce 18
Dern, Laura 11, 18, 20
Derricks-Carroll, Clinton 238
Desilva, Jason 235

Detroit, Michigan 15
Devlin, Dean 218
Dewitt, Joyce 28
Dial M for Murder 77
Diary of Anne Frank, The 79
DiCaprio, Leonardo 40-41
Dick Van Dyke Show, The ix
Dilbert 107
"Dilemma, The" 143
Directors Guild of America 68
Dishy, Bob 154
Diskin, Phil 218
Disney 31, 275, 288, 298
District, The 29
Dixon, MacIntyre 149
"Do You Take This Waitress" 208
Dobkin, Christi 286, 288
Dobkin, Kaela 286, 288
Dobkin, Kristy 286, 288
Doc Corkle 106
Doctor in Charge 30
Doctor in Spite of Himself, The 92
Doctors and the Nurses, The 78
"Dog Day Evening" 69, 184
"Dollars to Donuts" 228; photo 228
Don't Fence Me In (song) 191, 230, 289
"Don't Lock Now" 157
"Don't Play It Again, Elliot" 230
Doney, Randy 165, 170, 176
Donna Reed Show, The 106
Donovan, Martin 138, 143
Dorfman, Sid 226
Doris Day Show, The 146
Double or Nothing 94
Dowling, Chet 201, 204, 206, 209
Dr. Kildare 15, 266
Dr. Quinn: Medicine Woman 19
Drake, Jim 138, 140
Drama Desk Award 260, 269
Drama-Logue Award 258
Drescher, Fran 197
Drowning 18
Ducktales 100
Dugan, Dennis 137

Duke Ellington 51
Dukes of Hazzard, The 28, 71, 117, 219, 254
Dulo, Jane 150, 205
Dunn, Conrad 224
Durrell, Michael 232, 234, 237-238

"Each Dawn I Diet" 98
Earle, Merie 215
"Earthquake" 158, 243
Eastwood, Clint 257-258
Eaton, Evelyn 309
Ecobelli, Lora Lee 268, 308
Ed Sullivan Show, The 97
Edison, Thomas 266
Egan, Mark 176, 178, 184, 186-188, 191-192, 196, 198, 202-203, 205-206, 209-210, 215, 219, 222, 224, 229, 238
Egg, The 259
Eichholz, Mary 261
Eight is Enough 82, 268-269
Einstein, Albert 266
Eisenhower 33
El Chiquito Mexican Restaurant 304
Electra Woman and Dina Girl 142, 145
Elias, Hector 183, 199
Ellen Burstyn Show, The 17
Elvis 28
Elvis and Me 28
Embraceable You (song) 150, 222
Emmis Books 325
Emmy Award 19, 57, 73, 86, 102, 104, 255
"Enemy Below, The" 285
Englund, Robert 225-226, 284
Enlightenment 20
ER 29, 93, 264
Erdman, Richard 159
Eriks, Lynn 209-210
ESP 165
Espionage 30
Eurich, Robin 233
Europe 276

Evans, Mitchel 224
Every Day's A Holiday 321
Everybody Rides the Carousel 90
Executioners, The 40
Exorcist, The 2, 17
"Eyes of Texas, The" 153

Fabricant, Daniel 80
Facts of Life, The 88
"Failure, The" 145
Fair Game 15
Falcon Crest 257
Falling in Love 34
Fame 167
Family 24
Family Affair, A 78
Fanny award 268
Fantasy Island 90, 98
Fantozzi, Tony 2
"Farley, the People's Choice" 285
Farrington, Hugh 231
Fat Black Pussycat, The 257
Fat Man, The 93
Father Dowling Mysteries 19
Favorite Son 90
Feldman, Corey 164
Felsenburg, Rosa 93
Ferber, Mel 203, 207, 211, 213, 215, 218
Ferraro, Dolores 221
Ferrero, Martin 232
Fiedler, John 144, 148
Finley, Greg 291
Fiore, Bill 149
Fisher, Robert 63, 105-106, 151, 153-154, 156-158, 160-162, 164-167, 169-172, 174-176, 179, 181-183, 186, 189-191, 194-195, 260
Fisherman and His Wife, The 309
Fitzgerald, Ella 109
Five Easy Pieces 28
Flashdance 264
Flat Rock, Arizona 132
Fletcher, Aaron 235
Flightplan 32

Flippin, Lucy Lee viii, x, 232, 254, 262-264, 292; photo 263, 272, 284
"Flo Finds Her Father" 171
Flo viii, x, 36, 68, 86, 141, 232, 238, 242, 253-255, 257, 260-261, 264, 266-267, 269, 273, 277, 281, 297, 301, 306-307, 322; photo 272
"Flo's Chili Reception" 174
"Flo's Encounter of the Third Kind" 295
"Flo's Farewell" 179
Flo's Yellow Rose (song) 294
"Florence of Arabia" 155
Florida 103
Florida State University 84
Flory, Med 174
Flower, George "Buck" 281-283, 286, 288, 292-293
Flushing, Queens, New York 37
Flying High 56
Focus on the Family 308
Foofur 100
"Footloose Mel" 235
"Footsie" 294; photo 299
For She's a Jolly Good Fellow (song) 283
"For Whom the Belle Toils" 180; photo 180
Foreigner, The 260
Formula One race car driver 118
Forty-Second Street (song) 209-210
Foster, Alicia Christian 31
Foster, Jodie 5, 8, 31-32, 309; photo 32
Four Jills in a Jeep 95
"Fourth Time Around, The" 166
Fox, Fred S. 153
Francis 93
Frank, Bob 224
Frank, Dorothea Benton 309
Franken, Steve 163
Franklin Township Public Library vii
Fraser, Prudence 196-197
Frasier 29
Freaky Friday 31
Frederick A. Speare School of Radio and TV Broadcasting 20

Freeman, Marion 165, 171
Fried, Ian 239
Friedman, Kim 149-151, 153, 155
Friend (song) 189
Frischmen, Dan 238
Frizzell, Lou 165-166
From Dusk till Dawn 35
Front, The 264
Fujioka, John 285
Full Moon 26

Gallo, Lew 140
Gallup, Denise 285
Gallup, Dian 285
Gangs of New York 40
Garden District 88
Garfield Show, The 93
Garner, Jay 289, 295
Garrett, David 219
Garrett, Joy 216
Garver, Lloyd 139-140
Gautier, Dick 221, 236
Gay 59-60, 90, 138
Gazzo, Michael V. 151
Gehring, Ted 174-176, 178-181, 186-187, 189-190, 192, 195, 204
Geiger, George 283, 285-286, 289-290, 292, 295
Genius on the Wrong Coast 31
Geoff Levin Music 308-309
George, Joe 159
George, Susan Carr 209-210
Gere, Richard 263
German Shepherd 69
Germany 25, 74
Gershwin, George 109
Get Happy (song) 150, 187
Get Smart 99
Getchell, Robert 1-2, 5, 11, 13-14, 35-37, 53, 86, 137, 325; photo 36
Getting Married Today (song) 82
Getting Out 267
Getty, Estell 90
Ghostlight Records 311

Gibb, Donald 214
Gibbons, Kay 311
Gift of the Magi, The 176
Gifts of Greatness 266
Gilbert, Lois 105
Gilford, Jack 199
Gilliam, Burton 144, 148, 155, 242, 286, 288
Gillin, Hugh 180
Gillooly, Edna Rae 15
Gilman, Kip 181
Gilvezan, Dan 232
Girl from Ipanema, The (song) 80
Girlfriends 107
Giuliano, Geoffrey 310
"Give My Regrets to Broadway" 205
Glendale Community College 20
Glenn's Diner 301
Glover, Sue 306
Gold, Barry 214, 217
Gold, Gina vii
Goldberg, Gary David 145
Golden Girls, The 90, 233
Golden Globe Award 13, 19, 40-41, 69, 78, 83, 102, 104, 256-257
Golden Idol (song) 25
Goldenberg, Harvey J. 163
Goldfinger, Michael 203
Goldman, Danny 170, 224, 239
Goldoni, Lelia 5, 30; photo 30
Golonka, Arlene 146
Gone with the Wind (song) 6
"Good Buddy Flo" 67, 177; photo 67
Good Heavens 106
Good House for a Killing, A 307
Good King Wenceslas (song) 199
"Good Night, Sweet Vera" 57, 142, 231
Good Times 56
Goodbye Charlie 16
Goodfellas 40
Goodwin, Michael 239
Gordon, George "Buck" 294
Gordon, Hurst 158
Gordon, Philip 197
Gore, Nick 225
Gorman, Brad 153
Gospel Mission, The 278
Goulet, Robert 185
Gower Street Columbia lot 7
Grace under Fire 19, 144
Grand Budapest Hotel, The 35
"Grass Is Always Greener, The" 216
Grease 260
Great American Songbook 109
"Great Escape, The" 192, 291; photo 290
Great Falls, Montana 260
Green, Katherine 178
Greenbush, Clay 28
Greenbush, Lindsay 28
Greenbush, Sidney 28
Greene, Daniel 214
Greenwich Village 78
Greenwood, Loretta 232
Gremlins 86
Grey, Joel 133, 209-210
Griff 21
Grisham, John 37, 86
Groucho 105
Groucho: A Photographic Journey 105
Groundlings 100
"Guinness on Tap" 196; photo 70
Gun Shy 257
Gunsmoke 15, 21, 23, 293
"Gunsmoke at the Yellow Rose" 293
Gunter, Bob 190, 226, 239
Guthrie Theatre Company 268
Guthrie, Woody 35
Guy's Guide to Dating, Getting Hitched, and the First Year of Marriage, The 106
Gyatso, Tenzin 40

Hagen, Uta 88
Hahn, Phillip Harrison 288, 291, 294
Halop, Florence 148, 192, 221
Halvorsen, Steve viii
Hamilton, Kim 239
Hamilton, Murray 144
Hansen, Glade Bruce 266

Happiness Is Just a Little Thing Called a Rolls Royce 106
"Happy Birthday, Mama" 283
Happy Days 28, 98
"Happy Hoofers, The" 164
Hardin, Jerry 286, 288
Harkins, John 183
Harks, Bob 149
Harlem Globetrotter 216
Harold 260
HarperAudio 309
Harris, Christine 55, 301
Harris, Mark 96
Harrison, Lindsay 221
Harvey, Brian 141
"Has Anyone Here Seen Telly?" 172, 246
Hastings, Robert 170, 285
Hatful of Rain, A 17
Haufrect, Alan 162, 165-166, 174, 181, 202-203
Havel, Václav 269
Havinga, Nick 189, 195, 289
Hawaii 213
Hawker, John 183, 191-192, 212
Haworth, Sham 192
Hay Fever 260
Hay House Inc. 325
Hayes, Helen 264
Hayward, Chris 61, 154-155, 158-159
Hazel Boone Studio 81
HB Studio 33, 88
HBO 41
Heaton, Patricia 79
Hecht, Ken 198-199
Heckart, Eileen 143-144
Hedison, Alexandra 33
Heflin, Frank 142
Heimlich maneuver 285
Hell's Angels 252
Hello Dolly 96
"Hello Vegas, Goodbye Diner" 184
Henderson, Florence 222
Henley, Trevor 233
Henry, O. 176

"Henry's Bitter Half" 188; photo 188
Henschel, Tom 213
Hepburn, Katharine 92, 114, 133
"Here Comes Alice Cottontail" 183
Here Comes the Bride (song) 223
Here's Lucy 61, 102, 104
"Hero of Flo's Yellow Rose, The" 284
Hess, Doris 225
"Hex, The" 146
Hey Vern, It's Ernest! 163
HighBridge 310
Hill Street Blues 28, 91
Hill, Maurice 187, 210, 236
Hill, Rick 291
Hinckley Jr., John W. 31
Hiroshige, Kimiko 185
Hobin, Bill 144
Hochhalter, Paula 258
Hoffman, Dustin 84
Hogan, Robert 150, 165, 167, 172, 181, 211
Hogan's Heroes 99
Holahan, Dennis 221
Holiday on Ice 262
Holiday, Billie 109
Hollander, David 281, 286, 288
Holliday, Polly 19, 22, 55, 58-59, 68, 70, 83-84, 86, 152, 157, 164, 178-179, 253-255, 257, 264, 287, 290, 311; photo 66-67, 85, 108, 124, 138, 152, 156, 272, 282, 284, 287, 290, 298-299
Hollywood 22, 32-35, 53, 78, 82, 85-86, 88, 94, 99, 110, 115, 137, 262-263, 325
Home Improvement 86
Home on the Range (song) 289
Home, Sweet Home (song) 233
"Homecoming" 281; photo 282
Homefront 30
Honigberg, Gail 197, 200, 205, 208, 211, 215, 218-219, 224, 229
Hope, Bob 105
Horn, Lew 171

Horton, Lester 31
Hotel Lobby 270
House of Cards 17
"Houseful of Hunnicutts" 233
Houston, Texas 113, 179, 281
Hovis, Larry 149, 154
How to Stuff a Wild Bikini 99
Howard Johnson's 55
Howard, Bruce 150
Howard, Mann 183
Howland, Beth 55, 57, 66, 68, 70, 74, 80-83, 152, 164, 169, 171, 176, 178, 190-191, 193, 199, 202, 204-207, 209-210, 212, 214, 216, 230; photo 66-67, 70, 73, 81, 108, 152, 156, 173, 185, 195, 201, 220, 223, 228, 234, 245, 318
Howland, Holly 82
Huff, Howard Ray 192
Hughes, Howard 41
Hugo 41
Hunizar, Hugo 235
Hunt, Will 165, 176, 198
Hunter, Robert Charles 19
Hurricane Katrina 268
Hurst, Gordon 154, 281-283, 286, 288, 292-294
Hustler, The 40
Hyatt, Gail 230
Hyman, Charles 233

I Dream of Jeannie 99
I Got a Crush on You (song) 222
I Happen to Like Arizona (song) 210
I Happen to Like New York (song) 209-210
I Love Lucy 61, 64, 68, 102-104, 149
I Love You Truly (song) 236
I Love You, Ronnie: The Letters of Ronald Reagan to Nancy Reagan 309
I Only Have Eyes for You (song) 213
I Send a Voice 309
I Wanted to Go Home 79

I'm Looking Over a Four-leaf Clover (song) 169
I've Been Working on the Railroad (song) 157
I've Got a Right to Sing the Blues (song) 193
I've Got Rhythm (song) 222, 230
Icon Audio Arts 310
"If the Shoe Fits" 170
Illes, Bob 283-284, 286, 288-289, 291-293
Impossible Years, The 105-106, 260
In the American Grain: An Interview with Robert Getchell 325
Incredible Hulk, The 28, 269
Independent Spirit Award 19
Indian River Boys 236
"Indian Taker, The" 149
Indiana 71, 101
Indiana State Teachers College 96
Indiana University vii, 101, 103
Indy 500 118
Invasion of the Body Snatchers 30
Ireland 113, 245, 317
Irishman, The 35
Isaacs, Charles 161, 170, 172, 174-178, 194
"It Had to Be Mel" 221
It Had to Be You (song) 137
It's a Bird . . . It's a Plane . . . It's Superman 78
It's All in the Game (song) 204
It's Only a Paper Moon (song) 169
Italy 74
Its Bitsy Spider (song) 151
iTunes 307

Jacket, The 90
Jackie Gleason Show, The 15
Jackson, Michael 40, 248
Jackson, Sherry 177
Jacobi, Billy photo 248
Jacobius, Jerry 225
Jacobs, Seamon 153

Jamison, Richard 184, 198
Janis Joplin—Rock of Ages 310
Janovitz, Walter 289, 295
Jansen, Jim 214
Jarvis, Graham 158
Jason Goes to Hell: The Final Friday 28
Jasper, Alabama 83
Jataka Tales 309
Jayne, Billy 197
Jeepers Creepers (song) 193, 205
Jeffersons, The 106
Jenkins, Larry Flash 232
Jeris, Nancy 194
Jerome, Arizona 136
Jerry 78
"Jerry Reed Fish Story, The" 190
Jesus Was a Capricorn 25, 310
Jewel 310
JFK 47, 314
Jingle Bells (song) 152, 199, 203, 290
"Joel Grey Saves the Day" 210
Joelson, Ben 139, 145, 148
John's Diner 301
Johnny Dangerously 260
Johnson, Bruce 53-54, 56, 84, 142, 144
Johnson, Coslough 291
Johnson, Stephen 294
"Jolene and the Night Watchman" 214
"Jolene Gets her Wings" 221; photo 220
"Jolene Hunnicutt, Dynamite Trucker" 204
"Jolene Is Stuck on Mel" 229
"Jolene Lets the Cat Out of the Bag" 218
"Jolene Throws a Curve" 226
"Jolene's Brother Jonas" 211
Jolson, Al 94
Jones, Henry 283, 291
Jones, Mickey 237-238, 281-283, 285, 291-294
Jones, Patricia 141
Jory, Victor 149
Joy to the World 310
Jump Out Boys 26-27
Jump, Gordon 139

Just One of Those Things (song) 238
"Just What the Doctor Ordered" 294
Juttner, Christian 177

Kahn, Irene 105
Kammerman, Roy 145-147
Kane, Arnold 56, 142, 144, 146-148
Kane, Bruce 144
Kansas 313
Kansas City, Missouri 35
Kaplan, Marvin 74, 92-93, 153, 156-158, 160-163, 165-166, 169-172, 175-179, 181-183, 186-192, 194-196, 198-203, 205-213, 215-216, 218-219, 221-224, 231-232, 234, 236, 240, 307-308, 310-311; photo 92, 156, 188, 201
Karen's Song 91
Karmazin, Lisa 35
Kasem, Casey 222
Kasem, Jean 222
Kastner, Daphna 35
Kathryn, Reynolds 196
Kaye, Caren 139; photo 140
Keefer, Don 232
Keeler, Ruby 248
Keenan, Michael 148, 165, 169, 292
Keitel, Harvey 4, 9, 33-35, 38; photo 34
Kelley, Michael G. 214
Kelly Services 20, 22
Kennan, Michael 292
Kennedy, Robert 314
Kenney, Ed 165, 170, 176-177, 189, 194
Kenney, Wes 292
Kentucky 259
Kessler, Lee 159
Kessler, Zale 188, 203
Ketchum, Dave 151
Khan, Noor Inayat 309
Kimbrough, Charles 83
Kimmel, Bruce 151
Kimmell, Dana 213
Kimmins, Kenneth 235
Kind Hearted Woman Blues (song) 289

Kindle, Tom 189, 191
King Lear 262, 317
King of Comedy, The 40
King, Damu 183
Kingdom Hospital 20
Kirby, Bruce 167
"Kiss the Grill Goodbye" 236
Kite, Lesa 232, 236, 239
KJZZ 302
Klane, Robert 29
Knaub, Jim 214
Knight in Rusty Armor, The 106
Koock, Guich 175, 211
Kopell, Bernie 145
Korean War 20, 115
Krinski, Sandy 201, 204, 206, 209
Kristofferson, Kris 4, 11, 25-27, 310; photo 26, 42
Kruschen, Jack 176, 191
Kübler-Ross, Elisabeth 311
Kuby, Bernie 150
Kuhlman, Ron 203
Kundun 40
Kusatsu, Clyde 143
Kuss, Richard 229

La Cucaracha (song) 211
La Femme Nikita 37
La Mama Experimental Theatre Club 33
La Nuit de Varennes 34
La Vie en Rose (song) 172
Ladd, Diane 4, 10-11, 13, 17-19, 54, 68-69, 86, 181, 183, 189-192, 325; photo 10, 18, 180, 318
Ladies and Gentlemen, the Fabulous Stains 23
Lady from Dubuque, The 88
Lafayette Park 61
Lafferty, Perry 54
LaHendro, Bob 286, 292-295
Lake Havasu, Arizona 136
Lampert, Jeffrey 239
Land's End 258
Landis, Ed 28

Landon, Michael 264
Landry, Ron 283, 285-286, 289-290, 292, 295
Lane, Cassidy 23
Lang, Neal 94
Lanier-Bramlett, Suze 145
Las Vegas, Nevada 116-117, 184, 206, 247
Lashly, James 159
Last Movie, The 25
Last Night of Ballyhoo, The 88
Last of the Red Hot Lovers 78
Last Picture Show, The 16
Last Precinct, The 264
"Last Review, The" 141
"Last Stow It: Part 1, The" 169
"Last Stow It: Part 2, The" 124, 170
Last Temptation of Christ, The 34, 40
Last Waltz, The 39
Laughing with Lucy: My Life with America's Leading Lady of Comedy 63-65, 104, 325
Laurel Award 102, 104
Laurel, Stan 63
Lavin, Linda 22, 53-56, 61, 68, 70-72, 74, 77-80, 89, 137, 150-154, 157-159, 161-162, 164, 167, 169, 171-172, 175-176, 178-179, 181-185, 187, 190, 193-194, 196, 199, 202, 204-205, 207-210, 212-213, 216, 218, 222-224, 227, 229-230, 233, 238, 303-304, 311; photo 66-67, 72-73, 76, 108, 138, 140, 152, 160, 193, 200, 228, 243, 245, 248, 251, 318, 320
Lawlor, John 151
Lawrence, Hap 284
Le Lycée Français de Los Angeles 31
Leal, Pete 200
Lebanon 33
Lee, Gracia 296
Lee, Lora 308
Lee, Peggy 109
Leeds, Peter 164, 227
Leeds, Phil 178

Lefebvre, Jim 225
LeHendro, Bob 289
Lehman, Ted 165
Leibman, Ron 78
Leitch Jr., Donovan 235
Lemon, Meadowlark 216
Lenehan, Nancy 172, 185
Leno, Jay 200; photo 200
LeRoy, Gloria 150
Les Misérables 268
Lessons in Becoming Myself 6, 310, 325
Lester's Diner 301
Levin, Andy 235
Levin, Charles 90-91, 223-225, 227, 229-230, 232, 239; photo 91, 223
Levinson, Barry 28-29
Levy, Lew 216
Lewis, Geoffrey 140, 254, 256-259, 283, 308-309; photo 258, 272
Libertini, Richard 155
Liebling, Howard 207
Liebman, Steve 203
"Lies My Mother Told Me" 226
Life with Groucho 105-106
Life with Lucy 61, 98, 102, 105
Lifebuoy Program, The 94
Lilly Library vii
Liminal 270
Lincoln Center 263
Linda Lavin Arts Foundation 79
Linda Lavin Papers vii
Lindgren, Lisa 205
Lindsay, George 289, 295
Lippa, Jeffrey 230-231
Lipscott, Alan 106
"Little Alice Bluenose" 174
Little House on the Prairie 23, 28, 82, 167, 232, 264
Little Murders 78
Little Old Lady (song) 222
Little Women 266
Lloyd Bridges Show, The 30
Lloyd, John Bedford 226
Lloyd, Kenneth 232

Lochhead, Lee 169, 175-176, 181-183, 188, 288
Lockers 236
Loman, Michael 154, 159
Long Island, New York 305
Longfellow, Henry Wadsworth 111
Longhorn Lager 279
Longo, Tony 206, 212, 214, 219, 230
Look for the Union Label (song) 178
Looking Up 93
Loose Ends 88
Lord, Justin 203
Loros, George 155
Los Angeles, California 7, 20, 27, 31, 69, 80, 85, 92, 95, 97, 99, 263, 268, 325
Los Angeles Herald Examiner 325
Los Angeles Times 102
Lott, Bret 310
Lou Grant 257, 268
Louisiana State University 17
Louisville, Kentucky 267
Love and Death 24
Love Boat, The 19, 22, 90, 98, 146, 269
"Love is A Free Throw" 153
"Love Is Sweeping the Counter" 151
"Love Me, Love My Horse" 155, 171
Love of Life 259
Love Star 267
Love, American Style 82, 93
Love's Old Sweet Song (song) 236
Loveday, Denise 232
Lucas, Marcia 12
Lucky Day (song) 193
Lucy Calls the President 61, 102
"Lucy Changes Her Mind" 149
Lucy Show, The 61, 102
Lullaby of Broadway, The (song) 202
Lullaby of Flagstaff, The (song) 210
Lutter III, Alfred 4-5, 8, 24, 55-56, 137; photo 8, 24
Lykes, John 214, 230
Lynn, Loretta 246
Lyons, The 80

MacArthur, James 264-265
MacDonald, John D. 40
MacGyver 22, 93
"Macho, Macho, Mel" 191
Mackenzie, Rock 293
MacRae, Michael 177
Mad Show, The 80
Madden, Dave 96-98, 163, 165, 167, 170, 172-173, 177, 182, 187-188, 190-192, 197-200, 203-204, 211, 214-217, 224, 226-229, 236-237, 240, 308, 325; photo 97, 228
Madden, Tommy 225
Maher, Bill 236
Mahoney, Tom 146-148
Make Room for Daddy 93-106
Mallory, Edward 266
Mame 297
Man I Love, The (song) 182, 236
Man with Bogart's Face, The 310
Manchester, William 310
Manhattan (song) 210
Manhattan's Garment District 37
Mann, Howard 180-181
Manny's Orphans 261
Mantee, Paul 235
Many Loves of Dobie Gillis, The 93
Marcus, Richard 230
Marcus Welby, M.D. 99
Marion Dougherty Associates 4
Markowitz, Gary 158
Maroon and Gold (song) 214
Married with Children 98
Mars, Kenneth 147, 204
Marsh, Earle 325
Martha Raye Show, The 95
Martin Scorsese: Interviews 325
Martin, Dick 285-286, 288
Martin, Helen 218
Martin, Quinn 102
Martin, Sandra 98
Marvin's Room 88
Marx Brothers 104-105, 252, 322
Marx, Arthur 63, 104-106, 151, 153- 154, 156-158, 160-162, 164-167, 169-172, 174-176, 179, 181-183, 186, 189-191, 194-195, 260
Marx, Groucho 104-151
Mary and the Fairy 310
Mary Hartman, Mary Hartman 260
Mary Tyler Moore Show, The 28, 82
Masak, Ron 153
Mask, The 100
Mass, Audrey 54
Massey, Marie 120
Masters, Natalie 233
Match Game, The 266
Mathews, Walter 159
Matlock 28
Matthau, Walter 16
Matthews, Paige 237
Maude ix, 56, 106, 233
Mayberry RFD 31
Mayfield, Charlie 284
Mays, Dawson 169
McBride, Dan 293
McCabe, Shane 214
McCarren, Fred 170
McCary, Rod 149
McClanahan, Rue 233
McClean, Bill 157
McClurg, Bob 151, 153, 157, 160-162, 164
McClurg, Edie 202
McCook, John 213, 219, 230
McCullen, Kathy 283
McGibbon, Duncan Scott 227
McGriff, Steve 233
McHale's Navy 105-106, 265
McKay, Sheila 20
McKeesport, Pennsylvania 103
McKeon, Nancy 88, 164, 197; photo 248
McKeon, Philip 22, 24, 56, 60, 68-69, 73-74, 88-90, 139, 152, 164, 169, 172, 174, 179, 187, 197, 199, 207, 228, 230, 304; photo 72-73, 89, 152, 160, 173, 228, 234, 316
McLaughlin, John C. 194

McMahon, Jenna 281
McManus, Michael 237-238
McMilan & Wife 96
Mean Streets 2-3, 5-6, 33, 38-39
Medea and Jason 89
Medical Center 23
Meeks, Betty 260
Meet Millie 93
"Mel and the Green Machine" 183; photo 318
"Mel Grows Up" 66, 167; photo 168
"Mel Is Hogg-Tied" 219
"Mel Love Marie" 126, 172
"Mel Spins His Wheels" 230
"Mel Wins by a Nose" 204
"Mel, the Magi" 176
"Mel's Big Five-O" 157; photo 156
"Mel's Christmas Carol" 199
"Mel's Cousin Wendy?" 217
"Mel's Cousin, Wendell" 198
"Mel's Cup" 147
Mel's Diner viii, 51, 53, 55, 56, 110, 112-114, 116-118, 126, 128-129, 131, 133-134, 137, 139, 156, 226, 231, 247, 301, 303, 325; photo 302
"Mel's Dream Car" 214
"Mel's Happy Burger" 148, 242
"Mel's in Love" 145
"Mel's in the Family Way" 163
"Mel's in the Kitchen with Dinah" 175
"Mel's Recession" 158, 243
Memphis Beat 88
Mencken, Max 78
Mercer County Community College Library vii
Meridian, Mississippi 17
Mert & Phil 263
Metaxas, Eric 309
Meyers, Lisa 26
MGM 7, 105
Miami University 37
Michigan 96
Michtom, Rose 291
Mickey 105

Middle East 243
Midnight in the Garden of Good and Evil 258
Midsummer Night's Dream, A 93, 263, 308
Miller, Arthur 262
Miller, Denny 138-139
Miller, Dick 172
Miller, Stephen A. 282, 285
Milligan, Spencer 174
Mills, Stephen Keep 254, 268-270, 281, 283-284, 286, 289-290, 292, 295; photo 269, 272, 282
Milner, Jessamine 150
Milwaukee Repertory Theater 261-262
Minchenberg, Richard 235
Minkus-Barron, Barbara 162
Minnie's Boys 105-106
Mission Impossible 21
Mississippi 116, 317
Mitchell, Shirley 163
Mitchell, Ty 197
Mittleman, Rick 146
Mod Squad, The 23, 93
Modern Family 88
Mohawk 73
Molière 84, 92
Moll, Richard 217
Molloy, Terry 48
Mommie Dearest 36
"Mona Lisa Alice" 172
Monkees, The 21
Montclair, New Jersey 104
Monterey, California 1, 11-12, 43-44, 53
Montevallo, Alabama 84
Montgomery, Alabama 27
Montner, Simon 142
"Monty Falls for Alice" 206
Monument Records 310
Mordente, Tony 291
Morgan, Bruce 194
Moriyama, Rollin 185
Mork & Mindy 144, 257
Morris, Helen Schermerhorn 40
Morris, Linda 63, 177, 180-184, 186,

189, 192, 197-199, 203-204, 206, 216-217, 221, 235, 237, 239
Morrow, Karen 169
Morton, Howard 217, 225, 232
Morton, Mickey 181, 187
Moss, C.W. 82
"Mother-in-Law: Part 1" 143
"Mother-in-Law: Part 2" 144
Mothers-in-Law, The 102, 104-105, 146
Mott the Hoople 6
Mountain Greenery (song) 179
Mr. Hippity Hop Goes to the Fair 274
Mr. T and Tina 102
Mulligan, Archie 291
Mumford, Thad 175
Munsters Today, The 264
Murder One 144
Murder, She Wrote 22
Murphy, Charles Thomas 150
Murray, Arthur 322
Murray, Warren S. 151, 157
Murtaugh, James 194
Muscat, Mike 235
My Bonnie (song) 172, 233
My Client Curley 310
"My Cousin, Art Carney" 176
"My Dinner with Debbie" 229
My Fair Lady 99
"My Fair Vera" 171
My Favorite Husband 61, 65, 101, 103
My Four Hollywood Husbands 325
"My Funny Valentine Tux" 178
"My Mother the Landlord" 206
My Three Sons 31, 265
Myers, Pamela 175, 182, 205, 227
Myhers, John 139, 153
Myrtle Point, South Carolina 117

Nancy Drew and the Hidden Staircase 80
Nanny, The 197
Nashville, Tennessee 25, 69, 73, 110, 117, 192, 247, 319
National Freshman Intercollegiate Tennis 104

National Society of Film Critics Award 31
Natwick, Mildred 186; photo 185
Navarro, Chi Chi 145
NBC 19, 55, 68, 101
Neighborhood Playhouse 257
Nell 32
Nelson, Ann 291
Nelson, Frank 219
Nevil, Steve 162
New Dick Van Dyke Show, The 28
New Hope, Pennsylvania 264
"New Improved Mel, The" 186
New Jersey 109-110, 143-144, 211
New Orleans, Louisiana 276
New Temperatures Rising Show, The 260
New York 4, 20, 37, 56, 78, 80, 82, 89, 134, 257, 259-260, 262-263, 267-269
New York City 15, 17, 28, 30, 33, 40, 55, 77, 79-81, 84, 88, 104, 109, 212, 262, 276
New York University 37
New York, New York 39
Newhart 144
Newman, Paul 40
Newport News, Virginia 264
Next Cassavetes, The 31
Nielsen ratings 86, 255
"Night They Raided Debbie's, The" 238
"Night to Remember, A" 147
Nightmare on Elm Street, A 226
Nine to Five 29, 106
Ninety-Nine Bottles of Beer (song) 204, 230
Nite in the Nite Club, A 94
Niven, Kip 79, 198, 205, 217, 225, 237-238
No End Save Victory Vol. 1: Perspectives on World War II 310
"No Men's Land" 295
No, No, Nanette 96, 118, 249
Noah, Peter 224
Noland, Cornelius "Neil" Massini 259
Norman Corwin's 100th Birthday Tribute 310

Norman, John 26
North Carolina 87
Northwestern University 262
Norton, Cliff 139, 213
"Not with My Niece, You Don't" 201, 215, 291
Nurse 267
Nutty Professor, The 297, 322
NYPD Blue 91

O Christmas Tree (song) 290
O'Brien, Brian 198
O'Brien, Frank 150
O'Byrne, Bryan 171
O'Connor, Donald 196, 248, 319; photo 70
O'Leary, Jack 137
O'Neill, Eugene 268
O'Shea, Robert 95-96
O'Sullivan, James 212
Oakland, Texas 277
"Odd Couple, The" 146
Off-Broadway 17, 33, 78, 80, 257
Oh Susanna (song) 227, 286
Oh, George Burns! 64, 153
Oh, God! 64, 153
Ohmart, Ben viii
Old Man Music 259
Old West 293
Olkewicz, Walter 189
On a Clear Day (song) 184-185
On the Occasion of My Last Afternoon 311
Once upon a Mattress 82
One Day at a Time ix, 106
One Life to Live 102, 267
"One on One" 239
"One Too Many Girls" 181
Ontiveros, Lupe 145, 159
Open All Night 261
Operation Blue Bat 33
Oppenheimer, Alan 176, 289
Oppenheimer, Jess 149
Oregon Shakespeare Festival 260-261
Orloff, Rick 285

Orpheus Descending 17
Our Lady of the Freedoms 311
Our Mississippi 305
Out of Order 88
Out of Practice 29
Outer Critics Circle 78
Outer Limits, The 27
Ovation award 269
"Over-the-Hill Girls, The" 222
Oxford University 25
Oxford, Ohio 37

Padilla Jr., Manuel 196
Page, Patti 109
Paige, Janis 156
"Pain of No Return, The" 146
Paint Your Flag 194, 196
Painted Bird, The 35
Paisley Convertible, The 265
Palillo, Ron 200
Pallucci, Angie 146
Palme d'Or 13, 39
Panic Room 32
Paolone, Catherine 190, 203
Papp, Joseph 84
Paquin, John 212
Paramount Pictures 88, 94
Parfrey, Woodrow 289
Park, Sungmin vii
Parker Lewis Can't Lose 106
Parker, F. William 214, 217
Parker, Lara 141
Parsons, Kelly 179
Partners in Crime 143
Partridge Family, The 97
Party of Five 29
Pasquin, John 201, 203, 205, 211, 214-215, 217, 219, 225
Pat's Family Restaurant 301
Pataki, Michael 163
Patrick, Randal 233
Patterson, Lillian 86
Paul Lynde Show, The 106
"Pay the Fifty Dollars" 139; photo 140

Peachtree Special (song) 283
Pearl, Barry 236
Peirce, Robert 196
Pellow, Cliff A. 151, 166
Penguin Audio 310
People 69
People's Choice, The 106
Perkins, Kent 233
Perry Mason 15
Perry, Joseph V. 165
Perry, Roger 266
Persky, Bill 139
Peterson, Cassandra 214
Petticoat Junction 93
"Pharmacist, The" 154
Philadelphia, Pennsylvania 262
Philippines 105
Phoenix Books 309
Phoenix, Arizona viii, 52-53, 55-56, 59, 110-111, 116-120, 128, 132-134, 143, 178, 206, 210-211, 239, 246, 301-302, 320
Phyllis 28
Pic 'N' Save 85
Picardo, Robert 205, 213-215, 223-225, 235
Picerni, Paul 143
"Piece of the Rock, A" 139
Pierce, Stack 154
Pierson, William 161
"Pilot" 137; photo 138
Pitlik, Noam 154, 158-159
Place to Call Home, A 79
Plainfield, New Jersey 257
Planet of the Apes 26
Platt, Howard 174, 182
Play It Again Sam 88
Play of the Week 265
Please Don't Talk About Me When I'm Gone (song) 175
Plot to Overthrow Christmas, The 311
Plunkett, David Barry viii, x, 60, 303-304, 306-307; photo 304

Point of No Return, The 37
Polaroid 288
Polk II, Henry 145
Pollard, Michael J. 82
Pomona College 25
Ponca City, Oklahoma 13
Ponce, Luis Daniel 225
Porsche 214, 249
Porter, Cole 109, 224
Portland, Maine 77
Poryes, Michael 230
Possibilities 80, 311
Poston, Tom 144, 199, 206-207, 212
Prell, Jerry 296
Presley, Elvis 28
Prestwood, Hugh 80
"Pretty Baby" 291
"Price of Avocados: Part 1, The" 292
"Price of Avocados: Part 2, The" 292
Prince, Hal 78
Prince, Jonathan 233, 235
"Principal of the Thing, The" 165
Private Benjamin 86, 261, 267
Private View, A 269
"Profit Without Honor" 181
Prophecy 23
Prouty, Olive Higgins 36
Psychotherapist 107
Public Theater 84
Puff, the Magic Dragon (song) 216
Pulp Fiction 35
Putt, Barry viii
Putt, Judie viii
Puzzle solving 58

Quando, Quando, Quando (song) 289

Rabbit Ears Entertainment LLC 309
Rabin, Arthur 151
Rafkin, Alan 145-147
Raging Bull 39
Ramada Inn 47
Rambling Rose 19
Ramona from Arizona (song) 210

Rams 314
Ramsen, Bobby 169, 171
Random House Audio 309
Rauseo, Vic 63, 177, 180-184, 186, 189, 192, 197-199, 203-204, 206, 216-217, 221, 235, 237, 239
Raye, Martha 66-67, 93-96, 167-168, 175, 178, 187, 191, 202, 206, 211, 215, 222, 226-228, 311; photo 95, 168, 228
Rayhall, Tom 293
Reagan, Nancy 309
Reagan, Ronald 31
Recipes for Busy People 22, 325
Recorded Books 310
Red Barn Studio Theatre 79-80
Red Cross 116
Redford, Robert 250
Reed and Hooper 93
Reed, Jerry 158, 190
Reed, Margy 93
Reiker, Donald 141
"Reporter, The" 159
Reservoir Dogs 35
Restoration comedy 84
Reuben on Wry: The Memoirs of Dave Madden 325
"Reunion, The" 285; photo 284
Revenge of the Green Dragons 41
Reynolds, Debbie 16, 207; photo 208
Reynolds, Rebecca 291
Rhodes Scholarship 25
Rhodes, Donnelly 225
Rhythm on the Range 94
Rich, Allan 159, 196
Rich, John 57
Richarde, Tessa 208
Richards, Jennifer 213
Richards, Kim 201
Richards, Lou 184, 202, 286
Ridgewood, New Jersey 24
Rifkin, Ron 166
Riley, Jack 140-141
Riverhead Books 325

Roberts, Doris 198, 211; photo 320
Roberts, Paul 15
Robinson, Douglas 184, 190-192, 206, 209, 215, 218, 228, 231, 236, 240
Robles, Walter 192, 194
"Robot Wore Pink, The" 224
Roccuzzo, Mario 205, 217, 226
Rock-a My Soul (song) 193
Rock-a-Bye, Baby (song) 189, 207
Rococo 69
Rogers and Hammerstein 119
Rolike, Hank 206
Roll Away the Stone (song) 6
"Romancing Mr. Stone" 232
Romano, Andy 192
Romeo and Juliet 134, 205
Room for Two 79
Rooney, Mickey 105
Ropers, The 264
Rose, Alan 165
Rose, David 94
Rose, Reva 179
Rose, Roger 219
Ross, Shavar 187, 197
Rossellini, Isabella 39
Rounds, David 198, 217
Row, Row, Row Your Boat (song) 191
Rowan & Martin's Laugh-In 97
Rowan, Gay 159
Rowe, Vern 192
Rubin, Fred 165
Rubinstein, Paul 221
Rumor of War, A 269
Rupert, Michael 209-210
Ruskin, Bill 268
Russia 74

'S Wonderful (song) 227
Sabella, Ernie 225
Sabrina, the Teenage Witch 83, 98
Saga, Carl 309
Salem College 87
Same Time, Next Year 17
San Diego, California 35

Sand, Paul 212
Sanders, Richard 221
Sandman 90
Sands, Billy 147
Sanford and Son 102
Sarasota, Florida 84
Sargent, Dick 230
Sarnia, Ontario 96
Savalas, George 172
Savalas, Telly 172, 246
Sawyer, Mark 218, 222
Schachter, Felice 183
Schell, Ronnie 148, 175
Schilling, William G. 217
Schisgal, Murray 84
Schmidt, Arnold 234
Schmidt, Georgia 283
Schrader, Paul 39
Schuller, Frank 231
Schur, Silvia 325
Schwartz, Lloyd J. 143
Scorsese, Martin 2-14, 31, 33-34, 37-41, 325; photo 38
Scott, Christine 237
Scott, Fred D. 233
Scott, Oz 225, 228
Scranton, Peter 203
Scruples 30
Seaborn, Christian 150
Seals, William Neal 140
Sean Saves the World 80
"Second Time 'Round, The" 148
Secret Agent 30
Secret Love (song) 284
"Secret of Mel's Diner, The" 209
Secret Storm 19
Seduction of Joe Tynan, The 90
"Semi-Merry Christmas, A" 62, 152; photo 152
Sessions, Ida 19
"Sex Education" 141
Sexual revolution 1-2
Shadow Box, The 268
Sharma, Barbara 154

"Sharples vs. Sharples" 202, 207
Shaw, Joe 282, 297, 323
Shaw, Steve 163
Shayne, Alan 19, 54, 57-58, 61-62, 82, 84, 253
Shea Jr., William A. 11, 19
Sheehan, Doug 218
Sheldon, James 141, 143
Shelley, Dave 149, 163
Shepard, Sam 268
Sherman, Ellen 147
Shermet, Hazel 165
Sherwood, William 154
Shimerman, Armin 236
Shine on Your Shoes, A (song) 196
Shire, David 56
Shirnokawa, Gary 178
Shore, Dinah 116, 175
"Showdown at the Yellow Rose" 282
Shroyer, Sonny 219
Shuffle off to Buffalo (song) 193
Shull, Richard B. 174
Shutter Island 41
Sight & Sound 325
Silence of the Lambs, The 32
Silent Night (song) 176, 290
Silva, Steven Daniells 235
Silver Spoons 261
Silver, Diane 147
Silver, Joe 153
Silver, Johnny 235
Silverman, David viii, x, 106-107, 211-213, 228-229, 231, 233, 237
Silverman, Fred 78
Simon & Schuster Audio 309-311
Simon & Simon 261
Simon, Neil 78-79
Sinatra, Frank 97
Singer, Raymond 145
"Single Belles" 150
Sister Act 35
Sister Gretchen 80
"Sixty Minutes Man, The" 151
Skeleton, Red 105

Alice . . .

"Slight Case of ESP, A" 165
Smart, Jean 230
Smith, Donegan 288, 291
Smith, Paul 186, 192
Smokey and the Bandit 297
Smurfs, The 100
Snyder, Arlen Dean 285
"So Long, Shorty" 289
Socorro, New Mexico 1, 5, 8, 13, 43, 45-46
Solebury School 264
Solomon, Mark 176, 178, 184, 186-188, 191-192, 196, 198, 202-203, 205-206, 209-210, 215, 219, 222, 224, 229, 238
Someone to Watch over Me (song) 171, 222, 292
Something Wicked This Way Comes 19
Something's Always Cooking at Mel's Diner 325
Son of Groucho 105
Song of Hiawatha, The 111
Song Remembers When, The (song) 80
Songwriter of the Year 25
"Sorry, Wrong Lips! 207"; photo 208
Southampton, Long Island, New York 276
Southern California 25
Souza, Emory 140
"Space Sharples" 232
Space, Arthur 137
Spain 74
Spartanburg, South Carolina 87
Spatz, Gary 203
"Spell Mel's" 206
Spelman, Sharon 286, 288
Spiraling Through the School of Life: A Mental Physical, and Spiritual Discovery 19-20, 325
St. Mary's Academy 15
St. Petersburg Junior College 103
Stafford, Jo 109
Stahl, Richard 289
Stalag 17 20

Staley, James 295
Stanford University 25
"Star in the Storeroom, The" 157
Star is Born, A 26
Stardust Records 311
Starsky and Hutch 98, 242, 315
Statue of Liberty 314
Steely Dan 80
Stein, James R. 283-284, 286, 288-289, 291-293
Steinem, Gloria 54
Steinmetz, Dennis 159
Stella 36
Stella Dallas 36
Sternin, Robert 196
Stetson 299, 323
Stevens, Bob 221
Stewart, Lynne Marie 150
Still Standing 264
Stiller, Jerry 208
Stivaktakis, Christina 302-303
Stivaktakis, Emmanouil (Mano) 302
Stivaktakis, John 301, 303
Stoiber, Edmund 285
Stone, Leonard 145, 226, 231, 235, 291
Stoney Burke 27
Storm, Wayne 179
Stout-Hearted Man (song) 215
Strait, Ralph 294
Strange Affliction, The 311
Strasberg, Lee 4, 16, 33
Streets of Laredo, The (song) 289
Streisand, Barbra 26, 56
Strickland, Amzie 283
Strickland, Gail 205
Stripper, The (song) 283
Stritch, Billy 79-80
Stroud, Claude 174
Strouse, Charles 78
Studio audience 57, 60, 63, 66, 74; photo 59
Sturges, Preston 29
Suicide 57, 72
Summer and Smoke 88

350

Summers, Bunny 230
Sun Devils 111
Sunday Mornin' Comin' Down (song) 25
Susman, Todd 223
Susskind, David 2, 53
Sustarsic, Stephen 106-107, 211-213, 228-229, 231, 233, 237
Swanee (song) 164, 210, 235
"Sweet Charity" 166
Sweet Dreams 36
"Sweet Erasable Mel" 217
Sweet Georgia Brown (song) 216
Sweet Harmony (song) 238
Sweetening 66
Swem Library vii

Tacaremba la Tumba del Fuego Santa Maliga Zacatecas lo Onto del Sol y Cruz? 80
Take Her, She's Mine 265
"Take Him, He's Yours" 160; photo 160, 243, 316
"Take My Sister, Please" 283; photo 298
Talboy, Tara 162
Tale of the Allergist's Wife, The 79
Talented Mr. Ripley, The 88
Tales from the Darkside 22
Tales of the Unexpected 56
Tall Story 265
Tanner Alvin 24
Tanzillo, Pat 214, 228
Taps (song) 227
Tarantino, Quentin 35
Tarloff, Eric 159
Tarpey, Tom 263-264
Taxi Driver 31, 33, 39
Tayback, Christopher viii, x, 56, 183, 218
Tayback, Vic x, 4, 11, 20-22, 54, 56-57, 63, 65, 68, 71, 74, 80, 99-100, 126, 152, 183, 187, 189, 194, 196, 199, 209-210, 213, 215-216, 218, 222-223, 226, 228, 230, 293, 304, 307; photo 21, 66, 73, 108, 152, 156, 168, 188, 195, 200-201, 208, 245, 316, 318
Taylor, Curtis 186
Taylor, June Whitley 198, 217, 224, 236
Taylor, Tom 194
Tea for Two (song) 193, 209, 213
Teenage drinking 72
Teigh, Lia 159
Telephone Book, The 262
Temple, Renny 205
Templeton, Christopher 239
Terre Haute, Indiana 96
Texas 90, 253
That Girl 146
"That Old Back Magic" 151
That's Life 17
Theatre World Award 265
Thelma and Louise 35
There's a New Girl in Town (song) 56, 159
"Therese Raquin" 265
Third Side of the River, The 41
This Boy's Life 37
Thom McAn 218
Thomas, Melissa vii
Thomas, Peter 2
Thomas, Venus DeMilo 225
Thompson, J. Lee 40
Thompson, Richard 325
Thorton, Jim 165
Thou Shalt Not 268
Three Little Fishes (song) 77
Three Stooges, The 252
Three's Company 28, 266
"Th-th-th-that's All Folks" 240; photo 73
Thunderbold and Lightfoot 257
Tiano, Lou 162
Tibbles, George 151
Tilton Bass Publishing 325
Tip-Toe Thru' the Tulips with Me (song) 215
"'Tis the Season to Be Jealous" 224
Tobin, Michele 141

Tobolowsky, Stephen 237
Tollin, Red 268
Tolman, Steve 236
Tolsky, Susan 186, 202, 204, 213
Tom, Dick and Mary 265
"Tommy Fouls Out" 216
"Tommy Goes Overboard" 225
"Tommy Hyatt, Business Consultant" 218
"Tommy, the Jailbird" 213
"Tommy's First Love" 167
"Tommy's Lost Weekend" 72, 234; photo 72, 234
"Tommy's T.K.O." 186
Tony Award 17, 79-80, 86, 88
"Too Many Robert Goulets" 184
Too Marvelous for Words (song) 191
Topanga, California 106
Torpedo (song) 294
Touched by an Angel 19
Tovarich 259
Travalony, Treva 146
Trbovich, Tom 222
Tripoli, Libya 97
True Blue 268
True Love (song) 224
Tucci, Michael 184-185
Tucker, Forrest 71, 171, 286, 288; photo 287
Tucson, Arizona 1, 7, 12, 44, 47-48, 53, 313
Turf Paradise 136
Turkey in the Straw (song) 171
Turner, Lloyd 207
Tuttle, Lurene 139
TV Guide 58, 63
Twinkle, Twinkle, Little Star (song) 194, 209
Two Tootsies from Tucson (song) 210

UK 74
Uncle Bud (song) 117, 181, 190, 317
"Undercover Mel" 235, 252
Unfaithfully Yours 29
Unger, Joe 237

United Service Organizations Inc. (USO) 95
United States Air Force 97
United States Coast Guard 20, 105
United States ix, 34, 37, 71, 93, 95, 154, 197, 268
United States Marine Corps 33
University of California, Berkley 113
University of Denver 267
University of Miami 97
University of Missouri 35, 37
University of Montana 260
University of Southern California vii, 92
University Press of Mississippi 325
Urban Cowboy 268
Ursitti, Jennifer 225
US Army 25
US country music charts 26

"Valentine's Day Massacre, The" 203
Van Patten, Pat 159
Varady, Brien 191
Varney, Jim 163
Vaudeville 99, 104
"Vera Gets Engaged" 222
"Vera Goes Out on a Limb" 189
"Vera on the Lam" 217
"Vera Robs the Cradle" 174; photo 173
"Vera the Torch" 215
"Vera the Virtuoso" 212
Vera, Billy 236
"Vera, Queen of the Soaps" 202; photo 201
"Vera, the Horse Thief" 225
"Vera, the Nightbird" 237
"Vera, the Vamp" 181
"Vera's Anniversary Blues" 236
"Vera's Aunt Agatha" 186; photo 185
"Vera's Bouncing Check" 198
"Vera's Broken Heart" 169
"Vera's Fine Feathered Friends" 229
"Vera's Grounded Gumshoe" 239
"Vera's Mortician" 144, 242
"Vera's Popcorn Romance" 162

"Vera's Reunion Romance" 205
"Vera's Secret Lover" 219
"Vera's Wedding" 224; photo 223
VFW 112, 242
Vietnam War 261
Vocal & Big Band Jazz 311
Voland, Herb 296
Volz, Nedra 157, 184-185

Wade, Dixie K. 296
Wagon Train 139
Waikiki Wedding 94
Walcott, Gregory 233
Walker, Ann 294
Walker, Nancy 230, 236, 238
Walker, Texas Ranger 258
Wallace, Gary 266
Walls 56
Walterhouse, Annrae 174
Walton, Bernard 308
Waltons, The 116
Waltz of the Toreadors, The 259
Ward, Lyman 163
Warner Books 22, 325
Warner Bros. 2, 6, 12-13, 54, 60, 69, 88, 137; photo 305
Warner, Marsha 224, 236
Warren, Jennifer 83
Watch Out for Slick 93
We Gather Together (song) 287
We Were Strangers 30
We're in the Money (song) 228
Webster, Byron 196
Wedding Band 84
Weddle, Vernon 178, 186
Weinberger, Michael 200, 295
Weintraub, Sandy 4
Weird Science 266
Weitzman, Harvey 226
"Welcome to the Club" 287, 292
Wells, Derek 164
Welsh, John 150, 170, 288
Wendt, George 206
West Point 25

West, Adam 141-142
West, Isabel 225
West, Mae 321
Westbury, New York 88
Westchester, New York 88
Western Kentucky University 267
Westmore, Bud 94
Weston, Celia 69, 74, 87-88, 192-193, 198-199, 202, 204-205, 207, 209-210, 213, 216, 222-223, 230, 304, 309-310; photo 70, 73, 87, 220, 228, 234
Weston, Jim 289, 295
Wharton, Edith 40
What a Dummy 146
"What Are Friends For?" 293
"What Happened to the Class of '78" 162
What Now, My Love? (song) 236
"What're You Doing New Year's Eve?" 165
What's Happening? 235
Whedon, Tom 148-152, 155, 157-158, 162-164, 169-170, 172, 174-178, 194
Wheeler, Margaret 238
When Your Lover Has Gone (song) 6
Where or When (song) 6
Where's My Man 23
White House 61
White, John Sylvester 189
"Who Killed Bugs Bunny?" 143
"Who Ordered the Hot Turkey?" 164
"Who's Kissing the Great Chef of Phoenix" 194
Who's That Knocking at My Door 3, 33, 38
Why Me? (song) 4
Wilcox, Dan 175
"Wild One, The" 200; photo 200
Wild Thornberrys, The 107
Williams, Louise 139; photo 140
Williams, Tennessee 86, 88
Williams, Tom 165, 190-191, 194, 206, 209-210, 227
Williamson, Mykelti 211
Willingham, Noble 141, 143-144, 157

"Willoughby vs. Willoughby" 288
Wills, Terry 174, 179, 281-283, 291
Willy 106
Wilmington, North Carolina 79
Wilson, Dick 166-167
Wilson, Grant 233
Windsor, Ontario 15
Winnick, Jerry 163
Winter Wonderland 105
Winter, Edward 151
WIRE 101
Wisconsin 261
Wise Guys 34
With a Song in My Heart (song) 193
Witt, Howard 178, 187
Wizard of Oz, The 7, 93, 313
Wolf of Wall Street, The 41
Wolf, Susan 200, 225
Wolfe, Ian 219, 291
Wolff, Tobias 37
Woman of the Year 102
Women in the workforce 54
Women's movement 61
Wonderful Wizard of Oz, The 311
World War II 95, 101, 104-105, 315
World's Youngest Mind Reader, The 99
Worsham, Curry 236
Wrecking ball 65
Writers Guild of America (WGA) 14, 102, 104
Wulff, Kai 289, 295
Wyle, Frances 144
Wyner, George 183

Xiaolin Showdown 107

Yahr, Betty 217
Yale School of Drama 268
Yale University 31
Yankee Stadium 115
Yellow Rose of Texas, The (song) 167, 281, 284, 289
Yentl 56
You and the Night and the Music (song) 206
You Do Something to Me (song) 150, 183
You Don't Have to Die 83
"You Gotta Have Hoyt" 294, 322
You Wish 107
You'll Never Know (song) 6
You're the Top (song) 193, 207
You've Got Possibilities (song) 78
Young, Cletus 139
Young, J. S. "Joe" 149
Your Eyes Shine Like a Bunny (song) 183
Your Eyes Shine Like a Possum (song) 183
(Your Love Keeps Lifting Me) Higher and Higher (song) 238

Zadikov, Greg 218
Zaffina, Dino M. 226, 239
Zagon, Marty 150, 284
Zapp, Peter 143
Zee, Eleanor 159
Zing! Went the Strings of My Heart (song) 158
Zuanich, Barbara 325
Zwerling, Darrell 142

About the Author

Barry M. Putt Jr. *(Photo taken by Mandee K. Hammerstein.)*

BARRY M. PUTT JR. is an author, screenwriter, and dramatist. He has adapted over forty classic and modern stories into audio dramas for Colonial Radio Theatre in Boston, Massachusetts; Baicizhan Technology in Chengdu, China; and the weekly series *Radio Theater Project* for KSVR in Mount Vernon, Washington.

He was a staff writer for Ebru TV's Telly Award–winning series *The Wisdom Tree* and head writer for the children's show *In the Cellar*. Barry cowrote the script for the award-winning short film *Departures* (2011) and wrote the screenplay for *Maren's Rock: A Virtual Reality Film* (2019).

His stage plays have been performed in the United Arab Emirates, Canada, and throughout the United States. Barry's children's plays, *A Nutty Tale* and *All Is Fair in Show Business,* are published by Drama Notebook. Brilliance Audio published his audio drama adaptations of *The Holly Tree Inn* and *Wreck of the Golden Mary* as well as the forthcoming full-length adventure story, *The Mysterious Island.*

Barry holds a master of arts degree in English literature from Centenary University in New Jersey and a bachelor of fine arts degree in dramatic writing from New York University, where he runs an alumni group for filmmakers and writers. He lives in New Jersey with his rascally tuxedo cat, Ricky "McGillicuddy" Putt.

www.ingramcontent.com/pod-product-compliance
Lightning Source LLC
Chambersburg PA
CBHW071952220426
43662CB00009B/1103